AMERICA'S
MAIN STREET
HOTELS

C0-ASY-091

DATE DUE

SEP 0 7 2010			

Demco, Inc. 38-293

NOV 1 9 2009

AMERICA'S MAIN STREET HOTELS

TRANSIENCY AND COMMUNITY IN THE EARLY AUTO AGE

John A. Jakle and Keith A. Sculle

THE UNIVERSITY OF TENNESSEE PRESS
KNOXVILLE

Library of Congress Cataloging-in-Publication Data

Jakle, John A.
America's main street hotels: transiency and community in the early
auto age / John A. Jakle and Keith A. Sculle.
    p. cm.
Includes bibliographical references and index.
ISBN-13: 978-1-57233-655-1 (pbk.: alk. paper)
ISBN-10: 1-57233-655-2 (pbk.: alk. paper)
  1. Hotels—United States—History—20th century.
  2. Transportation, Automotive—United States—History—20th century.
  3. Architecture—United States—History—20th century.
  4. Roadside architecture—United States.
  I. Sculle, Keith A.
  II. Title.

TX909.J34 2009
917.306'217—dc22
2009001819

CONTENTS

Preface   xiii

Acknowledgments   xix

Introduction   1

1. Laying Out the House   23

2. The Business of Starting a Main Street Hotel   47

3. Hotel Management: From Front Desk to Housekeeper's Closet   69

4. Hotel Life   97

5. Food and Drink   119

6. Changing with the Times   137

Epilogue   159

Notes   183

Index   209

ILLUSTRATIONS

1. Terre Haute House, Terre Haute, Indiana, Circa 1940 2
2. The Relative Importance of the Hotel Industry State to State, 1929 5
3. Hotel Byers, Mattoon, Illinois, Circa 1950 12
4. Downtown Pocahontas, Arkansas, Circa 1910 13
5. Majestic Hotel, Oconomowoc, Wisconsin, Circa 1915 14
6. Hotel Dalles, The Dalles, Oregon, Circa 1920 15
7. Robert E. Lee Hotel, Lexington, Virginia, Circa 1930 16
8. Hotel McCartney, Texarkana, Arkansas, Circa 1925 17
9. Ground-Floor Plan, Hotel Van Dervoort, Paragould, Arkansas 26
10. Second-Floor Plan, Hotel Van Dervoort, Paragould, Arkansas 27
11. Plan for Third and Fourth Floors, Hotel Van Dervoort,
 Paragould, Arkansas 28
12. Basement Plan, Hotel Van Dervoort, Paragould, Arkansas 29
13. Hotel Wicomico, Salisbury, Maryland 36
14. Lobby of the Urbana-Lincoln Hotel, Urbana, Illinois 37
15. Lobby, George Washington Hotel, Washington, Pennsylvania 38
16. Office, Hotel Graham, Bloomington, Indiana 39
17. Portion of the Mezzanine, Hotel Ottumwa, Ottumwa, Iowa 40
18. Ball and Banquet Room, Hotel Robidoux, St. Joseph, Missouri 41
19. Pharmacy, Tallcorn Hotel, Marshalltown, Iowa 42
20. Barber Shop, Hotel Hayes, Jackson, Michigan 43
21. The Hotel Chandler in Chandler, Georgia 49
22. Temple, Texas, Skyline in 2007 Travel Literature,
 Showing Two of Its Hotels 57
23. Meeting of the Sedalia Business and Professional Women's Club
 in the Ambassador Room, Hotel Bothwell 58
24. Meeting of the Women's Auxiliary of the Pettis County
 Medical Society 59
25. The Hotel Bothwell's Congratulations of the Sedalia
 Rotary Club's Fiftieth Anniversary 60
26. Edwin A. Boss, Circa 1959 62
27. Cartoon Postcard Depicting Too Many Lodgers in a Room 71

28. The Front Desk   72

29. Graphs Presented by American Hotel Association's *Hotel Red Book*   75

30. Sign Boards for the Hotel Bucklen in Elkhart, Indiana,
      on the Lincoln Highway   77

31. Posters Assuring Comfort and Security for Traveling
      Mothers and Their Daughters   78

32. Illustration of the Unity Managers Were Intended to Find
      between the *Red Book* and Hotels   82

33. Every Hotel Service Shown Accountable to the Hotel Manager   84

34. Postcard Advertising for the Hotel Yancey in Grand Island,
      Nebraska, Featuring an African-American Elevator Operator   85

35. Cartoon Illustrating Hotel Industry Management's Belief That
      NIRA Codes Were Unfair   90

36. Lobby of the Rogerson Hotel, Twin Falls, Idaho   100

37. Lobby of the Woodworth Hotel, Robinson, Illinois, Circa 1900   101

38. The Traveling Salesman as Illustrated by David Robinson   103

39. The Ohio Hotel at Wooster, Ohio   108

40. Dining Room, Hotel Shepard, Union Grove, Wisconsin   121

41. An Attentive Dining-Room Wait Staff   123

42. Dining Room, Florence Hotel, Missoula, Montana   124

43. Kitchen, Hotel Vicksburg, Vicksburg, Mississippi   127

44. Kitchen Layout, Hotel Otsego, Jackson, Michigan   128

45. Advertisement for the Duparquet, Huot, and Moneuse Company   129

46. Men's Café and Bar, Leland Hotel, Springfield, Illinois   130

47. Coffee Shop, Baxter Hotel, Bozeman, Montana   132

48. Coffee Shop, Hotel Powers, Fargo, North Dakota   133

49. Street Entrance to the Coffee Shop, Powers Hotel,
      Fargo, North Dakota   134

50. Cocktail Lounge, Hotel Lancaster, Lancaster, Ohio   135

51. The Stoddart Hotel, Marshalltown, Iowa, in 1930   138

52. "Modernizing Treatment" of the Lobby of the Hotel Gardner,
      Fargo, North Dakota, 1941   140

53. Photograph and Diagrams of the Innovative Main Street Hotel
      Garage, Poughkeepsie, New York   142

54. The Hotel Anthes in Fort Madison, Iowa, Before It Was
      "Face Lifted" and Afterward   143

55. Renovated Lobby of Hotel Burlington   144

56. Comedic Postcard, 1910, Illustrating Vexations of the Shared
      Bathroom   146

57. Two Idealized Floor Plans Presented in *Hotel Monthly*, 1917   148

58. Representative Room in the Boss Chain, Circa 1940   150

59. Postcard View of the Doherty Lodging Alternatives   154

60. Advertisment for the Hotel Greystone, Bedford, Indiana   160

61. The Hotel Greystone in Decline, 1994   161

62. The New Southern Hotel, Jackson, Tennessee, 1928   169

63. Reconstituting Interior Moldings, New Southern Apartments,
      Jackson, Tennessee, 2004   170

64. Restoring the Hotel Mezzanine, New Southern Apartments,
      Jackson, Tennessee, 2006   170

65. Refurbished Mezzanine, New Southern Apartments,
      Jackson, Tennessee, 2006   171

66. Refurbished Lobby Viewed From Mezzanine, New Southern
      Apartments, Jackson, Tennessee, 2006   171

67. Atrium of the Windsor Hotel, Garden City, Kansas, 2006   175

68. The Vacant Terre Haute House, Terre Haute, Indiana, 1990   178

69. Sign for New Motor Inn under Construction on Terre Haute
      House Site   179

70. Hilton Garden Inn, Terre Haute, Indiana, 2008   180

PREFACE

A half-century ago, a time when the automobile's impact on landscape was just beginning to be fully recognized, John Brinckerhoff Jackson, writing in *Landscape* (the influential magazine he founded), defined the term *stranger's path*.[1] He was referring to routes that visitors to a town or a city might follow on foot, in a cab, or by bus or streetcar from a railroad station or a bus terminal to a downtown hotel. Along the way were clustered the pawn shops, cigar stores, bars, cheap eateries, and other establishments that serviced mainly the underclasses. But he also had in mind the new commercial strips that had sprouted along the nation's highways peripheral to towns and cities. Along these new paths of urban entry and exit were concentrated gas stations, fast-food restaurants, and, of course, motels that serviced not only travelers but, like the older routes downtown, locals also. Only now, customers—generally more affluent customers—arrived mainly by car. A new era of automobile convenience had arrived.

In an earlier essay, Jackson had focused on the important structural elements that typified the nation's commercial roadsides, coining the term *other-directed houses*.[2] In it he took umbrage with those who saw in highway strips only blight and ugliness, as many writers about landscape and place were apt to do at the time. Recalling his own experiences at traveling across the American West, he wrote, "I keep remembering the times when I have driven for hour after hour across an emptiness—desert or prairie—which was *not* blemished by highway stands, and how relieved and delighted I always was to finally see somewhere in the distance the jumble of billboards and gas pumps and jerry-built houses. Tourist traps or not, these were very welcome sights, and even the commands to EAT, COME AS YOU ARE, GAS UP, GET FREE ICE WATER AND STICKERS, had a comforting effect."[3]

When travel by railroad fully dominated, strangers to cities and towns found many of their needs anticipated by businesses located at or close to railroad stations. Indeed, in most urban places, especially the smaller ones, downtown business districts were fully railroad-oriented, most businesses being but a short walk from a railroad depot. On or near Main Street was where people of a small town or small city, as well as its surrounding hinterland, accessed the outside world. It was there that farm and other products were assembled for shipment to distant markets. It was there that the products and services that originated beyond a locality were made available for local consumption. Additionally, it was where strangers from other locales were hosted. Importantly, downtown was where hotels were located. In the early days of motoring, strangers arriving in a place by car invariably made their way to an urban center. For decades motorists remained very much dependent on facilities that had originated in the railroad era.

In coauthoring books over the past two decades, we explored various of the other-directed houses typical of stranger's paths that were fully auto-oriented. We looked in turn at the rise of the gas station, the motel, and the fast-food restaurant.[4] Additionally, we explored the rise of roadside signage and even the lowly parking lot.[5] In these efforts we emphasized entrepreneurship—the production side of roadside evolution, especially the practices of large corporations but also the practices of small business people. However, in a recent book, *Motoring: The Highway Experience in America,* we emphasized more the consumption side of things, specifically how it was that motorists through the first half of the twentieth century treated the roadside as a kind of place.[6] Accordingly, we dealt with an array of topics earlier slighted: the establishment of named highways (roads marked and promoted by private highway associations), the coming of the public highway system (which replaced named highways with numbered roads), the coming of toll highways and interstate freeways, the nation's flirtation with parkways, the rise of the automobile service garage (which preceded the gasoline station), roadside tourist attractions (from snake farms to history museums), travel by bus, the role of trucking, and, lastly, the rise of the convenience store (which today has largely displaced the gas station).

But there is yet another topic deserving of a book. It is a topic that speaks very much of the origins of auto-oriented landscapes and places—to the roots, if you will, of the stranger's path as it evolved in the auto age. It is a topic far too big for a mere chapter in an umbrella volume. That topic is the traditional Main Street hotel, the focus of this book. The Main Street hotel we take to be a kind of other-directed house not only worthy of exploration on its own merits but also as a very important contributor to early motoring. This focus on the traditional downtown hotel, we think, offers an important means of understanding how it was that travel by automobile became so impelling and ultimately so intrusive in the American scene. Few small-town and small-city hotels built before 1910 embraced automobility directly. However, by 1920 the inclusion of drive-up motor entrances and parking garages, among other auto-oriented features and services, had become standard. After 1930, of course, hotels found themselves competing against motels that were not only newer and located at the peripheries of towns and cities (thus to intercept motorists) but were also laid out to be fully automobile-convenient, with motel guests able to park directly at their bedroom doors. Traditional downtown hotels, nonetheless, remained substantially dependent on the automobile trade. Automobility and Main Street hotels remained integrally linked.

Pleasure tripping was important from the earliest days of automobile travel. Americans, at least those who could afford cars, took to the nation's highways with enthusiasm not only in search of release from everyday routines but in search of adventure through motoring as a kind of sport. Initially, motoring was very much an athletic event, given the primitive nature of the nation's cars and roads. Motoring was fraught with punctured tires and broken axles, not to mention the difficulty of obtaining gasoline, meals, and lodging in many localities, particularly across the western United States, a region especially attractive to adventure-seeking motorists for its relative emptiness and unusual scenery. Through mass production, motor cars became infinitely affordable, the pleasures of motoring diffusing rapidly to Americans of the middling classes. Once a majority of Americans came to enjoy car travel, clamor for highway improvement greatly intensified, as did clamor for improved hotels. The federal highway system may have been justified in Congress as a means of insuring military preparedness and as a means of stimulating economic growth, but what made highway improvement politically feasible was actually the widespread desire to motor, especially for pleasure. Probably nothing gave more pleasure than the "open road"—unless, of course, it was having a clean, comfortable hotel room to collapse into at the end of a travel day.

Automobility resonated well with established American values. Motoring struck responsive chords in the American psyche. It reinforced in a geographical sense the valuing of individual freedom of action. Car ownership quickly came to symbolize social success. The embrace of new automobile technology symbolized progress through change, something that also enhanced personal esteem. Not to drive became a form of social deprivation, a matter of being outside the social mainstream—of being "left behind." By the 1950s the vast majority of Americans found themselves "on the road," not just motoring for pleasure but also driving to work, driving to shop, and generally using their cars to run most of the errands that constituted modern life. The automobile loomed as more than a prized possession. It had become an absolute necessity. In accommodating the motor car and motor truck, the nation's geography was substantially reorganized. This was especially true at the peripheries of urban places—in the suburbs. There the auto-oriented stranger's path fully matured into the modern commercial strip, complete with shopping malls, office parks, residential subdivisions, and literally every other sort of land-use development oriented to it. There, indeed, did the new motels proliferate. Seemingly, many traditional things had been, or soon would be, left behind, including, it was becoming all too apparent, traditional downtown business districts along with their hotels.

People in every American small town, or so it might be argued, thought at one time or another that their town would surely become a big city. Accordingly, every town needed at least one up-to-date hotel, if not to symbolize success on the community level, then to help precipitate it. That was the nature of American optimism, the nature of local boosterism. But for the vast majority of America's towns, creatures mainly of one or another railroad development, sustained growth was difficult. Most towns served only limited hinterlands as farm trade centers. Towns that attracted industry tended to do better, but even most factory towns remained modest in size, stuck well down the nation's hierarchy of urban places. In small cities, as compared to small towns, train travelers and then motorists did encounter a wider array of hotel accommodation, including some hotels for which local citizens could justifiably be proud. Starting about 1910, new hotels, built mainly to attract an affluent motoring public, were, indeed, very much big-city-like. Many were actually quite cosmopolitan.

In every locality, towns competed with one another for economic advantage. In the nineteenth century, they competed to host county courthouses. They rivaled one another in attracting new railroad lines, if they were not, in fact, founded in conjunction with a new railroad development.

Early in the twentieth century, towns competed for improved roads. Then towns competed for motorists and the money they spent. To attract the tourist dollar, it was important that hotels not only be adequate but also fully comfortable and, of course, tastefully appointed. People "from away" needed accommodations where they might feel fully "at home." A town would certainly not become a travel destination, or even a mere overnight stop of convenience, if no modern hostelry was at hand.

Pleasure-seeking motorists, of course, were not the only ones to crowd the nation's highways. There were commercial travelers, especially sales people, who had traditionally traveled by train but who were, even before World War I, traveling more and more by car. Importantly, there were business owners on the lookout for new investment opportunities, perhaps to locate a new store or even a factory. Up-to-date hotels, community boosters asserted, were crucial if a town was to positively impress such people. How was a community to grow if it could not attract new business? Important also were conventioneers. How better to boost hotel trade, and thus a town's fortunes, than by attracting large congregations of people? Convention goers also spent money.

Early in the twentieth century, hotels were usually the largest, tallest, and most strategically located of a community's downtown buildings. As often as not, they were the most elegantly styled architecturally. In most places only bank buildings or, perhaps, a department store or two challenged them for attention. Even the old railroad-era hotels had stood out. J. B. Jackson, in still another classic essay, which he entitled "The Almost Perfect Town," wrote of fictional Optimo City. There downtown buildings of brick or stone stood with "cornices like the brims of hats, fancy drip stones over the arched windows like eyebrows; painted blood-red or mustard-yellow or white; identical except for the six-story. . . hotel and the classicism of the First National Bank."[7]

The new Main Street hotels made possible by the new motoring public put an even better "face" on community. But, more important, they served, it was argued, to reenergize community—not just in an economic sense but in a social sense as well. A quality hotel stimulated the kinds of social interactions that made a community a community. Did they not host a wide array of public events (political rallies, for example)? Did they not cater to social organizations (the Rotarians, for example)? Did they not host family-oriented activities (wedding receptions and anniversary parties, for example)? Much of a town's spontaneous interacting occurred in a hotel's public spaces: in the dining room, in the barber shop, in the beauty parlor, at the cigar counter, at the newspaper stand. Serving motorists, therefore, was not the lone rationale for new hotel development, but, as we argue herein, motoring did provide the major catalyst. Although not *on* the highway (or the roadside) per se, hotels of the early auto era were, in a sense, *of* the roadside. They anticipated roadside America. They were the first phase, so to speak, of the lodging industry's response to motoring. The were transitional from the old stranger's path to the new.

So widespread was new hotel development (and the refurbishing and expansion of old hotels also) that, indeed, a distinctive era of hotel architecture evolved: tall, architecturally styled buildings that for the most part anchored major downtown intersections. Most of those buildings remain as an important kind of architectural legacy, being fully visible in small-town and small-city business districts across the nation today. Now vintage, they stand fully reminiscent of motoring's early days, the era when people, even in the nation's smallest and seemingly most backwater places, could enjoy at least a momentary rebirth of optimism through embrace of renewed hotel development downtown. The story we tell in this book outlines how these hotels came to be. Our questions are basic: What were they like? Who financed and built them? How were they managed? Who patronized them? To what extend did they, in fact, function as community centers? To what extent did they meet the challenges of a new motor age?

In the introduction we define terms and provide historical context. In chapter 1 we treat the Main Street hotel as a building type, exploring, accordingly, hotel layout and logistics. In chapter 2 we outline how these hotels were financed and, in the process, begin our exploration of their community-building implications. In chapter 3 we look at hotel management and consider labor issues. In chapter 4 we emphasize hotel life, examining, most importantly, the typical hotel's customer base. In chapter 5 we focus on hotel food services. In chapter 6 we treat the changing fads and fashions of hotel furnishing, especially with regard to guest-room design. Finally, in the epilogue we draw our various lines of discussion together by exploring the uses that surviving Main Street hotels perform today. Although over the years numerous hotels have been demolished and many presently stand vacant or even derelict, the largest proportion continue to function in some way supportive of their localities.

We limit ourselves to small-town and small-city hotels for several reasons. First, they offer a clear view of the role that motoring played in early-twentieth-century hotel development, and vice versa. Second, they offer a clear view of how hotels contributed to community development. Urban places of relatively small size were, and are, simply not as complex as big cities, and thus sorting out the roles that hotels played, both for strangers from away and for local residents, is made all the easier. Third, past scholarship has tended very much to emphasize the nation's grand hotels in its biggest cities. Relatively little attention has heretofore been given to smaller hostelries. We seek to at least partially fill that gap. We focus our attention on hotels sized between 25 and 250 rooms and located in urban places of between some 600 and 60,000 people. We restrict discussion mainly to the period from 1900 to 1960.

There are additional topics that, perhaps, ought to be treated here, but space simply does not allow for that. Thus we leave aside the resort hotel, important as resort hotels were and are to the economic prosperity of many an American resort town. Our focus is very much the transient hotel where rooms were let more by the night than by the week or month, and certainly not by the season. Nor do we treat apartment hotels where suites of rooms were rented or leased to residents by the year. In concluding, however, we do discuss the many small-town and small-city hotels originally transient in nature that in recent decades have undergone conversion into, for example, assisted-living homes for the elderly or Section 8 housing for low-income families. It is through such redevelopment that many hotels dating from the early years of motoring continue to function.

ACKNOWLEDGMENTS

This book would not have been possible without the assistance of many individuals who graciously shared information both current and historical. In Alaska: Jill A. Galbreith of the Z. J. Loussac Library and Doug Gasek at the State Department of Natural Resources, both in Anchorage. In Arizona: Lynn and John Reilly of Scottsdale. In Arkansas: Hank McNabb and Cindy Robinett, both of Pocahontas. In California: staff at the Monterey Public Library. In Colorado: David Becker of Denver and staff at the Lamar Public Library. In the District of Columbia: Daniel Duggan of the National Trust for Historic Preservation. In Idaho: Dick Riggs of the Nez Perce County Historical Society at Lewiston and Jennifer Hills of the Twin Falls Public Library. In Illinois: Sue Jones of the Crawford County Historical Society in Robinson, Sue Richter of the Vermilion County Historical Museum at Danville, Jean Kay of the Historical Society of Quincy and Adams County at Quincy, Iris Nelson at the Quincy Public Library, staff at the St. Charles Public Library, staff at the Library of the University of Illinois at Urbana-Champaign, and cartographer James Bier of Urbana. In Indiana: Sarah Cody of the Bedford Public Library, staff at the Crawfordsville District Public Library, Brenda Legate of the Willard Library at Evansville, and Sharon Olson at the Evansville-Vanderburgh County Public Library. In Iowa: Jet Kafoot of the Algona Public Library, Joyce Ring of the Burlington Public Library, Bill Burch of Centerville, Marguerite and Don Boss of Des Moines, Jill Sanders at the Elkader Public Library, Mayone Costigan also of Elkader, and Ina Ward of the Marshalltown Public Library. In Kansas: Sarah Martin at the Cultural Resources Division of the State Historical Society at Topeka. In Massachusetts: Linda Dyndiuk of the Somerville Public Library. In Minnesota: Mark Diehl of the Clay County Historical Society at Moorhead and Randolph E. Stefanson, also of Morehead. In Missouri: staff of the State Historic Preservation Office at Jefferson City; staff at the Rolla Public Library; Pam Hunter of the Sedalia Public Library; and Don Barnes, William B. Claycomb, David C. Furnell, Rebecca Carr Imhauser, Don Morton, Jake Sommers, and Chris Young, all of Sedalia as well. In New Mexico: Jeanne La Marcia of Lordsburg and John W. Murphey, State of New Mexico Department of Cultural Affairs, Historic Preservation Division at Santa Fe. In North Dakota: Shane Molander of the State Historical Society at Bismark and Carol Bursack of the *Fargo Forum*. In Oklahoma: staff at the Elk City Public Library. In Pennsylvania: staff of the Tioga County Historical Society at Wellsboro and Evelyn James of the Dauphin County Historical Society and Jonathon Stayer at the State Archives, both in Harrisburg. In Oregon: Karen Bratton of the Douglas County Museum in Roseburg. In South Carolina: James Gahagen of the Colleton County Memorial Library and staff of the Colleton County Museum, both in Waltersboro. In Tennessee: Gina Gentry of the Erwin Public Library; Jacquetta Edwards and James A. Goforth, also of Erwin; Barbara Fagen of the Cleveland Public Library; Bob Cantler of Greenville; Connie Cobble of the *Greeneville Sun;* Madge Walker of the Greene County Public Library at Greeneville; Don Miller of the T. Elmer Cox Historical and Genealogical Library of Greeneville; Barbara Milsaps of the Harriman Public Library; Jack D. Wood of the Jackson-Madison County Library at Jackson; Hal Crocker, also of Jackson; and Claudette Stager of the Tennessee Historical Commission at Nashville. In Texas: Debbie Swendson of the City of Marshall, Ann Laird and Silvia D. Christy of the Seguin-Guadalupe County Public Library at Seguin, Kate Silvas of the City of Seguin, Craig Ordner of the Railroad and Heritage Mueusm at Temple, Nancy Glover of the Temple Visitor Center, and Julie Haag of the Temple Chamber of Commerce. In Virginia: Maria Longley of the *Staunton News Leader.*

Lastly, we thank Gene Adair for his capable editing of the manuscript. The reviewers' critical remarks as a result of their assignment by the University of Tennessee Press were invaluable.

We also owe a debt of gratitude to the publishers and editors of the *Hotel Monthly,* a trade journal that serviced the hotel industry through our study period. Founded in Chicago in 1892 by longtime publisher and editor John Willy, the publication was originally a hotel directory issued quarterly. In 1898 it became a monthly magazine targeted both at hotel operators and hotel suppliers. At the journal's thirty-eighth anniversary, bound volumes were said to take up some seven feet of shelf space. Published therein were some 18,000 illustrations, including the plans of some 450 hotels. As John Willy wrote, "It has been the policy of the publisher always to print on good quality of paper; to keep abreast of the times in the quality of illustrations; and these features supplemented with accuracy in the text matter. It has given to the publication an outstanding individuality."[1] With this we fully concur. The reader will find in the pages ahead many *Hotel Monthly* photographs and diagrams, as well as much quoted narrative. As Willy continued, "From the days of bowl and pitcher and one bath to a floor to every room with bath, with chromium plated fixtures and glass enclosed shower; from flickering kerosene lamps and gas jets to shadowless electroliers; from fireplaces or portable stoves which toasted the face and froze the back, to temperature controlled air; from stable to garage; from drudgery to the pushing of a button or the throwing of a switch, we have watched the [American] hotel industry grow to one of the world's greatest."[2] It is our intention to place that story in the context of the nation's embrace of motoring.

INTRODUCTION

Our concern with Main Street hotels derives from previous scholarship focused on the automobile's impact on American life, especially through the rise of automobile-oriented landscapes and places. For historian Keith Sculle, however, interest also stems from being a career preservationist, one concerned with such questions as: How might buildings such as old hotels be given extended life? And for what purpose? How might they be promoted even today as community resources? For geographer John Jakle, interest derives additionally from concern for small-town and small-city viability. What has been happening in small urban places, especially in their downtowns? Nostalgia also enters his thinking, particularly memories of childhood vacation trips anchored by overnight stays in small-town and small-city hotels. What became of those places? What is it that ought be remembered about them?

For both of us one small-city hotel has come to stand symbolic of the whole: the recently demolished Terre Haute House in Terre Haute, Indiana (fig. 1). Located but a few hours' drive from where each of us now resides, we have watched it slowly decay over the decades, first one and then another proposal for its reuse coming to naught. There has been a hotel on the site since the late 1830s. Terre Haute's two main highways (east–west US 40 and north–south US 41) once crossed in front of it, a downtown intersection still dubbed by locals "The Crossroads of America." Before the wrecker's ball began to swing some seven years ago, brick was cascading off the hotel's rear wall. Many windows, even across its facade, were broken, pigeons being the building's main tenants. There had definitely been better times—glorious times, as a matter of fact. When the last version of the Terre Haute House was opened in 1920s, it quickly became the most important building in town. As a landmark it long dominated the city's skyline. It was the town's principal social center, at the least the social center most frequented by

FIGURE 1. Terre Haute House, Terre Haute, Indiana, circa 1940. Authors' collection.

the most residents. Quickly was it gone. Today a new chain hotel stands in its stead, hotel function at least continuing in place.

There was that evening in the early 1950s when the Jakle family, traveling from Detroit, arrived with overnight reservations at the hotel's main entrance. With their luggage, they climbed down from the cab of a wrecker; their car, having broken down east of town, was hoisted up behind. The family looked bedraggled. But what greeted them, even at the hotel's sidewalk entry, was a gala event: men in evening jackets and women in fancy gowns. The Republican Party was ending its state convention in the hotel with a formal ball. Much to their chagrin, John's mother and father, having grown up in the city, began to encounter people they knew. Entering between giant limestone columns and passing through the revolving door, they passed offices of the local automobile club and Western Union. Then it was into the impressive two-story lobby with its marble columns and wood paneling. On the right hung an oil painting of Dan Patch, the famous trotter. Off to the left was the reception desk, but that evening the lobby seemed so packed with people that one wondered if one could get there. First encountered was a former high school friend of John's parents. And then a grandfather's former business associate. John's mother glanced at her son as if to say: "Put on your best face, be introduced, and for goodness' sake be polite."

Twenty years later John Jakle attended a regional meeting of geographers at the hotel. Times had changed. The Terre Haute House appeared rather rundown. The painting of Dan Patch was still there on the wall, but the lobby itself looked dingy. The formal carpeting and much of the furniture had been removed. Gone were the potted plants. Buildings adjacent to the hotel had been torn down for a parking lot, enabling the Terre Haute House to call itself a "motor inn." Highlights of the conference (are not professional meetings really about socializing?) included a happy hour in the Marine Room, a cocktail lounge off the main lobby. As its name suggested, the room was decorated in nautical motif, a decor more appropriate to maritime New England than to the Midwest. Nonetheless, the room did offer a kind of fantasy escape from local Corn Belt realities. And then late one night there was further socializing in one of the guest rooms high up in the hotel, the closing climax of which came with a colleague attempting to drop kick an ice bucket out an open window. For many years the Terre Haute House had been the venue for a grandfather's Tuesday night poker game. It was where John Jakle's parents, in their early married years, went for a "night out." Variously did the place resonate in family history long after the family had moved away.

Variously will readers remember their own experiences at one or another Main Street hotel. Those memories, however, may not all be old. Many a small-town and small-city hotel still welcomes guests. Some are refurbished and very much up to date. Some are not. Some no longer serve transients, but have been converted to apartment living. Some have been converted into office buildings. Some merely stand vacant. Most of them still make for a formidable presence in their downtown settings, be it facing onto an actual Main Street, a court house square, or a nearby thoroughfare. It is time, we think, that they be given their due as important architectural features. It is important that they be recognized for their role in promoting America's early embrace of automobility. It is time to recognize them for what they promised to be: important energizers of local community.

Main Street Hotels Considered

The history of the hotel in early-twentieth-century America remains a topic little explored by scholars, and this despite the fact that an abundant literature (mainly in the form of trade-journal and popular-magazine articles) and an abundance of advertising ephemera (including hotel guides and promotional pamphlets) exists to foster scholarship.[1] Numerous are the plan books once circulated by hotel outfitters and architects.[2] Numerous also are vintage "how to" guides, including training manuals and textbooks.[3] What historical scholarship there is tends to focus on the nation's larger hotels, especially those of its largest cities but also its leading resorts. Books about hotels can be conveniently categorized as follows: overview histories, histories of specific hotels, biographies of successful hotel entrepreneurs, and histories of important hotel chains.[4]

We focus on the nation's smaller hotels located in its smaller urban places. We emphasize the hotels once predominant on America's Main Streets early in the twentieth century. According to the American Hotel Association's *Red Book,* there were some 25,900 hotels in the United States in 1928, the approximate midpoint of our period of concern from roughly 1900 to 1960. They contained more than 1,525,000 guest rooms.[5] Their geographical distribution closely paralleled that of the nation's population, except in the American South where racial segregation operated to restrict hotel patronage, thus reducing hotel numbers (fig. 2). The first federal census of hotel properties conducted in 1926, being limited to hotels with 25 rooms or more, counted only 15,557. Uncounted were at least a third of the nation's hotel properties, most of them very small.[6] Trade organizations also tended to ignore the nation's smaller hotels. As one disgruntled hotel manager complained to the *Hotel Monthly,* "I do not hear anything that pertains to the small country hotel talked about at the conventions. All I hear is some agent trying to sell lunch counters or something of that kind. I do not care anything about after dinner speeches either. What I want to hear and know about is how to run and make money with a hotel of 50 rooms."[7] In order to fully understand how hotels once figured in the life of America, one has to embrace, it seems to us, the small as well as the large. Such a focus fosters understanding of how automobiles and motoring came to impact life in America. It fosters, as well, comprehension of how hotels contributed to a sense of community from locality to locality.

In the late 1920s, numerous small-town and small-city hotels were holdovers from the railroad age, but fully predominant were the new hotels built in response to evolving automobile use. For the most part, these hotels were conceived and financed by local investor syndicates formed around booster organizations. Modern hotels were needed, it was vigorously asserted, to keep small towns "on the map," particularly the nation's new highway map of increased automobility. Through em-

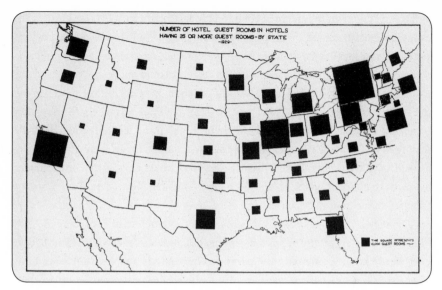

FIGURE 2. The relative importance of the hotel industry state to state, 1929. Proportional symbol at the lower right represents 10,000 guest rooms. From "Census Map Pictures Importance of Hotel Industry," *Hotel Monthly* 39 (July 1931): 54.

brace of motoring, even small towns might prosper. Modern hotels were critical to attracting transients and, of course, the money they spent. New hotels were critical to attracting new businesses to enhance a town's employment base and thus its general prosperity. Importantly, hotels could also function as a kind of community center. Typical of America were periods of boom and bust, booming optimism often resulting in overbuilding, including the placing of new businesses, such as hotels, on the nation's Main Streets. The hotels of the early auto era were quite numerous, and many, if not most of them, involved overextended booster confidence. Nonetheless, they were built. And most of them continue to stand today as important landmarks of Main Street America. Look around any locality across the United States and hotel buildings, especially of the 1910–1930 period, will come readily to view.

The Hotel Defined

It is, perhaps, best to start by defining what we mean by the word "hotel." It is, of course, a word of French origin which, for the French of the eighteenth century, denoted a large public building or a nobleman's residence. Adopted by the English to differentiate upscale coaching inns from those that were only ordinary, the word crossed the Atlantic to be adopted first in New York City. In 1790 Joseph Corre, a pastry cook and previously manager of the celebrated City Tavern, named a new enterprise, one with overnight accommodations, Corre's Hotel.[8] Over ensuing decades, designations such as "hotel," "inn," and "tavern" (what were defined in legal terms in most localities as "public houses of entertainment") tended to conflate in meaning. They designated places where transients could obtain not only food and drink but also overnight lodging, the latter often in open dormitory spaces rather than in private bedrooms. Toilet and bathing facilities, even where individual rooms were available, were usually shared in common and located "down the hall." Dining rooms, reading rooms, and other public spaces in hotels were open to locals as well as to transients. Hotels thus served, like the nation's early coffee houses, as places to conduct business, discuss politics, and generally socialize. They were thought of as community centers.

The very large hotels that evolved early in the nineteenth century, especially in the nation's largest metropolitan centers, did, indeed, deserve the élan that the new word "hotel" conveyed. Compared to European hostelries, they were quite impressive, being almost palace-like. Although private guest rooms—most of them usually quite modest— came to dominate upper stories, lower floors were usually given over to large, elegantly furnished public spaces. Perhaps the first purpose-built hotel of this type was the City Hotel in New York City, which opened in 1794. "Here," as historian Jefferson Williamson described it, "the gay New Yorkers, first to copy English and French fad and follies, danced the rigadoon, cotillion and *allemande,* and the 'plain and fancy minuet,' at weekly subscription dances given by 'gentlemen of the town,' who attended in knee-breeches, silk stockings, white dancing-gloves, London cocked hats and dress-swords."[9] The era of the truly grand hotel was launched in 1829 with the opening of the Tremont House in Boston. With its 173 guest rooms, it occupied an entire city block, its dining room able to accommodate two hundred diners at a single sitting. Holt's Hotel in New York City—six stories tall with 225 rooms—quickly followed.[10]

America, it could be said, invented the hotel, at least as it evolved through the nineteenth century worldwide. American hotels, especially the big-city hotels, tended to set international standards through constant innovation. An American hotel was first to provide electric lighting in every guest room (the Hotel Everett in New York City in 1882) and first to provide each guest room with private toilet and bathing facilities (the Victoria Hotel in Kansas City in 1888).[11] The new Waldorf-Astoria Hotel in New York City, opened in 1897, was seventeen stories tall, having adopted high-speed elevators. Guest rooms offered extraordinary views out over Manhattan. Europe had nothing like it.

What truly set American hotels apart from their European counterparts, however, was the simple fact that they were open to all. That is to say, they were open to all males (and escorted females) who could afford hotel services. Decorated in the height of fashion (thus providing many Americans with their initial encounter with the materialism of heightened gentility), they were not specifically restricted to a gentry class. Hotels were said to be "palaces of the people," and thus, in theory, everyone was welcome. As one historian put it: "The point was not that the 'society' contained in microcosm in the hotel dining room included everyone but that everyone had a chance to meet its criteria for membership. Those people who dressed, behaved, and ate genteelly were welcome at the table of any first-class hotel. Self-possession, not material wealth or birth, was the key."[12] Such was not a denial of republican egalitarianism but, rather, an award for it. It reflected the values of the increasingly affluent middle classes as well as the upper classes for whom refinement marked a successful combination of market and republican principles. The nation's hotels, and certainly its grand hotels, provided, in the words of one commentator, "the material and spatial arrangements" that corresponded to such values. "In turn, these arrangements enabled the hotel to create simultaneously a haven from the city and an exemplary, highly visible enactment of refinement."[13]

For European travelers, American hotels came to symbolize much of what they found distinctive about the United States. In mixing into the social swirl of hotel life, Europeans tended to see the American hotel as a kind of microcosm of American life. For one thing, hotel life seemed to symbolize the "fluidity" of a dynamic nation. This was especially true of the small-town and small-city hotels where travelers sojourned as they traveled west across the continent. "The European middle classes," noted historian Daniel Boorstin, "counted the right to be by oneself or alone with one's family or chosen friends among the amenities, a sign of civilized respectability." But a foreign visitor who found himself "sharing his dinner table, and called upon to chat familiarly, with a miscellaneous company of common soldiers, farmers, laborers, teamsters, lawyers, doctors, ministers, bankers, judges, or general, soon discovered that Americans considered the desire for privacy a vice akin to pride."[14] It seemed that Americans were, in the words of another historian, by nature a gregarious people who loved to live in public, to see and be seen, to hear and be heard, and to participate 'on the level.'"[15]

Something else differentiated American hotels in the nineteenth century from their European counterparts: the so-called "American Plan," whereby meals were included in the price of lodging. Rather than being prepared and served to order with guests seated at private tables, meals were prepared and taken at communal tables and only at set times each day. The dinner gong that announced meal servings was an important hotel accouterment. Key to making the system work was strong landlord paternalism. In the better-run hotels, owners or their designates orchestrated guest activities, benevolently directing them in the course of daily routines according to prevailing rules of refinement. Landlords traditionally greeted guests at a hotel's front door, sometimes offering them a drink. They undertook to help them register and saw to it that a bellboy escorted them, along with their luggage, to an assigned room. Landlords traditionally presided over meals, carving the meat, for example, in a kind of dining room ritual. In the 1850s the Metropolitan Hotel in New York City was the first to abandon a fixed meal schedule and to adopt the so-called "European Plan."[16]

It was with a strong, lingering sense of paternalism that the hotel industry in the twentieth century sought to precisely define the word "hotel." According to John Willy, editor of the *Hotel Monthly*, "A hotel is a house of public entertainment, with clean, moral atmosphere, where proper persons are received and furnished wholesome food and lodging for pay; the landlord (proprietor or manager) of the hotel holding himself at all times to do the best he can to insure the comfort, safety, and property of his guests." Willy called for a legal definition of the term. He suggested the following: "The word 'hotel' on buildings, signs, registers, letter-heads, or advertisements of any nature, shall be confined and restricted to the use of a licensed owner, lessee, proprietor, or manager . . . who shall be of good moral character and he or she shall be licensed by the same county court authorized to issue marriage licenses, to conduct and operate as a hotel a house of public entertainment for the accommodation of transient proper persons with wholesome meals and sanitary lodgings, for pay." For hotels to be hotels, he thought, they needed to have at least twenty-five guest rooms.[17]

The concern to fully define hotels in terms of social propriety stemmed from the fact that a wide diversity of lodging establishments, many of them in moral disrepute, were freely using the term also. It did not bother so much that inns and taverns residual along the nation's rural byways, many of which survived from the stagecoach era, were adopting the term in order to attract a new motoring public. It bothered more that the increasingly antiquated and rundown hotels surviving from the railroad era were continuing to use the term. Truly worrisome were the lodging or boarding houses that adopted the name, most of them being not the least hotel-like, especially the cheap "flop houses" that catered to society's truly down and out.[18] Then there were the guest houses and the tourist homes run, for example, by "gentlewomen who had fallen on hard times."[19] Such women might run reputable hostelries, but they did not run hotels.

The matter of definition assumed critical importance in the 1930s with congressional approval of the National Recovery Act, a major component in the Roosevelt administration's attempt to jump-start the nation's depressed economy. By then, tourist courts or motels had come to the fore to compete vigorously for the motorist's dollar. Many of them were called "motor hotels." Hotel interests, confronted with bond obligations and mortgages to pay off in the face of diminished business, were determined to deny motel owners any advantage, especially when it came to setting NRA operating and pricing codes. The settled-on definition for a hotel was as follows: A hotel was "any establishment operated for profit, which extends lodging to the general public; has at least ten guest rooms available for such lodgings in *one building* [italics ours]; charges not less than 50 cents per day per transient person; is equipped to provide lodging in at least 25 percent of its rooms without prior understanding or agreement as to the duration of any guest's stay."[20] The Supreme Court, of course, invalidated the National Recovery Act.

Collecting the 1930 Census of Population involved still another attempt at hotel definition.[21] However, census takers found it exceedingly difficult to sort out the many "hotel" variations they encountered. For the 1935 Census of Business, therefore, stricter definitions were adopted, hotels being defined not so much by what they were as by what they were not. As one authority reported,

> The Census includes, principally, establishments designating themselves as hotels and providing hotel accommodations as their major business activity. Establishments reporting a total of less than six guest rooms, or receipts from room rentals amounting to less than $500 for a full year's operation, [were] excluded. . . . Apartment hotels were canvassed and classified as hotels, provided a substantial portion of their receipts was derived from the accommodation of transient guests. Apartment houses, residential hotels catering exclusively to permanent guests, boarding houses, lodging houses, tourist homes or camps, resorts, Y.M.C.A.'s, Y.W.C.A.'s, dude ranches, club dormitories, and other similar establishments furnishing lodging and/or meals to guests [were] not considered hotels.[22]

Hotels in Small Towns and Small Cities

Many a frontier town grew up around a hotel. That is to say, in areas of new settlement, especially in the nineteenth century, once a new town site was staked out and lots put up for sale, many a town promoter opened, or had opened, a hotel.[23] A hotel not only served to host prospective buyers of real estate but also to persuade them as to the sincerity of a promoter's town-building intentions. Transportation was key to town prosperity, many a frontier settlement remaining little more than a "paper town" (a kind of speculative fiction), especially where competing places proved more successful at connecting with the outside world, whether by stagecoach, river, canal, or railroad. The quick and thorough settling-up of a surrounding locality, along with maturation of its transport linkages, fostered a town's prosperity as a farm trade center. Capturing county government was beneficial, and attracting a factory or two, of course, even more so.

Small-town hotels thrived, as did towns themselves, by aggressively competing with one another. Successful hotels were often enlarged or, as was sometimes done, replaced entirely by a new structure on site. Some of the small-town hotels encountered by early motorists, especially in the East and Midwest, originated as stagecoach inns. Such was the Nachusa Tavern at Dixon, Illinois, which remained, as late as 1918, the town's principal place of accommodation. A joint stock company was formed and a state license granted in 1837 to erect an inn at what was then Dixon's Ferry on the Rock River, a location midway on the wagon road that connected Peoria and another of Illinois's then-largest cities, Galena. The inn was enlarged in 1853. Closed during the Civil War, a new company was formed to refurbish and reopen it shortly after. In 1880, following the arrival of a railroad in town, the hotel was enlarged through the addition of a fourth story configured as a stylish mansard roof. In 1914 a matching addition was completed, doubling the building in size.[24]

By the 1920s old coaching inns were not only catering to motorists but to bus passengers also. The Wolf Creek Tavern at Wolf Creek, Oregon, built in 1861, enjoyed a brief renewal after World War I, mainly as a meal stop for motor bus passengers traveling between San Francisco and Portland. As the *Hotel Monthly* reported, "The building has been refurbished by its present owners in the simplest colonial style with excellent taste. While hosts of tourists in summer rob it of some of its charm, it is in winter that the motorist can best appreciate the cheery fireplaces and excellent meals. The building is a typical western . . . specimen with broad porches upstairs and down."[25] In Oregon other old inns were similarly operating at Canyonville and at Phoenix.

Railroading impacted towns variously. In the older parts of the country, where urban development preceded railroading, tracks were sometimes run along established streets directly to a town's leading coaching inn, the hotel then serving as a depot, linking, as it did, both coach and train travelers. In other instances, tracks were run along one edge of a town's street grid, necessitating a new depot, but one which, in the earliest years of railroading at least, was very much patterned after the traditional coaching inn. Purpose-built, track-side facilities combining station and hotel services enjoyed a brief period of popularity beginning in the 1850s. Examples on the Baltimore and Ohio Railroad included the Grafton House at Grafton, West Virginia, and the Queen City Hotel at Cumberland, Maryland. Still standing today is the Erie Railroad's Starrucca House at Susquehanna, Pennsylvania. In the West, railroad hotels and eateries immediate to the Atchison, Topeka, and Santa Fe

Railroad, run by its Fred Harvey subsidiary beginning in the 1880s, thrived through the middle of the twentieth century.[26]

After 1870 railroad-oriented hotels were increasingly moved away from track-sides, including the so-called railroad hotels that served train crews, as well as drummers and other travelers looking not only for convenience but also inexpensive accommodation. One such hotel, the Ayers Hotel at Harvard, Illinois, was opened in 1857 immediately across from the station of the Chicago and Northwestern Railroad. It contained fifty guest rooms in three stories. However, the bulk of its business came from food service, not so much in its dining room as in its large lunch room, which offered quick service to rail passengers disembarking during short train layovers.[27] The popularity of the nation's railroad hotels quickly eroded with the increased use of dining cars and sleeping cars on trains.

Most of America's small towns were laid out in response to railroad construction, street grids as often as not being oriented to a railroad's right-of-way. A town's Main Street either paralleled the tracks, often a block or two away, or crossed the tracks on the perpendicular. Most railroad-era hotels were located in business districts close to but, nonetheless, comfortably distanced from the smoke and noise of railroading. Although distances might be short, hotel-owned, horse-drawn "hacks" met all trains to solicit business and, importantly, convey would-be guests quickly and conveniently to a hotel's front door. Hotels might be within walking distance of a depot, but guests—at least the more affluent ones—seldom ventured to them on foot.

Through the nineteenth century, most small-town hotels, as well as many small-city hotels, were integrated physically into downtown business "blocks." They were housed, in other words, in a single building (or in a row or set of closely integrated buildings) containing a variety of functions: lodge halls, so-called "opera houses," and banks, but most frequently just retail stores. Such was the Hotel Byers at Mattoon, Illinois, a hotel built in the 1880s but pictured here in a 1950s postcard view (fig. 3). The Hotel Byers anchored one end of Mattoon's principal retail street, being immediately across from the depot of the Illinois Central Railroad but also on the new "Egyptian Trail" automobile highway (later U.S. 45). Additionally, the city hall, the public library, and the town's principal churches were all located close at hand. The hotel's large reception room and other public spaces were located on the second floor, accessed from the building's street-level entry both by a grand staircase and an elevator. Guest rooms were located on the hotel's third and fourth floors. The ground floor facing the street was divided into rental spaces for retailers. In the 1950s the businesses located there included a jeweler and optometrist shop, a drug store, a clothing store, and a store selling sewing machines (fig. 3). The development of a business block represented a grand gesture whereby a property owner could symbolize his or her importance as a community leader through both the upgraded look and the improved functioning of a town's business district.

Where a town's retail district was organized around a courthouse square, then inevitably its leading hotel faced the square, lesser hotels being relegated to side streets. Such was the case at Pocahontas, Arkansas. The accompanying map identifies the businesses extant around the town's square about 1910, at least as recalled by local residents some sixty years later (fig. 4). The St. Charles Hotel on the square's east side was the town's leading hotel. Immediately to the north, at one corner of the square, was Turner's Boarding House, obviously linked to Turner's Livery Stable adjacent. Note also that Bigger's Hotel and Bigger's Livery Stable, located to the north and farther off the square in the direction of the railroad depot, were also

FIGURE 3. Hotel Byers, Mattoon, Illinois, circa 1950. Here the postcard view places the hotel fully into the context of a town's Main Street. Authors' collection.

linked. Ease of entry and exit by visitors arriving and leaving town by train, as well as ease of access to hired carriages to convey them locally, is clearly implied. Also close to the square, but on the west, were two other hotels: Bank's Hotel and the Imboden Hotel. Downtown Pocahontas was a pedestrian place, the entirety of the town's business infrastructure being easily accessed on foot.

Integrated business blocks with hotel facilities typified Main Street America's so-called Gilded Age of the late nineteenth century. More commonly built after 1900, however, were stand-alone hotel buildings, such as the Majestic Hotel in

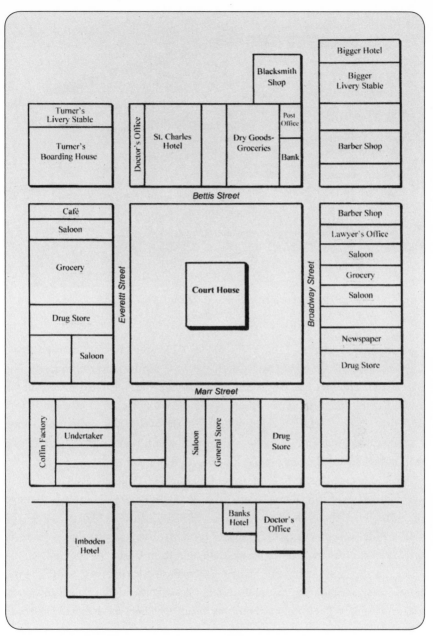

FIGURE 4. Downtown Pocahontas, Arkansas, circa 1910. Although made a county seat in the 1830s, with a new courthouse built in the 1870s, the town did not actually begin its vigorous growth until arrival of a railroad in the 1890s. From Catherine W. Deaver, "History of Hotels of Randolph County," *Randolph County Review* 1 (Apr. 1965): 42.

FIGURE 5. Majestic Hotel, Oconomowoc, Wisconsin, circa 1915. Authors' collection.

Oconomowoc, Wisconsin (fig. 5). The Model T pictured out front in an advertising postcard from about 1915 was clearly meant to signify auto convenience. The hotel's main entrance accessed a glassed-in veranda that supported an open porch at the second-floor level. Arriving guests entered a small lobby to face a reception desk to one side of which was located entry to the hotel's dining room. The hotel appears to be designed rather like a country inn, with some of the amenities of a resort hotel included—for example, the second-floor porch.

The same could be said for the Hotel Dalles in The Dalles, Oregon, pictured in still another advertising postcard, also from about 1915 (fig. 6). Located at the edge of downtown, rather than at its center as with Oconomowoc's Majestic Hotel, the Dalles Hotel was on the leading edge of business-district expansion. The town, located west of Portland in the scenic Columbia River Gorge, was not only on the Union Pacific Railroad but on the new Columbia River Highway, one of the nation's first scenic parkways to be purpose-built as such. Sections of the highway are still extant today. The hotel was built specifically to attract tourists arriving by car, although pictured in the photograph beside an automobile is a horse-drawn hack. There is only a token front porch.

After World War I new hotels in America's small towns and small cities were financed not so much by individual entrepreneurs as by investor syndicates often organized by local booster clubs or chambers of commerce. Once completed, operations tended to be handed over to a hotel-management firm, some hotels being

FIGURE 6. Hotel Dalles, The Dalles, Oregon, circa 1920. Authors' collection.

operated as part of a hotel chain. As hotels, they were fully intended to appeal to affluent motorists and thus to contrast, especially as self-standing buildings, with hotels left over from the railroad era. At the new Robert E. Lee Hotel in Lexington, Virginia, opened in the late 1920s, the symbolism of the traditional front porch was gone entirely. Instead the hotel sported a canopied front entrance very much intended as a welcoming gesture to guests arriving by car (fig. 7). Stationed there was a doorman, not just to open and close doors but also to help with luggage and arrange for parking.

In small cities, as opposed to small towns, investor syndicates tended to build at large scales, many a hotel being as impressive to the eye, both inside and out, as its big-city cousins. Hotels were often combined with parking garages, either immediately on site or located but a short distance away. In Texarkana, Arkansas, the Hotel McCartney was erected immediately adjacent to the city's Union Station (fig. 8). But clearly evident in the postcard view from the 1930s is the entry to its parking garage. Just inside that entry was the hotel's auto entrance, a place of arrival and departure fully protected from the elements. Ten stories tall and, therefore, one of Texarkana's tallest buildings, the McCartney stood out boldly, a clear symbol of community in a landmark sense.

Of course, places that were vigorous economically tended to garner most of the new hotel investments. Economic vitality fostered investment optimism. Travel writer Edward Hungerford wrote in 1913, "It is a pretty poor sort of American town

Robert E. Lee Hotel   Lexington, Virginia

FIGURE 7. Robert E. Lee Hotel, Lexington, Virginia, circa 1930. Authors' collection.

that cannot boast a new hotel these days. It may cling to old traditions in one case, and in another try to capitalize its hopes, but it is sure to boast on its Main Street somewhere a palatial sort of a box-like sky-scraper." Conjecturing for his readers a hypothetical town called Blissville, Hungerford continued, "The Blissville citizen who meets you at the train calls your attention to [the hotel's] unshrinking magnificence as you approach it from afar. 'The very pearl of metropolitan elegance,' he says slowly, thinking of his own stockholdings in the thing. 'It's the Waldorf of this end of the state.'"[28]

New hotels were logically located, or so David Ritchey, a consultant in hotel planning and operation, advised, on the "growth edge of downtown." "It is not only true that hotels should be located in the path of high class residential or business expansion," he wrote, "but also that in many instances the location of a new hotel will definitely encourage such growth."[29] In following the rule that real estate should not exceed 20 percent of the total cost of a hotel project, land just beyond downtown, especially that previously given to residential use, made economic sense. Real estate there was usually cheaper, and, as building sites, individual properties were usually larger. Being a residential land use of sorts, hotels, if carefully styled architecturally and, additionally, carefully landscaped, tended to blend into residential zones even along elite residential streets. Such was the case at Murfreesboro, Tennessee. The James K. Polk Hotel was "just removed" from the town's business section. "It sets back from the street to allow a grass carpeted lawn in front of the building. Large trees surround it, almost hiding it from view.

FIGURE 8. Hotel McCartney, Texarkana, Arkansas, circa 1925. Authors' collection.

The passing tourist gets snatches of views at the Colonial architecture of the brick building, and its white painted trim," the editors of the *Hotel Monthly* wrote enthusiastically. It was "in keeping with its surroundings," being "deeply shaded." "A small skyscraper," they concluded, "would have been an atrocity in this little town, whereas as the house built seems to blend in happily with the long established atmosphere of this old town."[30]

But other commentators argued that new hotels were best located at a major downtown intersection, even if several land parcels had to be purchased and several buildings had to be torn down at some expense to make way for it. "You ought to get the best corner in the city if you can," wrote H. L. Stevens, a member of the Kansas-Missouri-Oklahoma Hotel Association. "You need just as good a location as a department store, or an office building, or a five and ten-cent store or anything else." The reason was quite simple. Ground rents charged for retail space on the hotel's ground floor would cover the extra cost. "Theoretically," he argued, "the location should cost you nothing; the sub-rents should carry your lease, so you should have nothing to charge against your [guest] rooms."[31]

America's small towns were losing population, most of them by 1920 having reached (or passed) a population peak. More and more small-town people, and farm people also, were moving to the nation's cities where job opportunities were plentiful. Small towns remained very much dependent on railroading. In the nineteenth century, railroads had competed vigorously among themselves for geographical prominence, expanding branch lines, for example, into virtually every locality where farming, mining, or other economic activity was possible. In retrospect, they built too many lines, thus fostering too many towns. There was much redundancy built into the nation's urban infrastructure, a situation made painfully obvious with the coming of the motor car and motor truck. Already by 1920 auto use had discouraged retailing in the nation's smallest urban places, people being able to motor off to larger places where enhanced scale of business invariably wrought not only broader lines of merchandise but also lower prices. In many a village or hamlet, storefronts stood vacant or were only marginally utilized.

And in many a very small town, older hotel buildings stood vacant in the 1920s or were converted into apartment houses or given to other uses. By the 1950s their life as transient hotels could in many places barely be remembered. Historian Lewis Atherton reminisced of the Midwest: "Even hamlets were likely to have hotels because of the leisurely moving pace of travel. Some village hotels were two and three stories tall, with long porches, chairs and settees, where guests cooled off on drowsy summer evenings and lazily watched the parade of strolling villagers. Livery-stable advertisements above the registration desk in the main office called attention to facilities available for side trips. Sample room for drummers, perhaps a 'saloon parlor' with piano, and a dining room were common." On floors above, the guest rooms were furnished, he continued, "with bed, chairs, pitcher and basin, and a chamber pot."[32]

In towns with faltering economies, disinvestment rather than reinvestment was clearly the order of the day. If not physically run down, then the old railroad-era hotels of these places tended to lack modern amenities. They were functionally, if not physically, obsolete. Many proprietors through the 1920s were only holding on, delaying the inevitability of quitting business. As journalist Martha Haskell Clark wrote, "The American country hotel has won disfavor wherever the unwilling foot of the train-bound transient or the ubiquitous tire of the vacation motorist has paused. Its general aspect awakens little anticipation on the part of the entering guest, save the anticipation of a speedy release."[33] Such was the fictional hotel that Sinclair Lewis dubbed the "American House" in his novel *Work of Art:*

> The American House had thirty-four bedrooms; twenty-nine singles
> and five doubles. It was . . . a vigorously modern hotel; it had gas instead
> of kerosene lamps; and in the office was a telephone, in a long dark box
> like an up-ended coffin. Each of the single rooms . . . contained one
> wooden bed, the varnish a little cracked, one straight chair, one strip of
> carpet beside the bed, lace curtains, very dingy, a gas light in so crafty a
> position on the wall that it neither illuminated the mirror nor enabled

the guest to read in bed, one washstand with pitcher and bowl, painted with lilacs or a snow-scene, a slop jar standing on a strip of linoleum not very successfully imitating marble, with white oilcloth tacked on the wall behind it, one cake of streaky soap, one thin towel, and a concentration of the prevailing smell.

But the double rooms were more elaborate. They added an extra towel, an extra straight chair, a table, and usually a calendar on the wall.[34]

On the other hand, in small-town hotels that were new or had been substantially upgraded in catering to an automobile crowd guests often found themselves in surroundings very much equivalent to what most big-city hotels offered. Unlike most big-city hotels, however, guests still tended to receive personal attention. For the smaller scale of things, service tended to remain highly personalized. Of course, it was to big-city hotels that everyone looked when making judgments. Especially did the grand hotels of the nation's metropolises set hotel industry standards. Innovations tended to be introduced first in the big cities and then adopted later down the urban hierarchy in smaller places. But this was not always true. Charles Baur, a druggist in Terre Haute, Indiana, bought the city's leading hotel, the Terre Haute House, the rambling Victorian building that predated the hotel of the 1920s. In it he installed the first electric generating plant to operate in that city, making the hotel one of the first in the nation to be entirely lit by electricity. In the 1890s he was the first to introduce mechanical refrigeration into the hotel kitchen. He was first to place electric fans in guest rooms.[35] Perhaps, it was his way of extending to his guests small-town courtesy.

Hotels and Locality-Based Community

"We live in a changed world," exclaimed Illinois senator Harold Kessinger, speaking to the Executive's Club of Chicago. It was a world fraught with new technology, he said. It was a world dominated not just with new ways of doing, but of being. He argued: "We have the movie eye—we look without seeing; the radio ear—we hear without remembering; the newspaper brain—we read without thinking; the autoitis and mad desire to drive toward nowhere so fast you can't see anything on your way and when you get there cram a lot of food in your stomach, put a little gas in your car and drive back, and all for no reason at all except that we have a nervousness and a restlessness almost uncontrolled, seldom restrained, that we cannot stand to be by ourselves or quiet."[36] The hotel industry assigned many of these urges: certainly the constant coming and going of the American people, but also their need to congregate, associate, or, to put it differently, gather communally even if only superficially.

The nation's approximately twenty-six thousand hotels in 1930 contained some 1.5 million guest rooms, and were valued at some $5 billion, the hotel industry ranking ninth among the nation's industries with revenues well over a billion dollars annually.[37] It was not a bad return on investment. Hotel buildings, begun with optimism before the Stock Market Crash of 1929, continued to open to the public even as the Great Depression deepened. But by 1935 industry receipts had fallen by over 25 percent, although hotel employment continued to hold at about three hundred thousand people. Commentators stressed that the hotel industry primarily comprised small business operations, some 90 percent of all America's hotels having fewer than a hundred rooms.[38] The industry was also one of the nation's most evenly spread in geographical terms. There might be fewer hotels in the American South per capita, but otherwise hotels were distributed more or less in direct proportion to population density. The reason seemed obvious. No locality—no community of any size—could function, it was said, without the services that a hotel traditionally offered.

Community, at least locality-based community, was something that could either be ignored (and even denied) or embraced (and even fostered). By locality-based community we mean social interaction based substantially on people's geographical proximity: people in a locality forming lasting communal ties primarily on the basis of propinquity. Of course, a hotel was a place for transients. As strangers in a locality, they could (and, indeed, it was expected that they would) remain largely anonymous, both to one another and to locals. In a hotel's public spaces, relationships among transients tended to form spontaneously but also readily dissolve, all through the serendipity of chance encounter. Encouraged was the sort of exchange that foreign visitors to the United States had long described as socially leveling. Superficially at least, Americans in hotels accepted one another on equal terms, thus seemingly validating American democracy. And that encounter, as superficial as it might be, was indeed often quite gregarious. It was a gregariousness meant to be seen, to be heard, and to be thought about, but not one that was necessarily meant to be remembered. Social relationships quickly evolved only to dissolve just as rapidly once strangers went their separate ways.

On the other hand, a hotel was also a place for promoting community very much of a long-lasting, more tangible sense. Importantly, a hotel was a place for promoting social interaction among residents of a locality. Indeed, most of the new auto-era hotels originated with that idea prime in mind. True, localities needed to entertain strangers from away. In so doing, hotel proprietors stood to profit in a business sense. But an entire town could profit from a hotel also, at least in a social sense. Locals, as well as strangers, used hotel public spaces. For certain kinds of community initiative and social involvement, hotel meeting rooms, hotel dining rooms, and other facilities were often vital. They provided, for example, neutral ground whereby political and other social factions, despite their differences, might find an overarching sense of commonality. The hotel was not a church with a specific religious cause. It was not the town hall, where politics was expected. It was not a private club privileging some but not others. Its public spaces, in other words, did not necessarily sustain predetermined social agendas, save, perhaps, the need for decorum and gentility under the patronizing gaze of a business proprietor.

The word "community," like the word "hotel," is also something of a chameleon term that has been variously stretched in meaning over time. Sociologist Suzanne Keller saw community as "akin to an organism where the whole is more important than individual members."[39] That is how we see it. The kind of community that we emphasize is that of locality where members share, for whatever reason (residency, work, and the like), an identifiable territory. It is territory easily taken for granted but also territory that inspires passionate defense when demeaned. It is where people sense they belong. It is where they feel comfortably "at home." Locality-based community may not be as important as it once was. Peoples' lives are no longer so limited geographically as, for example, in the railroad era when it was relatively expensive and inconvenient to leave a town's geographical confines with regularity. Most socializing, therefore, was locality-based. In other words, localities were substantially turned in on themselves. Today, we live in an age of vastly enhanced geographical mobility. "Physical and social impediments to spatial mobility once restricted almost everyone's activities and personal relations to a single place," sociologist Claude S. Fisher observed, "and thus consigned [people] to be a member of a local corporate group." But today people in a locality can pick and choose their involvements one with another. They have more leeway to interact or not. People thus live more in localities of "limited liability," he argued.[40]

Literary historian Park Dixon Goist asked, "If community consists of people in a given geographic area interacting together and sharing one or more common tie, where should we look to find it actually functioning?" Where in modern society are we most likely to find people binding together in feelings of territorial solidarity? Where is it, in other words, that community, especially locality-based community, tends "to happen?"[41] For America's small towns and small cities, at least early in the motoring age, the hotel was one important place to look. It is, therefore, something that very much needs exploring when considering America's Main Street hotels. The nation's new automobility extended the geographical reach of the typical American, thus breaking down the restricting ties of locality. But all across America automobility also renewed hotel development, giving localities new venues for socializing.

* * *

Importantly, a new kind of hotel, as well as new hotels, opened in America's small towns and small cities, especially between 1910 and the Great Depression. These hotels were intended for a new clientele: the nation's affluent motorists. Built to be up-to-date, and thus attractive and comfortable, they did not, however, fully embrace what is now recognized as automobile convenience. They were not, in other words, fundamentally auto-oriented. Most were programed and configured rather like the hotels of the railroad era except that they were much larger, better equipped, more luxurious, and located well away from the noise and commotion of railroading. Importantly, they tended to stand alone and not as part of a business "block." Through the 1920s, more and more small-town and small-city hotels provided separate automobile entrances. And they provided parking garages also, if not directly on-site then but a short distance away, arriving and departing guests being served by parking valets. If hotels did not fully embrace motoring convenience, as the new motels surely did in successfully diverting patronage away from hotels, they did embrace motorists, giving them comfortable and reasonably convenient overnight accommodation.

Importantly, hotels also served their localities as upscale community centers, especially through their dining rooms, event rooms, and (after Prohibition) their cocktail lounges. These venues were meant not only to service transients from afar but to attract locals as well. Indeed, community boosters, it could be argued, actually targeted the new motoring public as a means of creating for their localities community resource, the motoring of transients thus turned to community benefit. Small-town and small-city hotels were very much conceived and operated as community amenities, a kind of benefit from the early days of motoring largely forgotten and thus little appreciated today. In America today, private rather than public purpose seems increasingly to prevail, at least with regard to the way society plans and manages space. The automobile, along with television, the personal computer, and many other recent technological innovations, seems more to champion individual benefit over collective good. And yet there was a time when automobility, for all its support of individual prerogative, was also turned to community purpose.

LAYING OUT THE HOUSE

As the new twentieth century dawned, most of America's small towns continued to rely on hotels built in decades after the Civil War, America's so-called Gilded Age, when railroading became the nation's predominant form of transportation. Storefronts shouldered one another in Main Street business blocks. Hotels, if only by their size, stood fully noticeable. Such was the case in Gopher Prairie, the fictional Minnesota town that Sinclair Lewis described in *Main Street*. Lewis's heroine, Carol Kennicott, just arrived as the new bride of the town's doctor, walked the streets of Gopher Prairie to get her bearings: "She glanced through the fly-specked windows of the most pretentious building in sight, the one place which welcomed strangers and determined their opinion of the charm and luxury of Gopher Prairie—the Minniemashie House. It was a tall lean shabby structure three stories of yellow-streaked wood, the corners covered with sanded pine slabs purporting to symbolize stone. In the hotel office she could see a stretch of bare unclean floor, a line of ricketly chairs with brass cuspidors between, a writing desk with advertisements in mother-of-pearl letters upon the glass-covered back. The dining-room beyond was a jungle of stained table-cloths and catsup bottles."[1] Such was Lewis's way of introducing his readers to the typical American small town.

There were far too many railroad lines built, especially across the Midwest and, accordingly, far too many small towns established at intervals along them. Competition town to town, locality to locality, was intense, creating something of a scramble, town to town, to stay up to date. That meant that towns needed to orient themselves more to the automobile and the hotels in them to guests who arrived increasingly by car rather than by train. Not only was it important for small towns to be located on at least one improved automobile road and have garage facilities available, but a quality hotel was also needed to tend appropriately to motorist needs. Economic growth in the nation's small cities, sustained by industrial expansion and the rise of regional wholesaling among other commercial activities, readily fostered hotel renovation and, more to the story we tell here, new hotel construction. In small cities, hotel development very much emulated what was going on in the nation's big cities. As Theodore Dreiser wrote in traveling across Upstate New York, "We were having breakfast at Elmira, a place much like Binghamton, in the customary 'Rathskeller-Grill-Café de Berlin.' This one was embossed with gold paper and Teutonic hunting scenes, and contained the usual heavy mission tables, to say nothing of a leftover smell of cigarettes burned the night before."[2] It was easy, of course, to treat small hotels in small places, even in small cities, satirically. Small-town and small-city hotels, especially the new ones, were, after all, largely imitative of the grand hotels—if not of Berlin, then certainly of New York City or Chicago.

Thus did motoring stimulate a new round of hotel building. Nonetheless, most of the new hotels remained traditional in layout, only larger and grander. Attracting the motoring public led to hotel renovation and to new hotel construction, but the formulas for hotel success worked out in the railroad era remained very much in force. Public spaces might be larger and certainly fancier in their furnishings. Guest rooms might be better equipped. But not until after World War I was the automobile itself deliberately accommodated, although more through hindsight than through forethought. Motorists were welcomed to secondary auto entrances where, informally attired (and, indeed, usually physically tired and emotionally drained), they could alight from their cars beyond formal public scrutiny. And, of course, there were the new parking garages where vehicles might be stored overnight under roof, something especially important before enclosed auto bodies were popularized. Even then, parking garages were usually located at some distance away, even when owned and operated by a hotel itself. Full auto-orientation was something that motels would embrace.[3]

The architectural firms that specialized in hotel construction were numerous. Also, hotel outfitting firms evolved to specialize in furnishing and equipping hotels. Trade journals, such as the *Hotel Monthly* published in Chicago, carried feature articles and advertising copy to fully illustrate emergent hotel fads and fashions. Consequently, much standardization came to the fore, the new hotels being built across America coming to share much in common. Nonetheless, each hotel project, irrespective of its size, stood very much as a unique enterprise. It was intended that each hotel property, even those owned and/or managed as part of a hotel chain, should have distinctive personality: character conducive to a distinctive sense of place. Hotels were to reflect their localities, many being named and deliberately "themed" accordingly. The nation's hotels, including its small-town and small-city hotels, embodied a kind of difference through sameness. While sharing much in common, hotels were still intended to be distinguishable one from another. Ultimately, it would be the motel chains that would embrace near absolute sameness from one location to another.

Laying Out the Small Hotel

The *Hotel Monthly,* as with most trade journals serving the hotel industry, tended to emphasize big-city hotel development and thus big hotels. But in 1906 its editors admitted that the majority of their readers were, in fact, more interested in the "plans, furnishings and methods" of the "consistent two-dollar-a-day country hotel" than those of "the big and swell Waldorf-Astorias and Bellevue-Stratfords." The reason was quite simple: "There are one-hundred small country hotels to one big metropolitan hotel of the first class."[4] There followed an annual design contest, one that invited architects to submit plans for workable hotel buildings of modest size. The 1912 contest laid out the following design specifications—specifications which, in and of themselves, suggested what a small-town or small-city hotel might be. Called for was a fifty-room hotel costing no more than one hundred thousand dollars, a hotel "adapted for commercial and automobile patronage":

> The conditions are:
> A CORNER LOT fronting 100 feet on the main street, and with depth of 150 feet; an alley to run in back of the lot; the main street front to be built in the adjoining building line.
> THE GROUND FLOOR to have:
> A lobby, approximately 50 x 40 feet;
> A dining room to seat 50;
> A lunch room with ten stools;
> Kitchen with storeroom and ice boxes adjoining arranged for the control of stores;
> Five combination sample and sleeping rooms, 15 x 20 feet, to be equipped with wall beds;
> A barber shop;
> Two business stores for rent, and basement space for them;
> No bar; no billiard room;

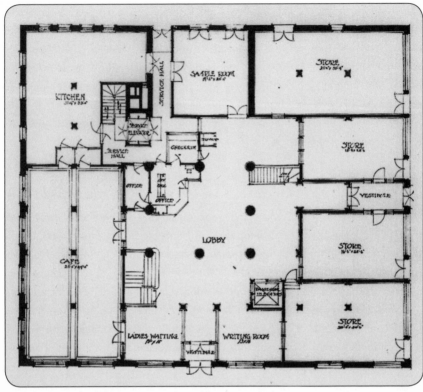

FIGURE 9. Ground-floor plan, Hotel Van Dervoort, Paragould, Arkansas. From "New 50-Room Hotel in Arkansas Town of 7,500 Population," *Hotel Monthly* 22 (Oct. 1914): 80.

> A garage with capacity for two cars. . . ;
> There should be a commodious porch.
> The writing room to be in the lobby; also a long distance phone.
> A small parlor and retiring room for ladies on the office floor, so as
> to be under control of the desk.

All plans submitted were to be published, but the winning entry would also command a prize of one hundred dollars.[5]

More important, the *Hotel Monthly* published more and more articles featuring hotels either planned for or recently opened in small towns and small cities. Articles were highly visual, including diagrams, photographs, graphs, and tables as appropriate. For example, featured in the October 1914 issue were the plans for the fifty-room, four-story Hotel Van Dervoort to be built in Paragould, Arkansas.[6] The ground-floor layout was to be organized around a lobby with registration desk,

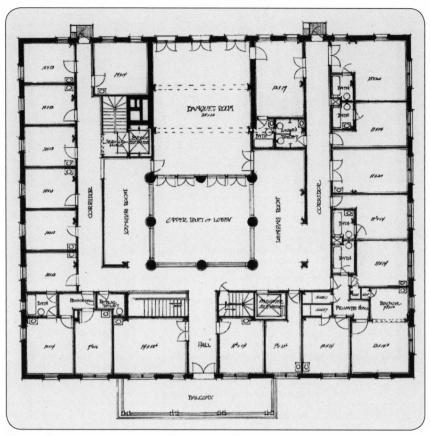

FIGURE 10. Second-floor plan, Hotel Van Dervoort, Paragould, Arkansas. From "New 50-Room Hotel in Arkansas Town of 7,500 Population," *Hotel Monthly* 22 (Oct. 1914): 81.

check room, and elevator connected by a short hallway and small vestibule with the street (fig. 9). A "ladies waiting room" would be located to one side of the front entrance and a "writing room" on the other. A sample room, four retail spaces for renting, and a café and kitchen would complete the ground-floor arrangement. Sample rooms were spaces where a sales person could display wares during the day and, in some hotels at least, also sleep at night. A large banquet room was to be located on the hotel's second floor, along with several small reception rooms, twenty guest rooms (six with private bath and toilet), and two public toilets (one for men and one for women) to service the remaining rooms (fig. 10). Guest rooms were to be accessed off long linear hallways; a short hallway would give access to a small outside balcony perched over the front door.

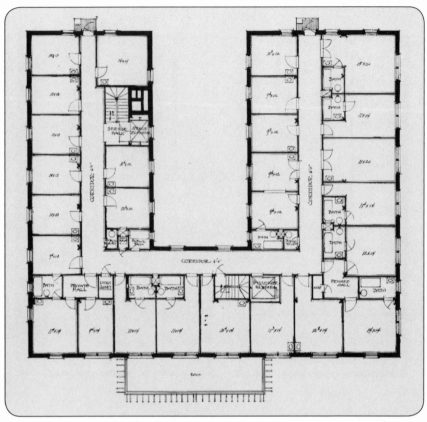

FIGURE 11. Plan for third and fourth Floors, Hotel Van Dervoort, Paragould, Arkansas. From "New 50-Room Hotel in Arkansas Town of 7,500 Population," *Hotel Monthly* 22 (Oct. 1914): 82.

The *Hotel Monthly* provided the following specifications for the two upper floors. They were

> to be devoted almost entirely to bed rooms, every room to have abundance of outside light, and to be equipped with hot and cold running water, a clothes closet, but no telephone.
>
> Ten of the rooms to be considered as court rooms to rent for 75 cents.
>
> Fifteen rooms without bath or toilet to rent for $1.00.
>
> Ten rooms with toilet (a few of them may also have shower) to rent for $1.25.
>
> Ten rooms with bath and toilet at $1.50 (All baths, toilets and showers to have outside window light.)
>
> Separate public toilets for men and women, but no public bath.[7]

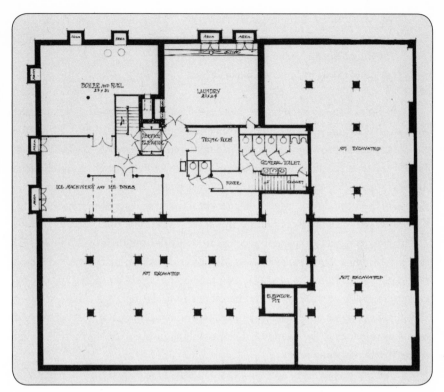

FIGURE 12. Basement plan, Hotel Van Dervoort, Paragould, Arkansas. From "New 50-Room Hotel in Arkansas Town of 7,500 Population," *Hotel Monthly* 22 (Oct. 1914): 83.

Since much of the Hotel Van Dervoort's second floor was to be given over to public space, two additional floors of guest rooms were called for (fig. 11). On each of these floors, seven of the guest rooms were to have private baths, and two would share a bath and toilet. However, fifteen rooms would be without either amenity, two public toilets being provided accordingly.

The Hotel Van Dervoort was to occupy an 85 x 100 foot lot, only one-third of which was to be excavated for a basement. That space was to be divided between a boiler room with coal bin, a refrigeration room with ice boxes and an ice-making machine, a laundry, a trunk-storage facility, and a small foyer connected directly to the lobby above, off of which was to be placed a coat closet and a "general toilet" for men (fig. 12). Women were to use the ladies' toilet situated on the second floor, the facility also intended to service guest rooms on that floor.

Basement specifications for the *Hotel Monthly*'s 1912 design contest were minimal:

THE BASEMENT to contain a small laundry;

Public toilet and lavatory conveniences in limited quantity;

A heating plant and cellar storage room.

The hotel to buy its light and make its heat. [8]

Every hotel had its "back regions," areas closed to guests where hotel logistics were overseen. For example, hotel basements tended to be off-limits, at least in part. Many hotels provided bedrooms, a lounge, and sometimes dining facilities for employees, thus guaranteeing that adequate help was on the premises at all times. At the Hotel Russell-Lamson in Waterloo, Iowa, quarters for the "help" occupied a section of the second floor closed off from guest rooms and accessed by a restricted stairway rising directly from behind the hotel checkroom. But only female help was housed; men were expected to commute to work from their own homes. Men as well as women, however, were accorded their own separate dining and lounge facilities.[9] Located close at hand was the office of the hotel's housekeeping department, along with storage closets for linen and janitorial supplies. A service stairway and service elevator offered access throughout the building. Service stairways in hotels were usually "fireproofed," thus providing guests with alternative escape routes in times of emergency.

Hiring an Architect

Investors in new hotel projects invariably employed architects, as was generally true of any expensive building project even in the smallest urban places. The Hotel Van Dervoort, for example, was estimated to cost fifty-five thousand dollars, an amount that provided neither for land purchase nor for furnishing or equipping the building once it was completed.[10] Before hiring an architect, however, investors needed a business plan, one that would fully inform the architectural program. Procedures for developing a "functional plan," as it was called, were outlined in *Hotel Planning and Outfitting: Commercial, Residential, Recreational,* an idea book edited by C. Stanley Taylor and Vincent R. Bliss for the Albert Pick Company, a firm merged in 1928 with one of its competitors, the Barth Company, to form the industry's leading supply house. Clear justification, they said, needed to back up every anticipated expenditure. In other words, everything in a hotel needed to be fully rationalized. The first step was to consider carefully a town's local economy, especially with regard to its carrying capacity for hotel services. The second was to select an appropriate site. The third was to determine which hotel services were to be emphasized. Finally came the financial plan. Up front, investors needed to make a direct connection between each anticipated revenue stream, the planned space that would sustain it, and overall debt retirement. Each profit center needed to return its share on total investment. Only then could the elements of the architectural program be outlined so that once an architect was hired, he or she might concentrate on planning "a building rather than a business."[11]

Location was important. Not any site would do. The best situation, of course, was close to the center of business activity. C. Stanley Taylor, writing on his own in *Hotel Management,* another leading trade journal of the day, emphasized the need for "a nice balance between the requirements of traveling men and automobile tourists." The site needed to be "in a good developing business district, within easy distance from the principal railroad station but not near enough to subject patrons to the nuisances of noise and smoke." The site also needed to be "accessible to the important routes of tourist traffic." "Find the right site and pay the price," he advised.[12]

Hotels of differing size varied not simply by scale but according to the types of revenue-producing space they were to contain—the kinds of "front regions" they were to provide. In its planning and outfitting guide, the Albert Pick Company suggested a checklist for hotels sized at 75, 150, and 225 rooms respectively (table 1). As hotel buildings needed to be carefully scaled to anticipated revenue streams, another checklist was provided in elaboration (table 2). It is important to note that hotel profits tended to derive more from services rendered in hotel public spaces (dining rooms, banquet rooms, and so on) than from the renting of private guest rooms. Before national prohibition set in following World War I, sale of food and drink represented the largest single hotel revenue stream, as it would for most American hotels after the lifting of Prohibition in the 1930s. Indeed, it could be argued that before and after Prohibition the typical hotel in the United States rented guest rooms primarily as a means of guaranteeing restaurant and bar patronage. Public spaces in hotels tended to be spacious. Guest rooms, on the other hand, tended to be very small, just large enough to contain a bed, nightstand, chest of drawers, and a chair. In popular parlance, they were barely large enough to "swing a cat."

With impressive hotel lobbies and dining rooms, hotel proprietors hoped to attract guests out of the narrow confines of their private rooms to spend money. Nonetheless, hotel planners could not simply lavish money on public spaces thus to make them attractive. Investors especially needed to watch the non-revenue-generating space they allowed. Utility rather than amenity needed to drive the bottom line always. Lobbies, dining rooms, and ballrooms, for example, might be spectacular to look at, but they could also be expensive to heat, cool, and otherwise maintain as a part of normal hotel operations. It was important to remember that hotel operating costs varied according to building volume, and not just according to

TABLE 1. Types of Revenue-Producing Space in Commercial Hotels*

Average 75-Room Hotel	Guest rooms (with and without bath)
	Sample rooms
	Concessions, lobby stand, and 1 or 2 shops
	Restaurant (often omitted in small hotels)
	Private dining rooms
	Club rooms (under local management)
Average 150-Room Hotel	Guest rooms, suites, and sample rooms
	Restaurant and coffee shop
	Concessions, news, cigars, etc.
	Barber shop
	Stores and shops
	Banquet and ballroom
	Club rooms, private dining rooms
Average 225-Room Hotel	Guest rooms, single and double
	Sample rooms and suites
	Concessions
	Barber shop, beauty parlor, Turkish bath
	Stores and shops
	Restaurant, grill room, coffee shop or tea room
	Banquet and convention room
	Club rooms and private dining rooms
	Garage space (separate building)

*This checklist indicates the various uses of hotel space from an earning viewpoint as based on general experience in hotels of different sizes. Adapted from C. Stanley Taylor and Vincent R. Bliss, eds., *Hotel Planning and Outfitting: Commercial, Residential, Recreational* (Chicago: Albert Pick-Barth Companies, 1928), 15.

building square footage. If, for example, a 10-percent reduction in a planned hotel's public spaces appeared necessary, given, for example, a recalculation of anticipated revenue, much of that space might be gained by cutting down ceiling heights rather than by eliminating floor space. All such decisions, of course, had trade-offs. Every change in a plan had to be carefully assessed in terms of potential impact.

The architect, once hired, had the responsibility of developing architectural drawings capable of sustaining the business plan. He or she was responsible for providing reasonable cost estimates and overseeing construction in cost terms. That is, it was the architect's duty to insure that contractors abided by the building plans and in ways that stayed within cost estimates. To the extent that unfore-

TABLE 2. Average Sources and Values of Commercial Hotel Revenue

Sources of Revenue	75 Rooms	150 Rooms	225 Rooms
Rooms[a]	$57,480	$114,960	$172,440
Restaurant[b]	52,600	108,000	167,000
Concessions, all types	1,800	3,600	6,000
Service[c]	8,000	20,000	38,000
Sub-rentals, stores, shops, etc.	4,000	5,000	21,000
Total	$123,880	$261,560	$404,440

[a]Average $3 per day estimated on basis of 70 percent occupancy.
[b]Including all forms of food service.
[c]Barber shop, manicure, valet, laundry, etc.
Adapted from C. Stanley Taylor and Vincent R. Bliss, eds., *Hotel Planning and Outfitting: Commercial, Residential, Recreational* (Chicago: Albert Pick-Barth Companies, 1928), 15.

seen problems were encountered in the building process, it was the architect's responsibility to provide the client full information relative to remedial action. Most architects worked in tandem with architectural engineers, heating and plumbing contractors, and interior decorators. Contingencies that needed anticipating were both diverse and complex, as outlined by C. Stanley Taylor in *Hotel Management* (table 3).[13]

It was desirable to find an architect fully experienced in building hotels. Many complaints were leveled at architect incompetence—for example, the walling-in of bathrooms and subsequent discovery that bathtubs would not fit through finished door openings, or the installation of windows of varied sizes that inflated the costs of shades and curtains.[14] But very pleased was the owner of the new Hotel Altamount in Hazleton, Pennsylvania. "I want to congratulate you," he wrote his architect in 1924, "on the success with which you have worked out the problems in connection with the Hazleton Hotel. Personally, I am much pleased with your arrangement of the public space. This arrangement not only gives a light interior and the maximum of income producing space, but you have so arranged your exchange that you can reach every portion of the building from it, with the minimum of effort and inconvenience."[15] The hotel's manager-to-be elaborated in a complimentary letter of his own: "The interior of the hotel has been worked out to the best advantage possible. The main lobby is reached by a short stairway from each entrance and this floor is so arranged that the main dining room and banquet hall at each end

TABLE 3. Plans and Specifications

Architecture	Construction	Equipment	Decoration
All floor plans	General type[a]	Plumbing	Designs and plans
Type of construction	Floors	Heating	Floor coverings
Exterior design	Partitions	Ventilating	Drapes and covers
Windows, shades, screens	Roofs and roofing	Electric wiring	Wall hangings
Entrances—doors	Fireproofing	Telephone system	Curtains
Exterior architectural accessories	Acoustics	Inner-communicating system	Decorations
Store fronts	Plastering	Lighting	Lighting fixtures
Architectural details	Exterior metal work	Elevators	Public room furniture
Ground improvements	Tank housing	Fire protection	Bric-a-brac
Interior architectural design[b]	Skylights	Power plant	Office furniture
Standard and special design[c]	Shafts and ducts	Pumps, tanks	Wall finishing
Wall finishes	Fire escapes	Refrigeration	Decorative tile, marble, etc.
Floor surfacing materials	Stairs	Food preparation	Ornamental metal work
Special problems of design	Window openings	Food service	Guest room furniture
	Door openings	Office	Guest room accessories
	Water proofing	Barber shop, valet, etc.	Paintings, murals, etc.
	Built-in furniture	Laundry	Restaurant furniture
	Closets, cabinets, etc.	Room service	Restaurant decorations
	Special construction[d]	Bathrooms, lavatories, etc.	Shop and store interiors
	Chimneys and stacks	Special service	Mirrors and glass work
	Vaulted ceilings and special structural effects		Cabinet workspecial structural effects

[a]Includes steel or concrete, etc.
[b]Applies to both public and semi-public rooms.
[c]Applies to guest rooms.
[d]Applies to kitchens, bathrooms, etc.

Adapted from C. Stanley Taylor and Vincent R. Bliss, eds., *Hotel Planning and Outfitting: Commercial, Residential, Recreational* (Chicago: Albert Pick-Barth Companies, 1928), 15.

of the building are easily accessible from the kitchen, which is located between the two rooms. The general arrangement of this floor is admirable for the handling of conventions or functions of any kind."[16]

Public Space

"Back regions" might enable a hotel to function, but "front regions" were what sold the hotel services. It was there that the skill of the architect as designer was, perhaps, most important. But the architect's role as artistic stylist was most visible in a hotel's exterior, especially its facade. Whereas hotel buildings of the railroad era tended to be quite utilitarian in appearance, or were styled to blend into Main Street building blocks, most of the new hotels of the early twentieth century stood quite alone, configured to look fashionable following one or another popular design motif. Early in the twentieth century, tall buildings—those that displayed definite verticality—tended to be divided into three sections through alternate use of various cladding materials, and/or introduction of ornamentation. It was the modern tripartite building scheme first perfected in Chicago by architects such as Louis Sullivan and based on the ideal of the classical column with its base, shaft, and capital. It was a scheme especially appropriate to buildings supported by steel-girder frames, as were most tall buildings after 1910, including hotels. Buildings so supported were lightly clad in brick, stone, tile, or terra cotta, building weight being carried down through a steel frame rather than through the walls.

The ground floor of the Hotel Wicomico in Salisbury, Maryland, was clad in sandstone, its distinctive window and door treatments fully differentiating it from upper floors (fig. 13). Above, the building was evenly clad in brick, the much smaller windows of each floor sized and regularly spaced in a distinctive rhythm. Only the top floor was set apart by additional stonework, including that of the ornamental window hoods. For further emphasis, the building was topped by a bracketed cornice. The building carried so-called Beaux Arts styling, the architect having taken many of his design cues from traditional classicism as expounded by the influential École des Beaux Arts in Paris.

Low-profile buildings—those that displayed clear horizontality—tended to be styled in one or another period motif. Especially popular was the Georgian Revival, along with its watered-down Colonial Revival version: classicism merged with historical romanticism to suggest a kind of pastness or historicity. Through the first two decades of the twentieth century, the Arts and Craft movement inspired "mission-style" buildings imitative of buildings in Spain's New World colonies, especially in California and the American Southwest but in Florida also. Common elsewhere was use of English Revival styling. One such hotel was the Urbana-Lincoln Hotel

FIGURE 13. Hotel Wicomico, Salisbury, Maryland. From C. Stanley Taylor and Vincent R. Bliss, eds., *Hotel Planning and Outfitting: Commercial, Residential, Recreational* (Chicago: Albert Pick–Barth Companies, 1928): 57.

opened at Urbana, Illinois, in 1923. According to the *Hotel Monthly,* architect J. W. Royer "kept as far away as he could from the box idea" in "producing a Tudor-Gothic structure, eye-pleasing, [and] typical of the old-style inns of England."[17]

The central space of every hotel was its lobby. This was where guests entered. It was where first impressions were formed. Consequently, a lobby needed to fully reinforce the guest's proclivity to be a guest. Thus a lobby had to be not only reasonably spacious but also aesthetically impressive. At the Urbana-Lincoln, the English Revival theme was carried throughout the hotel's interior public spaces (fig. 14). "The lobby 25–16 feet is entered thru a loggia," reported the *Hotel Monthly.* "The room is Tudor-Gothic, the walls oak paneled to a height of nine feet, plaster to the ceiling; the ceiling is supported by wood beams. The furniture is walnut, upholstered. Grouped around the lobby are the desk, check rooms, manager's office, news and cigar stand, phone booths, and the usual metropolitan conveniences."[18]

Buildings that displayed Beaux Arts tendencies on the outside also tended to display them on the inside. At the twelve-story George Washington Hotel in Washington, Pennsylvania, the two-story lobby was surrounded by a mezzanine floor

FIGURE 14. Lobby of the Urbana-Lincoln Hotel, Urbana, Illinois. From "The Urbana-Lincoln Hotel in Urbana, Illinois," *Hotel Monthly* 32 (Apr. 1924): 71.

supported by square columns, the base of the mezzanine carrying a classically in-spired frieze (fig. 15). Similar ornamentation played out on the woodwork of the registration desk. Located over the desk was a large portrait of George Washington in a pose reminiscent of the heroes of ancient Greece and Rome. Adjacent was an American flag.

The eleven-floor Hotel Vicksburg in Vicksburg, Mississippi, was fully contem-porary on the outside but historically themed on the inside. Occupying a sloping site, the building sported two main entrances, one on the south and one on the west, each providing distinctive entry to the hotel. From the south, one walked directly into the lobby. On the west, however, one could either go up a short flight of steps into the lobby or down into a hallway that accessed the hotel's barber shop, men's wash room, and men's grill room. Over the stairs was a niche where Union and Confederate battle flags were floodlit at all times. Mounted nearby was a map of Vicksburg's Civil War battlefield. The *Hotel Monthly* reported: "The major por-tion of the lobby is used for lounge. It is of two-story height and has a mezzanine on three sides. It was designed to represent a baronial hall in an English manor house. The walls are paneled in dark oak squares to the height of the mezzanine and above this they are surfaced with caen stone finish. A carved oak balustrade borders the mezzanine. The ceiling is coved and from it hangs three large silver chandeliers of 'candelabra type.'"[19]

FIGURE 15. Lobby, George Washington Hotel, Washington, Pennsylvania. From "The George Washington Hotel, Washington, Penn.," *Hotel Monthly* 31 (Oct. 1923): 25.

The new Hotel Julien-Dubuque in Dubuque, Iowa, replaced an earlier hotel of the same name destroyed by fire in 1913. Opened two year later, its exterior was covered in buff Indiana limestone on the two lower floors and with a combination of brick and stone across the upper six stories. Reported the *Hotel Monthly*: "The lobby is a magnificent room with floor area aggregating 100 x 60 feet. The section within the mezzanine well rises to a 25-foot ceiling. The glory of the room is in the wealth of South American mahogany in wainscot, pillars, trim, fixtures, and clerk's desk. This is further enhanced with rich and tasteful furnishings of the Louis XIV period; the furniture of mahogany, upholstered in fabrics of varied kinds; the room centered with large tables embellished with wealth of hand carving; these graced with art lamps. Scattered about the rooms are jardinieres, vases, flower boxes, and ornaments of peculiar interest."[20] The floor was of pink Tennessee marble upon which lay a large blue, red, and gold carpet. A unique trim wound around the top of the room: a frieze of scalloped brocade in blue and gold.

The registration desk was every hotel's command center. It was always readily visible when entering a lobby. And entering guests were always readily visible from it. The lobby of the Hotel Bothwell in Sedalia, Missouri, was furnished as a lounge. Overlooked by a mezzanine, it also was a high-ceilinged, two-story space with registration desk located immediately across from the front entrance. To the immediate left of the desk was the hotel check room, and to the immediate right the manager's office. Farther to the right were the hotel's two elevators for guests,

FIGURE 16. Office, Hotel Graham, Bloomington, Indiana. From "Yes:—A Satisfactory Country Hotel," *Hotel Monthly* 38 (Feb. 1930): 43.

and farther to the left, entry to the hotel's dining room as well as entrances to three stores, each, of course, with its own outside door to the street beyond. Also located there was the stairway to the mezzanine. Farther to the left were entrances both to the hotel barber shop and to a waiting room set aside for bus passengers. A few steps from the main entrance, the *Hotel Monthly* reported, "is the bus station, which makes this location important as a travel terminal, particularly since . . . bus travel service is so extensively developed."[21] Under the surveillance of the desk clerk, all of the various entries were, in effect, "controlled." No one could come and go without scrutiny. Formality was expected. Guests were to abide by dress codes and polite rules of comportment.

Hotel offices were sometimes integrated with the registration desk but, more often than not, located behind it. Such spaces could be quite utilitarian, function being more important than appearance. Rarely was any hotel "back region" extensively decorated, strict utilitarianism tending to prevail. Such was the manager's office at the Hotel Graham in Bloomington, Indiana, (fig. 16). Visible in the photograph are the hotel's arrival-and-departure book, file slots for business forms, a registration card rack, time clock, house telephone, key cabinet, calendar, information board, cash drawer, and telephone switchboard.

FIGURE 17. Portion of the mezzanine, Hotel Ottumwa, Ottumwa, Iowa. From "Hotel Ottumwa of Ottumwa, Iowa," *Hotel Monthly* 26 (Apr. 1918): 64.

Hotel mezzanines served several purposes. They enhanced lobbies visually, especially when guests looked up upon entering. They provided overflow space for lobby functions when large crowds gathered. In this regard, they usually provided entry to ballrooms and meeting rooms. Importantly, they, like the lobby floors below, were often furnished as lounges and often in what was termed "parlor style." Such was the case at the Hotel Ottumwa in Ottumwa, Iowa, one section of its mezzanine being set aside as a writing room and another as a ladies lounge (fig. 17). At the Hotel Vicksburg, a beauty parlor occupied a portion of the mezzanine floor, the parlor area immediately adjacent to it functioning as a ladies lounge.[22] Public space reserved for the use of women and children guaranteed degrees of protection from what was, usually in the evening hours, boisterous male behavior. Women (at least unescorted women) were often provided (or restricted to) their own dining rooms, and even their own separate hotel entrances, although such was more common in big-city rather than in small-town and small-city America.

A hotel's main "event space" was often located off the mezzanine. Entry to the "ball and banquet room" at the Hotel Vicksburg, for example, was located immediately at the top of the formal stair leading up from the lobby. A checkroom was

FIGURE 18. Ball and banquet room, Hotel Robidoux, St. Joseph, Missouri. From "New Crystal Ball Room of the Robidoux, St. Joseph, Mo.," *Hotel Monthly* 26 (Mar. 1918): 58

located at the foot of the stairs with the hotel's two elevators close by. The banquet room was relatively modest, measuring only fifty-eight by sixty-eight feet, its ceiling being a normal fourteen feet high. But at the Hotel Robidoux at St. Joseph, Missouri, the ballroom was very impressive indeed, being quite up to big-city standards in all regards. Depicted is the gala held at the hotel's dedication in 1918 (fig. 18). So also at the Hotel Ashtabula in Ashtabula, Ohio, was the banquet room quite large. It was hung with Italian damask, its woodwork, wainscoting, and pilasters finished "in antique blue with gold glazed effect."[23] Room decor was meant to make it seem "other worldly." Banquet rooms and ballrooms were potentially "fantasy" spaces—places where people might on special occasions break with the usual in life.

At the Hotel Fowler in Lafayette, Indiana, the combination banquet/ballroom/convention hall was located on the hotel's top floor, seven stories up from the lobby, and was accessed directly from the lobby by special elevator. "It is 100 x 45 feet, and carries thru two stories," the *Hotel Monthly* noted. Decoration was in white and gold. A gallery overlooked the hall at the north end. There was a serving pantry at the south end with a freight elevator connecting it with the kitchen located on the ground floor. A roof garden over the ballroom was serviced from this same pantry.[24] From the rooftop hotel patrons could look down into downtown, at night the lit streets being especially impressive. A guest was thus offered the opportunity

FIGURE 19. Pharmacy, Tallcorn Hotel, Marshalltown, Iowa. From "Hotel Tallcorn of Marshalltown, Iowa, Newest of the Eppley Chain," *Hotel Monthly* 37 (Jan. 1929): 59.

to play the nighttime sightseer, something that, in itself, could greatly romanticize an evening event.

At the Lincoln Hotel in Danville, Illinois, the "event room" was in the basement. It was seventy-two feet long, twenty-two feet wide at each end, and forty feet wide at the center, the center section "forming a sort of parlored alcove, its far wall ornamented with a huge mantel." The first function held in the room was a Kiwanis Club luncheon honoring Jospeh G. Cannon, longtime Speaker of the House of Representatives. The room was to be named the Cannon Room in his honor. As the *Hotel Monthly* reported, "Over the mantel there will be a life-size portrait of Mr. Cannon, who is Danville's most famous and beloved citizen. On the mantel itself there will be placed a miniature cannon as significant of the name." Upwards of two hundred people could be accommodated in the room for formal dinners.[25]

Most hotels built after 1910 included ground-floor rental spaces to be leased to retailers. In some instances a hotel might actually manage one or more of those stores itself. For example, cigar and newspaper stands were often hotel operated, as were coffee shops, which, once Prohibition set in, came to replace the hotel bar in complementing hotel dining rooms. A pharmacy was a highly desired tenant. Indeed, a drugstore with a soda fountain (or lunch counter) largely negated a hotel having to provide a coffee shop. So also might a drugstore negate need for a separate newsstand. At the Hotel Tallcorn in Marshalltown, Iowa, on the other hand, the pharmacy was hotel operated (fig. 19). Occupying a corner location in the build-

FIGURE 20. Barber shop, Hotel Hayes, Jackson, Michigan. From "Hotel Hayes of Jackson, Michigan, 200 Rooms," *Hotel Monthly* 35 (Mar. 1927): 39.

ing, it had its own street entry with outside signs and display windows, it being substantially dependent on walk-in custom. "The walls are lined with showcases of extra quality cabinet work," observed the *Hotel Monthly*. "The soda fountain has 12 stools. Behind it is a steam-table supplied from the kitchen; salad pantry with refrigerators, toaster, and ice cream cabinet."[26] Other retailers commonly found in hotels included jewelers, haberdashers, and clothiers. It was not unusual to find the office of the local automobile club at a hotel location, usually at street level. It was not unusual to find the local chamber of commerce occupying an office either, usually off a hotel's mezzanine. Both functions reinforced (and were reinforced by) hotel activity.

Barbershops were also found in most hotels, and more so than beauty shops, given that hotels were thought to be, in general, male places. If not at street level with an outside entrance, they were usually ensconced in the basement, often with entry by way of an outside stair directly from a public sidewalk. The barbershop of the Hotel Hayes in Jackson, Michigan, was on the ground floor, its floor of black and gray tile and its wainscoting of gray Tennessee marble (fig. 20). "Above the wainscot," the *Hotel Monthly* noted, "the wall paper is what is called modern in cream background and black figure with black and brilliant blue diagonal strip."[27]

The six barber chairs were upholstered in dark blue leather. Completed in 1926, the Hotel Hayes, centrally located as it was in Jackson's downtown, quickly became the city's leading hotel, its barbershop quickly becoming premier in the city.

Public Space as Social Space

The barbershop at the Lincoln Hotel in Danville, Illinois, never opened. No barber could be induced to rent it. For one thing, the hotel was located at the edge of Danville's downtown and thus away from local customers. As one journalist reported, the hotel manager "showed us a room that was originally intended for [a] barber shop, but which is to be converted into a tourist rest room, mainly for day accommodations—that is, it will be equipped with showers and other conveniences that people traveling by motor will appreciate." The manager's intent was to cater to motorists "breaking a journey for a few hours to clean up, be refreshed with a bath, and enjoy a meal."[28] At issue, therefore, was not just a disappointing barber-shop venue but also another kind of problem universal to every hotel manager: how to profit from those attracted to a hotel's public spaces, including motorists, but who were not likely to be paying guests, or, at least, paying overnight guests?

Hotel lobbies and lounges, with their luxurious appointments, came to serve small towns and small cities very much like public "living rooms." Hotel lounges were places of comfort where people, both locals and strangers from away, could feel "at home." Lounges offered respite from sightseeing, shopping, or other activities. For locals arriving downtown by public transit, and even those motoring downtown, hotel lounges were places to rendezvous conveniently and comfortably with others before going on. How might such "walk ins," however, be encouraged to spend money before departing? And how might that be done without sacrificing the impression that a hotel's public spaces were just that: "public"? Hotels could not charge admission for lobby use. Lobbies needed to remain free in access, and, in theory at least, open to all.

Most hotels promoted themselves as community centers—places where people in large groups could gather for planned events but also where people could gather spontaneously in pairs or in small groups. Necessary to a sense of community in any locality were public places for socializing. In America's small towns and cities, hotels usually provided the venues supportive of such socializing, at least socializing beyond town hall, church, and private club. And yet, in a social sense, a hotel's public spaces were not really public. They were private spaces that fostered public ends. They were private spaces designed to deliver goods and services for private profit. Community benefit was a plus—an important plus.

Not everyone was fully welcome at the typical hotel irrespective of how large it was or where it was located. African Americans, especially across the American South, were generally denied access except insofar as they worked as employees. Increasingly problematical for hotel managers were people waiting for bus connections, bus travelers tending to be less affluent than motorists, for example. In the early 1920s, when intercity bus travel initially became widespread, many hotels agreed to become de facto bus terminals. Bus operators set up offices in rented hotel storefronts, often loading and unloading buses at curbside under a hotel canopy. Such practice seemingly offered logical business symbiosis. The hotel became a destination for a new kind of traveler. Bus operators were able to forego the expenses of opening terminals. However, it quickly became evident that bus passengers and traditional hotel guests, especially motorists, did not mix well. Of differing social backgrounds, they felt "out of place" among one another. It was the motorist, however, that hotels needed to attract. Certainly they could ill afford to alienate their most affluent guests. Thus social-class differences loomed large. In commenting on his proposed "comfort station for motorists," the manager of Danville's Lincoln Hotel emphasized the hotel's parking rates. The hotel garage, he said, charged fifty cents for housing Fords overnight, and seventy-five cents for "more expensive and larger cars."[29] Even among motorists, it seemed, social differences were important.

* * *

Social class and status were something necessarily assigned when a hotel's business plan was formulated. They were something that architects necessarily had to consider in "laying out the house." Perhaps it was best to fall back on proven formulas. Perhaps it was best not to take risks in innovating—by planning lounges for bus passengers, for example. This was especially true in small towns, and perhaps in small cities also, where the carrying capacity both for hotel renovation and new hotel construction, relative to that of big cities, was limited. It was best that hoteliers, and their architects, assume a wait-and-see stance, adopting, for example, only those innovations fully proven in the large hotels of the big cities. But if most new small-town and small-city hotels were not on the absolute leading edge of innovation, both in a social and in a functional sense, they were relatively up to date physically. They were very much capable of meeting contemporary travel and community needs. They had most of the requisite features found in the grand hotels of the big cities but very much scaled down to fit the smaller communities that they served.

Not only were transients well served in the new hotels, but so also were local residents. Locals had a place to come to for organized social events, be they on a weekly, monthly, seasonal, or other cycle, or special events one of a kind. They had a place to host family affairs. Hotels provided spaces to just plain relax in, places to meet friends merely to socialize. Not only were hotels functional in this regard, but they were also fully symbolic. Whether or not a local resident frequented a hotel regularly, there was always opportunity to do so. That was something more than just self-referential: it sustained a sense of belonging to a community collective. Hotels also represented impressive venues where out-of-town dignitaries, for example, might be welcomed and entertained, very much without local embarrassment. Up-to-date hotels were something to be proud of collectively. Their aura potentially graced everyone, transient and local resident alike.

THE BUSINESS OF STARTING
A MAIN STREET HOTEL

Who perceived a need for a hotel in a small town or city? Did they see only the possible income? How did they go about raising the construction funds for such a costly business and oversee its birth? At the very outset of attempting to understand the business of Main Street hotels, we enter on some of the most fabled ground in United States history, richly predisposed to the limitations of small-town life rather than its own set of options. Novelist Sinclair Lewis's *Main Street* most especially evokes impressions of bumpkins groping for economic salvation in falsely fraternal clubs often convened in their town's or city's hotel dining room. For a most memorable scene, Lewis creates a guest of honor seated at the Commercial Club Banquet at the Minniemashie House, an occasion for menus printed in gold (but injudiciously proof-read): "for free cigars, soft damp slabs of Lake Superior whitefish served as filet of sole, drenched cigar-ashes gradually filling the saucers of coffee cups, and oratorical references to Pep, Punch, Go, Vigor, Enterprise, Red Blood . . . One Hundred Per Cent. Americanism, and Pointing with Pride."[1] The truth, in fact, is more complicated.

Entrepreneurship

Hotel entrepreneurs in small towns and cities operated within an especially circumscribed market. Profit potential there did not foster plans of large-scale ambition compared with those in big cities. Hotel founders more commonly grew up and remained in the towns where they began their business than did big city operators, although men from bigger cities were attracted when they branched out looking for new markets. That is to say that the hotels of small towns and cities took to a niche and, in so doing, further reinforced the definition of those towns and cities as a distinctive class. Derivative of high-style architecture embodied in the big cities' luxury hotels, the buildings designed for small towns and cities were successful financially where they satisfied the entrepreneur's need for flexibility in physical arrangements, spaces that could be expanded or contracted upon public demand. A minor note in the architectural narrative was building for future enlargement, as in the case of the Hotel Ashtabula opened in 1920 in Ashtabula, Ohio, where the architect explained that the over-large lobby for the 110-room facility would be appropriate when two more floors were added, bringing the total capacity to 151 rooms atop an especially strong foundation in the initial construction.[2] Whether or not it demanded "a bigger and better man to successfully build and operate a hotel in a small town than a city," as the owner-manager of the Irvin Hotel in Kenmare, North Dakota, claimed in 1921, the business certainly depended upon a wider clientele. The small-town hotel entrepreneur has, the owner-manager of the Irvin Hotel elaborated, "to build his place to suit the rich man, the commercial man, the railroad man, the farmer, the farmer's daughters and sons, his hired man, the clerical man, the school teacher, the shop girl, the show girl and many others that he does not know who or what they are." The business head had also to be his own attorney, real estate agent, broker, architect, and decorator, the North Dakotan advised.[3] Small meant less possible specialization even if it was not an ironclad prescription in every case.

In their keener attention to their comparatively precarious market, entrepreneurs of these hotels in small towns and cities seemed strangely no more attuned to automobile travelers. Even automobile taxi service dedicated to the hotel was exceptional, as in the case of the Farragut Transfer Company in Knoxville and Nashville, Tennessee, in 1919.[4] A few played to its consumers' special needs and expectations early. In Mason City, Iowa, the Eadmar's managers were foresighted in 1921, maintaining numerous uncommonly large rooms, spacious enough for three to five people arriving in auto tours.[5] Most did not respond until the mid-1920s when the *Hotel Monthly* began featuring hotels adapting to the automobile trade and still courting local patronage.[6] Most of those keying on the automobile trade at first were simply aware that improved highways through their town or city promised a new set of lodgers.[7] Through the 1920s, emphasis shifted in favor of the transient rather than the local trade. In 1928 Albert Pick–Barth Companies published a planning guide that gave equal weigh to "traveling men and automobile

FIGURE 21. The Hotel Chandler in Chandler, Georgia, was located on the Bankhead Highway, between Atlanta and the Stone Mountain Confederate Memorial. From "Hotel Chandler of Decatur, Georgia," *Hotel Monthly* 36 (Aug. 1928): 26.

tourists" but discouraged space assigned to "local, social, and fraternal activities" unless the demand was "clearly evident or long term leases are offered." [8] Anecdotal evidence confirms that small-town and small-city hotel men were convinced by the late 1920s that their future lay with auto and some even with plane traffic (fig. 21).[9]

Spatial availability for automobiles played more easily to the motoring travelers because, owing to cheaper land, curb and off-street parking space was less expensive than in big urban centers. At most, local drivers competed with travelers for parking, and hotels remedied the problem relatively simply through parking regulation, which the local police exercised.[10] Parking garages with attendant mechanical repair and washing services seldom were built and instead left to other entrepreneurs. Entrepreneurs rarely built garages within their hotels.[11] Government too lightly taxed in small towns and cities—usually ideological bastions of Jeffersonian principles—to even contemplate city-run parking structures and lots. Still, the Hotel Burlington built in 1912 in Burlington, Iowa, was portrayed in *Hotel Monthly* thirty-five years later as an exemplary business restructuring in part because the owner also acquired an adjacent two-floor parking garage for his customers. The *Hotel Monthly* took an opportunity in the article to lecture that hoteliers should restrict an area in front of the exit for guests arriving by car and see that violators parking there be arrested.[12]

In the early twentieth century, a feeling of inferiority and decline among small-town and small-city merchants with regard to large and growing corporations structured the birth of the hotels in their midst.[13] Voluntary associations of businessmen bypassed in numbers the older clubs of purely fraternal purpose to ally in defending, if not expanding, their town's economy. They emerged in tandem with chambers of commerce or founded them. Their principles of collegiality, cooperation, and materialism focused on hotels built to prime the economy and provide public space for their gatherings. Hence the scene from *Main Street* located at the start of this chapter. Women, too, although initially in separate organizations, joined to enrich local culture and enhance the quality of local life.[14] Real estate most clearly unified all social elements, although not every person, in a perceived improvement. Hotels made unquestionably important capital investments.[15] Small-city leaders, especially, engaged them in the constant remaking of their cities that hinged on diversifying the local economy.[16]

It is their showmanship, perhaps bravado in some cases, that accounts for the characteristically grandiloquent descriptions of new hotels just prior to their equally gala grand openings. In Lordsburg, New Mexico, a quietly prosperous economy derivative of mining and ranching from the outlying areas was awakened to new opportunities with the advent of Highway 70/80 in the early twentieth century. El Paso banker Charles N. Bassett envisioned Lordsburg as a conduit from El Paso for auto travelers through the Southwest.[17] When Bassett opened the Hidalgo Hotel on May 28, 1928, in Lordsburg, the local press ushered curious visitors in melodramatic prose to arouse their visual sense and grip their imagination: "On entering the lobby one is struck with the feeling of entering the living room of one of the old haciendas of Spanish days. The beamed ceiling, the red Spanish leather upholstered chairs and draperies all contributing to this effect. . . . On the extreme right is the entrance to the coffee shop through a colonnade and the rich looking draperies on the left. . . . On entering this room the first thing that attracts the eye is the huge fireplace all in harmony with the architecture of the building. The room itself is furnished in luxuriously velour upholstered chairs and right in front of the fireplace is a most inviting lounge."[18] The memory of would-be and actual patrons alike might well have been firmly cast by such wondrously scripted descriptions for public consumption.

Entrepreneurs tailored their enterprise within a framework of boosterism and competition with other small towns and cities. Building a hotel where a house once stood or razing an obsolete hotel readied investors to maximize profits from land deemed underdeveloped and to ballyhoo progress.[19] The frenzy for hotel construction reached an extreme in Seguin, Texas, where business factions with the town built separate hotels simultaneously.[20] Chambers of commerce usually became natural allies of the whole business community launching a hotel. These collective businesses not only symbolized ascent of the civilization scale but magnetized other financial investments. A small town or city could only grow bigger and be a better place to live if a hotel were built, it was argued. One worked the hotel for the small town or city and the business reciprocated.[21] Subscription campaigns for the townspeople's investment, no matter how small the sums given, embodied a civic esprit de corps. There were rituals commonly attendant regarding the balance left to be subscribed, tactfully nagging subscribers to actually give their money, and celebrations of the final achievement in a formal dedication and opening.[22] American entrepreneurial élan put the nation's hotels in the vanguard of the industry worldwide, and one of the reasons was entrepreneurs' saturation of small, local markets in the early twentieth century.[23]

Four kinds of entrepreneurs became apparent in retrospect. The contemporary trade literature coined the term "community hotel" for the creation of civic-minded groups that coalesced, not without heed to keeping the project solvent, to be sure, but because they saw the hotel as an asset for the small town or city and themselves as residual beneficiaries. Sentiment may have inspired some solely, but often they had businesses elsewhere in the town, city, or region that were due to benefit from the hotel's facilitation of business. Some "community hotel" entrepreneurs had no other significant investments. In Olympia, Washington, the Pierce brothers, as they were called locally, raised $225,000 in comparatively small sums ($200–$2,500) and added $90,000 of their own money to build and open the Olympia Hotel in 1920. The hotel was a critical feature for the city because it was the state capital, but the state legislature threatened the capital's relocation unless better accommodations became available. Thad and John Pierce had grown up in the hotel trade; John operated their father's hotel in Olympia. Entrepreneurship was not novel for them, and they turned ably to managing the Olympia upon its opening.[24]

In Sedalia, Missouri, John H. Bothwell, former state assemblyman, prosecuting attorney, judge, and prosperous businessman, spearheaded the campaign to provide the town with the latest in public lodging. The Bothwell, opened in 1927 and named for him, was fireproof; the several other hotels in town were of an earlier vintage and were not fireproof. The big-city press held Sedalia accountable for a higher quality of lodging because of the annual state fair held on the city's southwestern fringe.[25] Bothwell and other businesspeople rightly calculated that, with automobile traffic streaming over Missouri's incipient highway system due to federal aid (US 50 and US 65 crossed in town), Sedalia could benefit.[26] Against the city's entrenched hotel interests, which took out advertisements in the local newspaper in opposition to Bothwell's project, Bothwell tried to attract local contributors.[27] Bothwell's community spirit made a stratagem of the hotel.[28] "His first idea was for the erection of a modern hospital," the local newspaper reported, "but feeling that Sedalia needed adequate hotel facilities to care for relatives and friends who would accompany patients to Sedalia, changed his plans to make possible the erection of a modern fireproof hotel also."[29] John H. Bothwell's work as a public benefactor definitively exemplifies the small-town and small-city entrepreneur who led, redefined, and persisted in drawing others into one model of the "community hotel."[30]

More commonly, this hotel type was the object of individuals and organizations alike. Collective initiative and responsibility set this type apart from all other hotels in conception. In Cleveland, Tennessee, the city's newspaper editor and the newly formed (1925) chamber of commerce promoted and 225 stockholders financed the Hotel Cherokee, which opened in 1928 and was untaxed for ten years. The Penn-Wells in Wellsboro, Pennsylvania, is the direct descendant of an honored lodging lineage linked in local people's minds. A newspaper account in 1976 traced the hotel's origins to the Cone House that opened ninety-four years earlier on the same parcel of land. Although several fires and substantial remodelings intervened, the hotel that opened in 1926 with none of its forerunner's physical features except the walls was portrayed as fulfillment of a constant commitment to the community: "When asked why they [the local stockholders] would leave their money invested in a company which has not paid a dividend in the last five years, Dale [secretary-treasurer of the Penn-Wells company] . . . said, 'The Hotel has always been a community enterprise. There are probably sentimental reasons for it and the stockholders are hopeful that someday they will receive a dividend.'" This testimony to community was made only less simple by the degree to which the practical consideration was admitted that because many held the stocks, every stockholder could afford to hold on for a long time without profiting.[31] The St. James Hotel built in 1875 for Red Wing, Minnesota, similarly left no trace of a key individual nor of a single event standing forth in what is one of the best-documented founding chronicles.[32]

Entrepreneurs dedicated principally to profit exhibited varying degrees of interest in community and operated largely on their own financing. W. G. Hutson was born in Lawrence, Kansas, and was a veteran manager for the Fred Harvey houses west of Albuquerque and the manager of the Union Station restaurant in Detroit as well as a worker in Wabash Railroad dining cars and the Albany Hotel in Denver. Between 1925 and 1928, he remodeled the Eldridge Hotel when he returned to his birthplace.[33] Abner Palmer Woodworth, a successful businessman typical of many nineteenth-century American moguls, had structured much of the banking, railroad, petroleum, and farming sectors of Crawford County in Illinois when he launched his Woodworth Hotel venture in 1907 in the town of Robinson.[34] Donald T. Knutson entered his father's Standard Construction Company into the hotel industry as a risk taken in defense of the $500,000 the Knutsons already invested in the Frederick Martin Hotel in Moorhead, Minnesota, when the community-based corporation for the hotel failed.[35] Knutson completed the hotel in 1958 and also ran it successfully for twelve years. The regional newspaper stated bluntly, "As an absentee landlord who took over a local project, Knutson hasn't won the hearts of his involuntary associates but his success with the FM Hotel has won respect— grudging in a few cases—and gratitude."[36] The secretary-manager of the Moorhead Chamber of Commerce elaborated that the hotel was second only to the railroad in defining the town's economy: "The hotel contributed real impetus to Moorhead and 'people saw what could be done to make Moorhead a modern city.'"[37]

Financing

Hotels devoured huge capital investments. The pinnacle of the American hotel hierarchy, after all, was the luxury hotel prominently featured in hotel trade publications and subsequently in scholarly literature. Small-town and small-city hotels, while not designed to stand out vis à vis high-rise architectural symbols, as hotels were required to do against churches and skyscrapers in big cities, nonetheless had to be pretentious if their founders hoped for success. Financing such a gigantic undertaking required feasibility studies, subscription campaigns, and oversight by professionals in the case of small-town and small-city hotel projects. Architectural plans had to be carefully coordinated with expenses and anticipated profits, thus making the look of the place a careful calculation, hardly an act of architectural license for the sake of art or opulence.

While the final edifice and its trappings often awed the public, that same public did not always readily contribute the means. The Umpqua Hotel in Roseburg, Oregon, opened late due to the reluctance of local citizens to fund the furnishings of the hotel after it was ready for occupancy. The Hotel Bothwell in Sedalia, Missouri, cost $400,000 for the building, the tallest in town including the adjacent Pettis County courthouse, and $90,000 for furnishings. Bothwell challenged his townspeople to pledge an identical amount to his ($150,000) to make the hotel a reality. Against the contesting hotel owners already in business, the Community Hotel Corporation, which headed the Bothwell project, had to persist. One month before the deadline Bothwell set for withdrawing his money if members of the executive committee did not pledge the required sum, the corporation's executive committee was forced into a long and contentious meeting before the money was finally pledged. A hotel finance company based in Harrisburg, Pennsylvania, the Hockenbury System, Incorporated, was retained to manage the funding. Community finance meant firm and substantial commitment before anyone could bask in civic glory. In financing the new Eldridge Hotel in Lawrence, Kansas, the Hockenbury System withdrew from an agreement to organize a stock-subscription drive because of poor stock sales and further prospects of them. W. G. Hutson's aforementioned personal investment alone brought off a successful resolution. At a banquet in 1916 in Charleston, Missouri, Congressman Joseph J. Russell pledged to build the Russell Hotel if the people there would give the required site plus invest in stock equal to the value of the lot. In less profitable cases, investment houses bought the bonds issued to fund many community hotels in the 1920s and in the 1930s became overzealous generators of expansion that ended the subject hotels in receivership.[38]

Attendees at the Northwestern Hotel Men's Convention in Minneapolis in 1917 were sternly lectured contrary to the fulsome ethos of the luxury-hotel paradigm. "The hotel man of today," they were told, "is a merchant and operating a modern hotel is not essentially different from operating a department store." Every step of conceptualization before construction was best taken with extreme care, the attendees learned. Ground-floor stores and shops were not only convenient and polite services flattering guests and their associates: "It is one of the first principles of hotel financing that the stores and other sub-rents of a modern commercial hotel should at least take care of the interest and taxes on the investment in the ground, leaving only the business investment to be taken care of by the earnings of the hotel."[39] Money was available at a charge beyond the cost of repayment because bond houses charged discounts and agents obtaining funds charged commissions. Those services drove the price of money higher than the interest rates charged by most banks because banks were not ready to loan money for hotel projects. Moreover, taxes and interest on money during construction and various legal fees had to be paid.[40]

Securing investors also entailed not only the latest in architecture and technology, such as central heating and showers, but also human competence on the job. This helped assure the judgment necessary to make the complex interworking scheme, which the hotel manifested, a working success. Managers (most always men) with extensive hotel experience were announced as part of the ensemble when the hotel opened. When Knute Bjorkland and David J. Nolan came to manage the Hotel Okmulgee in Okmulgee, Oklahoma, in 1920, the *Hotel Monthly* reported, "Mr. Bjorkland has been with the Chicago and University Clubs and the Great Northern Hotel, Chicago, Toledo Club and Boody Hotel, Toledo and is new manager of the St. Louis Club, St. Louis. Mr. Nolan is assistant manager of Hotel Statler, St. Louis, and past president of the St. Louis Greeters."[41]

Community

Tension, in fact, ironically strained at the heart of small-town and small-city hotels. The town's establishment impressed their values on them; whatever divisions existed were only extended to them, not bridged, because they were the most coveted public spaces in most locales. Even commerce between members of the establishment could be contended at the hotel. Its very existence and a certain percentage of its business stemmed from local demand, but beside the narratives of hotel businessmen in felicitous bond with fellow townspeople, dissenting voices sensed separation instead of rapport. F. Harold Van Orman, head of his hotel chain, warned others in the hotel business to strive hard to relate to the community in which they did business. Not long before a 1919 speech by Van Orman entitled "Hotel Man's Relation to His Community," the manager of a small-town hotel told him, "Oh, I don't bother about the town people; what do they do for me?" Most of the small-town hotel's profit came from the transient trade, not the townspeople.[42]

Members of the town, for their part, were suspicious of the local hotel and its manager, Van Orman revealed. "They can't help it—the old jokes about 'Leave your valuables at the desk because the proprietor will get them anyway' and 'Why don't you use a gun in holding us up?' are instilled in the hearts of the babies."[43] Too few local businesses appreciated what a good hotel meant to the place where they lived, Van Orman insisted. Outsiders with a strong understanding of how the highly mobile clientele passing through town perceived a good hotel, however, uttered sentiments like this one from Professor John W. Cook of De Kalb University, commenting in 1902 on the opening of the new Illinois Hotel in Bloomington: "If you wish to give the world a good impression of your city, all you have to do is have a first class hotel in every sense of the word and you may be sure the fame will spread to the four corners of the earth."[44] In Roseburg, Oregon, the local newspaper, a key to the community, periodically published a list of all the recent registrants in the local hotels. Such means implied to the townspeople how attractive to outsiders, in fact, the hotels had made Roseburg.[45]

Verifications of Van Orman's adage are largely fugitive anecdotes or scattered citations in travel accounts but no less valid. Communities did touch travelers at hotels, and such was the case in Erwin, Tennessee, of a serviceman in World War II staying overnight at the Erwin Hotel. Lodged with his fellows at the hotel because snow blocked their trip from Fort Campbell, Kentucky, to Asheville, North Carolina, the serviceman recalled the local women who brought cakes and cookies to them on the evening of their stay. One of the group remembered this kindness about a quarter-century later when, as a cab driver in Hawaii, he attempted to repay the gesture: he purchased two leis for a distraught customer who had just visited with her serviceman-husband on his "R and R" in Hawaii during the Vietnam War and then stayed with her at the airport until her flight departed. How people remembered communities was strongly influenced by how they were received in the hotels located there.[46]

Did an inherent disadvantage to either the hotel man or townspeople impede practice of the ideal dynamic? In fairness, it appears that while some hoteliers may have been self-centered, others clearly were not. Henry Scharf, owner-manager of the Hotel Gettysburg in Gettysburg, Pennsylvania, one of the most widely renowned small-town lodgings, breached the distinction between his private business and his community. Before Scharf became president and publisher of the *Gettysburg Times,* the local newspaper, he wrote articles to promote the town's fame and eventually became involved with numerous voluntary organizations, including not only the Gettysburg Chamber of Commerce but also the Gettysburg Baseball Club. In the 1950s, during the presidency of Dwight David Eisenhower, Scharf made it possible for the hotel to gain attention from afar as the president's convalescent home and vacation White House.[47] It functioned as an ideal showcase to the world.

Expanded self-interest among other businesspeople in the small town or city could turn to the hotel's benefit. This was especially true initially among the numerous local suppliers and tradesmen whom the hotel entrepreneurs employed to build the hotel and who, as standard practice, advertised in the local paper to wish the new business well. News articles routinely accompanied grand openings and named all the local businesses employed in the hotel's construction.[48] Here the local press performed its role in bonding the new business with the existing businesses. Businesspeople on the board of the community hotel corporation also implied an enduring commitment by their existing enterprise to the incoming one. For instance, the three presidents, vice presidents, and cashiers of the banks in Holland, Michigan, acted as trustees and building board of the city's Warm Friend Inn, assuring their loyalty at least until their work was complete at the time of the opening in 1925. The $550,000 required for construction was subscribed without requiring a fundraiser's commission.[49] City-to-city competition augmented some promoters' successful appeals to townspeople. For example, as *Hotel Monthly* reported, promoters of the Hotel Tallcorn in Marshalltown, Iowa, pointed to the success of the Chieftan in Council Bluffs, which had opened because a special fund had been raised to retain a capable operator, and declared "that what Council Bluffs had done Marshalltown could do."[50] Newspaper publishers assured their readers

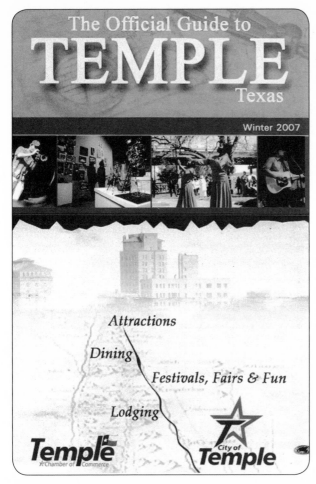

FIGURE 22. In its 2007 travel literature, Temple, Texas, proudly displays its skyline, two of whose three tall buildings are hotels: the Hawn Hotel (originally the Doering Hotel), left, and the Kyle Hotel, center. From *The Official Guide to Temple[,] Texas,* Winter 2007. Courtesy of the City of Temple and the Temple Chamber of Commerce.

that events of interest to the town, such as club functions and private parties, would be held at the hotel, making it much more than just a stop for people traveling through town.[51] Before naming the Lewis-Clark Center in Lewiston, Idaho, local business leaders invited names from the townspeople and the 110 submitted alternatives were proof of the town's collective "culture, education, and refinement," in the estimation of one member of the local elite. The process of naming thus became a means of engendering shared interests and paying self-praise.[52]

Community materialized in the hotel's very location and prominence on Main Street. Block-long facades of individual buildings joined side by side created an ensemble that Richard Francaviglia has articulated as an essential American type of landscape. In these ensembles, hotels stood forth, often as the tallest member mid-block or poised at the end, catching one's eye along two facades at key

FIGURE 23. One of the frequent meetings of the Sedalia Business and Professional Women's Club in the Ambassador Room, Hotel Bothwell. From the *Sedalia Democrat,* Mar. 21, 1937, A8. Courtesy of Rebecca Carr Imhauser and the Sedalia, Missouri, Public Library.

intersections.[53] Then, from miles beyond in terrain of especially low surrounding topographic relief, their dramatic verticality, accompanied occasionally by business buildings, signal still the approaching view of a town's center (fig. 22). These hotels as primary visual definers were integral to people's memory of Main Street for long periods. To the degree that Main Street symbolized community, the hotel was an imperative, even though it stood forth from the architectural stage.

Completed and opened, the small-town and small-city hotel usually functioned well, if at all, due to an owner-manager. The *Hotel Monthly* in 1940 commended Warren N. Woodson of the Hotel Maywood in Corning, California, as an exemplar, quoting in toto his speech to the local Rotary. "This dug-out or room or hall, as you may prefer to call it," Woodson told the assembled Rotarians, "has, for many years, supplied the setting for many commendable forward-looking community endeavors. In fact, it might truly be said to have served as the community incubator for the hatching of plans and activities calculated to contribute to better living—the life more abundant."[54]

The small-town or small-city hotel functioning as did Woodson's may be called the epicenter of community, both enabling it and symbolizing it. The International Order of Odd Fellows, the Sorosis, the Benevolent and Fraternal Order of Elks, the Masons, the Kiwanis, the Lions, and many others, no matter their dismissal as quaint by urban people and often travelers through small towns, spoke, according to John Stilgoe, "of instantaneous acceptance, of an immediate meal,

FIGURE 24. A meeting on November 1, 1942, of the Women's Auxiliary of the Pettis County Medical Society, honoring Lucille (Mrs. C. Gordon) Stauffacher, wife of a doctor who entered World War II service. Courtesy of Rebecca Carr Imhauser and the Pettis County, Missouri, Medical Society.

probably free, for members, of men still intrigued in civic duty, charity, morality-based self-improvement efforts."[55] Rotary often won attention as the representative community-service organization and likely grew to be the largest in the early twentieth century; thus, it was not surprising that Woodson spoke to a local Rotary in cataloguing the numerous civic and commercial organizations founded at the Hotel Maywood.[56] His hotel's community services also extended to a branch post office, local phone office, telegraph office, and de facto branch bank. Woodson actually disliked the loss of money from travelers, about half of them, who passed bad checks, but he did not stop check cashing. He was willing to cooperate with the traveling salesmen who ordinarily asked the hotel to write checks in exchange for cash collected from their customers in order to bring their collections to the home office.[57] Woodson observed that his hotel also sent lodgers clothing to be cleaned and pressed by local merchants. Strangers always required information about unfamiliar surroundings, "and the hotel is a public bureau of information," asserted Woodson.[58] And, lastly, especially in the region's hot summers, the hotel catered to sick travelers.[59]

The Bothwell further typified how hotels and communities bonded (figs. 23–25). Ten years after it opened, the local paper cast a fond retrospective glance by recalling

FIGURE 25. The Hotel Bothwell's congratulations of the Sedalia Rotary Club's fiftieth anniversary. From the *Sedalia Democrat*, Nov. 7, 1971, 7C. Courtesy of Donald Barnes.

how the hotel was booked to capacity for the state fair crowds well before the event.[60] Good times were equated with a full house. Amid the Great Depression, it was especially heartwarming news a month after that retrospective view appeared in print that over two hundred people in the Standard Oil Company came from inside Sedalia and the outlying area to fill the Ambassador Room and mezzanine, overflowing into the main dining room, for instruction about a new sales campaign.[61] The unity of Sedalia and its surrounding areas was tangible in this setting. In late 1937, an advertisement of the hotel as the town's premier showplace, one in a cycle of ads about the hotel's various services, touched seemingly every function a hotel could perform. It was not only a hotel for "traveling men," the ad proclaimed; rather, "everyday, every week, every month, hundreds of Sedalians make use of The Bothwell's better accomodations," holding afternoon bridge parties, evening banquets, family dinners, retreats for friends, nightly dancing for the "younger set," and shoppers' luncheons. "Yes," the advertisement concluded, "The Bothwell is a Sedalia institution."[62] These were the glories common to Main Street hotels across the country. During Sedalia's robust economy of the mid-1950s, the local paper ran an article about Kathryn Davis, who had earned advancement through the Bothwell's job hierarchy to run the "day desk" because of her skills. Her resilient and winning personality put a good face on the entire city, for the Bothwell, after all, was the principal point of contact between Sedalians and their visitors.[63] The good life was personified in a key hotel employee.

Chains

Chains targeted small towns and cities beginning in the 1910s at the earliest but expanded rapidly in the 1920s. Only the few that grew to ten or more hotels rooted their market exclusively in these places. Edwin A. Boss created the Boss Hotels System in Emmetsburg, Iowa, starting with a small hotel (thirty-six rooms) whose lease he bought in 1916 (fig. 26). His father had owned a hotel in Sparta, Illinois, but operated it indifferently. Edwin, in contrast, appears always to have been of a mind to do well at whatever he undertook and seriously honed his skills for the hotel trade by on-the-job training. While a teenager, he trained in the Maryland Hotel in St. Louis and learned a patented food-control system. He also took work in the food services department at the Union League in Chicago, the Hotel Sherman in Chicago, and as a railroad dining car steward. He started his chain in Iowa because he worked there for the railroad, made friends there, and was tipped off that the Waverly Hotel in Emmetsburg, Iowa, was for sale. An Emmetsburg building contractor, who frequently traveled on the railroad through Iowa with Boss, helped arrange a loan for the purchase.

FIGURE 26. Edwin A. Boss, circa 1959, remembered for the courtly manners he learned as a porter at his father's hotel. Courtesy of John Patrick Reilly.

Boss owned two small town hotels in Iowa before he served in World War I, added four more in the state before his term ended, and returned home dedicated to further building his chain. He predicated it upon the geographical knowledge that Iowa's county seats, linked by railroads, could provide him voluminous business when he applied his practical experience. Through the early 1950s, all of the hotels he acquired were small-town and small-city hotels originally railroad based. Sellers came to him with these properties because they learned of his growing aggregation of such hotels and likely because their owners faced the costs of remodeling if they stayed in business. Boss never intended at the outset to target the small-town and small-city market so much. By the early 1930s, he gained the attention of the hotel industry. By 1931 the chain numbered eighteen hotels, only a few of them leased, and included thirty-eight at its height. Although Boss regularly toured his hotels to oversee the conditions in each and personally knew the staff, he gave nearly complete latitude to his managers to purchase commodities from local merchants. In part to put on the best face for the towns where he did business, he prided himself on the best service and latest technology (especially private baths) in his hotels and remodeled their facades in keeping with the latest architectural styles.[64] Of course, these strategies also gave his chain appeal and consequent profit.

Boss was not entirely flexible, however. Even wedded to his original geographic scheme, he never fully embraced the possibilities of a new chain based on automobile travel. Dirt roads long plagued early automobile travel in Iowa, and Boss personally preferred the comparative convenience of railroad travel. In a brief retrospective written late in his life, he noted, "I have often told the story somewhat in jest, but equally true, that I never owned an automobile until I was 35 years old, which was 10 years after starting my business. For every time I thought I could afford an automobile, which at that time cost only $1,200 for a Buick, someone wanted a cook stove, or the roof was leaking, and it took that long to have the money to buy an automobile, as the hotels came first."[65] Eventually Boss extended the chain into big towns and cities such as Beloit, Wisconsin, Des Moines, Iowa, and Rockford, Illinois, which did not rely only on railroads, but his grandson, who frequently traveled with him, wrote, "One of my first memories was Ed saying to me that these Holiday Inns will never last."[66]

This best-documented small-town chain is peculiar to its founder's methods and cannot be taken for representative of the type, for two others in the same market exclusively deviated in several regards. W. H. Van Orman and Son started with Fred, who began in 1904 with the McCurdy Hotel in Evansville, Indiana, and operated what was credited by the *Hotel Monthly* as probably the first chain.[67] Unlike the Boss chain, the Van Orman business stretched over four generations with W.H. beginning in 1857 in Warsaw, Indiana. Son Fred articulated a system of hotel management that his own son, Harold, in turn further refined and published under the title *Van Orman System of Hotel Control*. While building their chain in three states—Illinois, Indiana, and Ohio—Harold and his son mixed politics with business, serving as an Indiana lieutenant governor and state legislator respectively.[68]

Extending through New England, Treadway Inns was the creation of Laurus G. Treadway, who started in 1912 with an aggregation of coach inns. The Lord Jeffrey Inn in Amherst, Massachusetts, embodied the model of newly constructed hotels that Treadway added to his chain. It simultaneously embodied historical references in a colonial decorative motif but also was situated with the chain's other five on an automobile highway between Amherst, Massachusetts, and Middlebury, Vermont.[69] Shortly after the Jeffrey Inn set the standard for Treadway's chain, he incorporated the Consolidated Hotel Service to guide future growth.[70] Whereas the Van Ormans hewed a modernist way by practicing, perfecting, and publishing their method of central management, and Boss fostered a federated scheme between himself and each local manager, Lauris Treadway espoused an ethos of Americanism and the contributing role of the New England inn.[71] By the early 1960s, Treadway's chain included twenty-eight lodgings, some renovated inns and some motels, still concentrated in New England but extended in Texas and Virginia. He staged a nostalgic charm, masking overt references to automobility by advertising "first class accommodations."[72] Treadway, like Boss, remained dedicated exclusively to hotel entrepreneurship.[73]

The United Hotels Company formed the subsidiary American Hotels Corporation to operate its larger hotels in larger places—hotels of 100–150 rooms in cities with populations under 100,000. J. Linfield Damon, who headed American Hotels Corporation until 1924, was credited with "many contributions in the way of scientific management" to reflect the prevailing paradigm in hotel management of the early twentieth century.[74] By 1943, Damon's successor, James Leslie Kincaid, built the chain to sixty hotels totaling 10,500 rooms in fifty-nine cities. They existed in nineteen states evenly spread throughout the nation. Although small towns and small cities remained the focus, company pride lay in big size in big cities: St. Petersburg (100 rooms) and Tampa (300 rooms). Kincaid's military experience informed both his persistent use of the title "General" after his service ended and adherence to it in administration: "The central office organization of this company closely follows military lines, and we never lose sight of the old adage that nothing in warfare succeeds save that which is simple."[75] He also kept to a winning personal style and adjusted each hotel's management to local circumstances.[76]

None of those bigger chains dedicated to small-town or small-city markets, none of those chains that included small-town or small-city sites as well as big cities,[77] and none of those numerous chains of two to five sites in those small locations[78] paid any more attention to nurture a hometown feeling or adapt to their special setting than did the large-scale operations in big cities. "Community hotels" occasionally fell into chain management and ownership after the initial fund-raising and construction. These adhered to the town's interests. Successful chains did adjust according to their understanding of local needs. As noted above, the United Hotels Company executive espoused a management policy in keeping with local circumstances, and Boss eschewed the financial savings of centralized purchasing for purchase from local merchants. Others seemed to emphasize more centralized authority, as did the Van Orman chain noted above, and they also profited. The Knott Hotels' management alone prided itself on sensitivity to each place's peculiar circumstances but, even in the twenty-seven hotels they operated by 1930, they distinguished five building types.[79]

By the mid-1920s, when small-town and small-city hotel entrepreneurs finally caught onto the motoring market, they rapidly overbuilt. This repeated the trend of a century before, when unfounded optimism had precipitated local projects and railroads that foundered as quickly in the Panic of 1857.[80] The hotel trade literature in the 1920s was not alone in warning against further building, the hotel construction boom of the twenties having occurred so quickly and dramatically. The *Saturday Evening Post* editorialized in 1926 against overbuilding and itemized the causes of misguided entrepreneurship: "The automobile has intensified the demand, and it is a common saying that motor travel will go where good hotel accommodations are to be found. . . . Yet misguided local pride, the desire of almost every community to become great, forces the creation of a larger and more imposing as well as more expensive structure than conditions warrant."[81]

The rapidity of the cautionary shift was palpable. Only three years before the *Saturday Evening Post*'s words, a Main Street hotel owner predicted to the local Rotary, "The hotel business is increasing far more rapidly than the population is increasing, and this is because of the great increase in the wealth of the people and the rapid improvements in our means of transportation. . . . The hotel business is just in its infancy and although today we are building many new and fine hotels, they are only a suggestion of what will be built by the generation that will come after us."[82]

By 1928, many of the big hotel companies decided the problem had to be addressed.[83] An editor of the *Hotel Monthly* looked further into the crisis to explain its origins before a meeting of the Illinois Hotel Association in 1928: Operators of older hotels tended to exaggerate the vitality of the business. Communities envied the hotels in neighboring towns, and it had become too easy to raise funds and sell bonds. The automobile also contributed to the undoing because the traveling salesman found less reason to travel; chain stores and mail-order houses provided new sources of supply. Furthermore, "the hotel man competes not alone with hotels in his own town, but with hotels in his territory, as the automobile is not like a train schedule, and road conditions are apt to make wide fluctuations in patronage."[84] Horwath and Horwath, the foremost accounting firm for hotels, on the eve of the stock market crash of 1929, attributed bad financing to the origins of overbuilding. Architects were warned against their involvement in a community hotel in return for stock and especially advised to look critically at the business's prospectus rather than at the stock offer.[85] Optimism and self-confidence imbued the new crowd of hotel men because they had emerged from the ranks of hotel employees and lacked the necessary understanding of finance.[86] Refinancing was the only remedy, as Horwath and Horwath saw it.[87] Shabby rooms from old and worn hotels yield "a run-down air of ill-kept grandeur," the *Saturday Evening Post* had warned in the heyday of construction and occupancy percentages.[88] No single reasoning commanded unquestioned authority, for amidst the overbuilding controversy the hotel planners Albert Pick–Barth Companies contended "that the hotel industry is not overbuilt. . . . The real trouble which shows up so plainly on the ledgers is that in many instances these hotels are in the wrong places and of the wrong kinds."[89] Not "very large city hotels" but "hotels of average size and of smaller types" were best designed to satisfy the travelers' demand.[90] Reason fell on deaf ears in both the hotel building boom and bust.

Conditions deteriorated in the 1930s during the Great Depression. Small hotels suffered most of all. In retrospect it was understood that civic pride had resulted in too much spent on promotion and structures too big for their locations. Hotels in receivership tended to charge rates below those of hotels run by their owners before the crisis, producing what some called unfair competition. The Chicago Title and Trust Company, receiver for many failed hotels, countered that people did not patronize distressed hotels. Virtually no new hotels were built for six years after 1930; occupancy averaged 51 percent in 1932, the lowest in the industry's history; and 80 percent of the nation's hotels were in receivership by 1935. An end to Prohibition and a gradual economic recovery nationwide witnessed improvement by the late 1930s. In 1938, in at least fifty selected cities, small transient hotels led the way, according to one report. Nearly full occupancy during World War II enabled some recovery throughout the hotel industry.[91]

Economic conditions following World War II caused extensive reshuffling of the entire hotel industry. Chains came out ahead. Hotel industry analysts had viewed single ownership and partnerships as passé even while they were common in the 1920s. None of those dedicated to small towns and cities emerged among the hotel leaders; that title went to Hilton and Sheraton, running twenty-four hotels in twenty-one cities and forty-two hotels in thirty-one cities, respectively. Motels made the most inroads against the small-town hotels, the Boss chain shifting belatedly to include Voyager Inn motels, but only three. Remaining a hotel man through his final days, Edwin Boss noted how motels grew to be like hotels in their size and luxuries. Independently owned hotels suffered at the bottom of the hotel hierarchy, which was fully chain dominated by the 1960s. Knott Hotels Corporation's management of the largest chain in the 1930s slipped to seventh rank, not because it was incapably managed but because it was satisfied to keep doing as it had done. Boss oversaw substantial remodelings in his chain and remained convinced that hard work would outdo his competition. The large convention hotels he acquired in Des Moines, Iowa, and Clearwater Beach, Florida, subsidized the chain.[92]

By the 1960s, chains in small towns and cities became historical artifacts. Van Orman sold his last hotel in 1969. Boss followed ten years later.[93]

* * *

Hotels came to people's minds in small towns and cities in various ways, no one of which fully explained what those hotels were or what they induced. Railroads had given birth to many of these towns and cities, and then, confronted by the even greater mass mobility afforded by automobiles, hotels built for railroad travelers gave way to those conceived for motorists. Entrepreneurs intervened at this juncture from different backgrounds in the early twentieth century. Some were civic-minded people inside their community, people who were also bound to profit in their own business if a good hotel could attract and serve travelers overnight. Some came from outside, attracted to a market niche of modest but measurable profit if the hotel was carefully conceived; some among these wanted immediate returns and had no intention of staying in the community. Some turned to benefactors, others to professionals to lead the fund-raising drive. Out of these circumstances arose the "community hotel" in the 1910s–20s, a noteworthy institution in the nation's past. Surely, undertakings of substantial financing reliant upon public help were not new, but never had they been so prominent as with the "community hotel" of the early twentieth century. Big chains and motels ultimately took over the small-town and small-city niche but not without opportunities envisioned first by individuals and small chains.

HOTEL MANAGEMENT: FROM FRONT DESK TO HOUSEKEEPER'S CLOSET

Management, it has been argued, took precedence in whether or not a hotel succeeded.[1] Hence, Main Street management demands study. Between art and science the sequence of developments regarding management in small-town and small-city hotels oscillated. If one understands "art" dictating behavior from a subjective premise with highly variable results in contradistinction with "science" guiding through formulaic procedures, the history of hotel management can be understood within this framework. It arose as art and remained so largely for small-town and small-city managers, while their counterparts in bigger-city hotels moved sooner toward scientific management.

The small-town hotel specialist Laurus Treadway, for one, was convinced that, as late as 1935, when the Depression had winnowed out many small hotels, too many unsystematic and badly managed ones unaccountably remained. "Mine Host," early hotel-trade press argot for the house manager, may be taken to symbolize the eventually laggard practices among small operators before the trade press pushed them to systematization and after big-business hoteliers operated chains and developed their management systems.[2] By the middle of the twentieth century, profit-making managers partnered their art with science. Mine Host became a creature of an antiquated past.

Mine Host and Scientific Management: Part I

Managing a small-town or small-city hotel remained throughout the institution's duration something done thoughtfully if it was to be a profitable business, but it was less something managers reflected upon systematically. Pervasive adoption of the "European Plan," one of the effects of scientific management most notable to hotel customers, seems to have happened because hoteliers in small towns and cities wanted to keep current with the precedents set by their big-city counterparts, rather than because astute cost analysis revealed the "American Plan" to be too expensive. Chicago's hotels adopted the "European Plan" just before the turn of the nineteenth century, and except for most resorts, the industry largely followed.[3] Not all small-town and small-city operators followed blindly, for in the early 1920s, the *Hotel Monthly* reported two small-town hotel managers who returned to the "American Plan."[4]

Scientific management was often promoted in print and made it clear that principles, not personality, reigned. The manager whose regular appearance in the barroom enabled him to spy on barkeepers to prevent theft, or whose natural social skills made for congenial hospitality, were two common practices of Mine Host, contrary to those of scientific managers.[5]

The half-century operation of the Hotel Gettysburg (1914–64) by the Scharfs, a German family, epitomizes what an uncommonly aggressive Mine Host might achieve but also illustrates the procedures of that increasingly outdated model. The Scharf patriarch, Henry Sr., learned on the job what he practiced, beginning in 1882 at the Bellevue Hotel in Philadelphia. He subsequently managed the White House Inn during the World's Fair in Chicago in 1893 and, thereafter, other hotels in Omaha and, again, in Philadelphia. Lacking a trained staff at Gettysburg, for whose management he was solicited, the senior Scharf relied heavily on his wife, one daughter, and two sons. After he died in 1922, his twenty-year-old son, Henry Jr., announced plans to enlarge and renovate the hotel and include a 1,500-seat auditorium, financing the expansion with locally sold bonds. Gettysburgers had long wanted such an auditorium for community functions. The young dynamo also hired a man to head a public relations department, and together they visited cities throughout Canada and the eastern United States to convince people to stop in Gettysburg. The Gettysburg battlefield's historical significance provided a reasonable platform for Scharf's mission, but he apparently never flagged in his promotional labors, which extended into the 1950s, when President Eisenhower regularly used Scharf's hotel for a retreat and a pressroom in an annex and, on one occasion, during physical recovery. Scharf always worked on drawing motorists and conventioneers. None of this required theoretical speculation or resorting to trade textbooks although Scharf stands prominently among the gifted hotel men in the trade's history. It all seemed an obvious series of steps if "Mine Host" Scharf was to profit in his business and publicize his community base.[6]

John Willy's exhortations in the *Hotel Monthly* and a wealth of advertisements throughout the publication show how the more common practitioners were taught to manage their business. It was a poorly managed small-town hotel that Willy described at length in hope of guiding others away from certain practices.[7] The founder of the Van Orman chain thanked Willy and other trade-related publishers for carrying advertisements on the latest products.[8] Above all, Willy wanted to inspire hotel managers, characterizing their potential in hyperbolic terms. To the Illinois Hotel Association in 1918, he concluded of managers, "They have opportunity to make the earthly habitation of travelers so near like heaven as it is the privilege of mortals to try to do."[9] Recalling the average wayside inn at mid-nineteenth century, he cited passages from Winston Churchill's *The Crisis* to invidiously contrast the "old days" with the potential of modern improvements. For example, about cramped quarters, Willy quoted one scene: "'Now, Ben, 'taint no use getting mad. You, and Joshway, an' Will, an' Sam the Cap'n, an' the four Beaver brothers will all sleep in number ten. What's that, Franklin? No, siree, the Honorable Abe, and Mister Hill, and Judge Oglesby is sleepin' in seven.' The smell of perspiration was stifling as Stephen pushed up to the master of the situation" (fig. 27).[10]

FIGURE 27. Hotel managers still routinely booked too many lodgers in a room, as this postcard's cartoonist contended. Authors' collection.

FIGURE 28. The front desk was the hotel's foremost public introduction once one came inside. The caption read in part, "Manager's desk is located directly back of room clerk's stand, so he can quickly serve the guest when clerk may be busy with his other duties." From "Hotel Holst of Boone, Iowa," *Hotel Monthly* 30 (Jan. 1922): 55.

Willy regarded Sinclair Lewis's *Work of Art,* published in 1934, as an accurate, yet fictional account of "the average hotel, as is, or as it has been in the United States during the last forty years."[11] There, one manager spouted generalizations lacking practical implementation—for instance, "The heart of a hotel is its kitchen; the Front Office its nervous system."[12] It sounded astute but lacked specifics. Lewis's novel treated the consumption of trade magazines as a potentially important educational resource for hotel managers.[13] Willy published numerous articles on exemplary hotels where managers, he wrote in 1934, guided "the period of transition from the crude to the scientifically equipped and operated house of commercial hospitality of today."[14] He picked out unique practices such as the program at the General Shelby Hotel of putting new wallpaper in one-third of the rooms every three years, hoping this example in Bristol, Tennessee-Virginia, might set a pattern elsewhere.[15] He dovetailed illustrations with pointed captions into the written text, maximizing every means to lecture (fig. 28). Moving from the rude past into the efficient present required the most progressive management to clearly delineate responsibilities and acquire knowledge through reading, participation in professional organizations, and ascension through a succession of increasingly larger hotels. When the Lincoln-Douglas Hotel in Quincy, Illinois, opened in 1931, the local newspaper reported its boasts of having both a managing director and a resident manager.[16] Myron Weagle, the protagonist of *Work of Art,* demonstrated the growing desires and expectations of lodgers, adding the pressure of popular culture to the evolving trade literature. Weagle started in 1894 at a hotel with thirty-four rooms in a small Connecticut town and reached the summit of his professional odyssey in the management of a hotel with eleven hundred rooms in New York City. In the Great Depression he returned to a Main Street hotel in Kansas.

The scientific management trend relieved managers of the stress from having to improvise in identifying and then performing the tasks of oversight, whatever the size and location of the hotel for which they worked. Small-town and small-city hotel managers still faced the peculiar need to be "jacks-of-all-trades." John Ostrow, who owned a hotel in Fredericksburg, Texas, was also his own manager, and to his state's hotel convention he remarked, "The man who owns a hotel in the country is at the same time, his own manager, general manager and assistant; he is his auditor, bookkeeper, clerk, porter, chief cook and dishwasher. Sometimes he has to clean up rooms and other places. He has to wait on the table."[17]

The specialization of tasks and the specialist's perfection in them that comes with repetition were hardly allowable during the fray of daily work. Periodic circumstances caused temporary difficulties, but solutions promised relief. Small-town and small-city managers at the Illinois Hotel Association meeting in 1923, for example, were dogged by coal prices, agreed that oil burners should be installed in future cold seasons, and anticipated a long reign of prosperity due to their state's early construction of an extensive concrete-highway network.[18] Small hoteliers less given to the new systematic-management approach, but still in business, bravely clung to aphorisms that now began to sound platitudinous or obvious. For example, in 1927, well into the ascendancy of the new paradigm, C. N. Ball of the Marietta Hotel in Rock Rapids, Iowa, counseled the Northwestern Hotel Association: "Service is the thing.... Courtesy opens every gate.... Honest service we often and unthinkingly call commercial cleverness, but, after all, it is nothing more than business built on honor." Technical knowledge found no place in his scheme. He instead summarized, "These principles, coupled with a lot of hard work, will surmount a mountain of difficulties. The power to do, the patience to endure, can only be acquired by hard work." It is not surprising in the early twentieth century, when the hotel trade embraced big-business techniques, that a manager like Ball declared no interest in owning a hotel chain: "I am contented to operate a country hotel."[19] Mine Host Ball helped define the past in the present. The latest technology could serve guests' convenience and comfort while at the same time improving the manager's profits. However, the small operating scale alone in small-town and small-city hotels permitted a more personal relationship between guests and managers, who could attend to the needs of individual guests.[20] Main Street managers perhaps took refuge in defending their practices against proponents of scientific management but only to the degree that they were aware of such claimed advances. Many simply ran their businesses more casually. John Ostrow, at the Texas hoteliers' conference two years earlier, spoke for what he believed to be the mass movement of small-town and small-city hotel managers: "The days of the old roadhouse tavern and the famous innkeepers are in the past. Today the country hotel is like the hotel in the city. . . ."[21] The Van Orman family's small-city hotel chain was built in part on regularized practices published in a manual to insure identical management from unit to unit.[22] The likes of Edward Cornelius Berry became rare. One of the few African Americans who owned and operated a hotel, he later became a celebrated hotel man who opened a house with his name in 1893 in Athens, Ohio; operated it until 1921; and introduced there several "firsts": Bibles and closets in every room and needle, thread, and buttons for all lodgers.[23]

Art no longer sufficed. The new learning entailed the science of accounting vigilantly applied. It was not enough to record and trace expenses because hotel men began to calculate the future. Most important was how to profit from a business package—the hotel's building, machinery, and continually trained staff—that did not remain useful for more than thirty-two years.[24] Others stretched it to fifty years.[25] Rigorous accounting yielded these calculations after the imposition of the income tax in 1913 and the concept of "depreciation" became important to reduce taxable earnings. Before then, "depreciation" was a highly variable figure each accountant assigned as they wished.[26] William J. Foster, a founder of the accounting firm of Harris, Kerr, Foster, said that at least before 1910 records were not well kept, including those related to the control of funds and materials.[27] Foster chaired a committee of accountants which, in 1925, proposed the Uniform System of Accounts to the American Hotel Association, and it was widely adopted. By the late 1950s, two firms performed most of the industry's accounting: Harris, Kerr, Foster and Horwath and Horwath.[28] Aggressive managers were those who paid careful attention to accounting. E. M. Statler wanted "accountants to know the danger signal and put up a red flag for the proprietors. They should not simply compile the reports and place them on the hotel operators' desks. They should make a special note of those matters which deserve attention."[29] In the 114-room Hotel Dunlap in Jacksonville, Illinois, manager Wilbur H. Kurtz practiced the Uniform System of Accounts despite his house's small size because "the information it provides us—daily, weekly, and monthly—is so useful in knowing trends and in adjusting our operation to meet conditions as they occur."[30] Accounting extended to other Main Street businesses enabled managers to help owners attempt to redress perceived inequities—for instance, that hotels should pay most of the cost of tourist

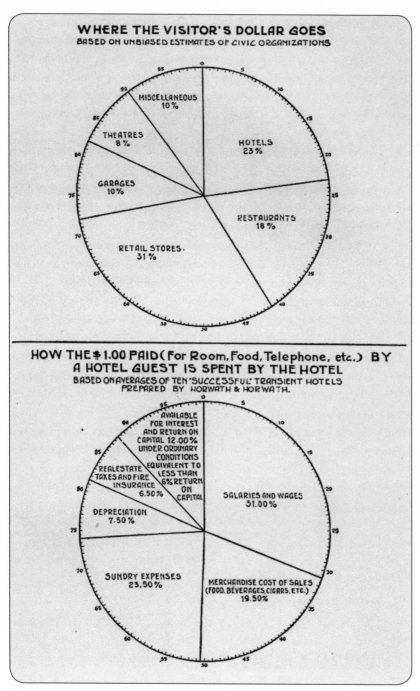

FIGURE 29. The American Hotel Association's *Hotel Red Book* presented the graphs above. From *The Official Hotel Red Book and Directory* (New York: American Hotel Association Directory Corporation, 1930), 831.

and convention bureaus because they induced business from which hotels earned the greatest share (fig. 29). Greater self-awareness also flowed from scientific management. Whereas the call to service sufficed in the past, the vice president and director of sales for the Drier Hotels wrote in 1941 that "nothing is more perishable than rooms, the principal hotel commodity. Some say that all a hotel has to sell is service." Keen profit-mindedness taught, "That is a pleasant fallacy." Tangibility superseded sentiment: "Service is not our stock. . . . you don't *sell* service—you give it away. Service is the invisible packaging that makes the product more acceptable."[31] Systematic management dictated attention to details, no matter how small; failure to do so "is one of the dangers in factory methods of extending service," especially among "the reliable repeater whose dusty luggage and familiar features turn up every few months."[32] Hence, continual diligence hovered over every decision: "Public hospitality that pays is inevitably the result of planning, knowledge, imagination, and sincere determination to please the guest-customer. This can be accomplished only through unceasing effort and constant study."[33]

The results showed themselves in intangible ways. "Check into a typical hotel, *incognito*," a *Hotel Management* columnist advised in 1953. "See if it has some vital spark, some engaging force of management." The origins of that "spark," however, were in rationalized management, not in some vague feeling for good will. A manager, the columnist preached, should even teach the entire staff the definition of the historical figure for which the hotel was named.[34] Legal considerations fostered education in the special realm of "hotel law" because, as the American Hotel Association's lawyer lamented in 1928, "there are a few elementary legal principles connected with the operation of the hotel concerning which many hotel keepers are even yet not clear as to their scope and limitations."[35] Should hotel registers be kept indefinitely? As a "quasi-public" space, what were the manager's limitations in dealing with people in his hotel?

Marketing

Hotel advertising also grew increasingly important throughout the twentieth century. Nationwide hotel directories first appeared in the 1870s, and small-town and small-city hoteliers did not fail to include their houses.[36] They also included themselves in other directories—for example, in the Travelers Hotel Credit Letter's pocket-size hotel directories. The Travelers Hotel Credit Letter was a company that certified commercial travelers' credit upon presentation of a check to hotel cashiers and simultaneously promoted their own services along with those of the hotels participating in their system of credit letters.[37] Like directories, signboards

Figure 30. The Hotel Bucklen in Elkhart, Indiana, on the Lincoln Highway built sign boards like this one only a few years after the highway's conception. From "Finger Posts in Automobile Highways," *Hotel Monthly* 27 (Oct. 1914): 59.

along roadsides also dated from before the turn of the twentieth century, but by at least the 1910s, with the advent of the automobile, came hotel managers eager to turn the old visual medium to their profit (fig. 30).[38] The depressed economy of the 1930s pushed managers to desperation. Advertising budgets doubled to approximately 4 percent of sales during the early 1930s.[39] Van Orman's budget for the McCurdy Hotel in Evansville, Indiana, was singled out for praise because it spent slightly more than 4 percent on promotion.[40] No longer did locational information on billboards seem enough; slogans were encouraged.[41] Notwithstanding the high costs of "direct mail," it was heralded in the early 1930s as "one of the most efficient" advertising techniques, and its proponents stipulated the components in great detail.[42] Emphasis on advertising persisted throughout the 1930s

FIGURE 31. Posters assuring comfort and security for traveling mothers and their daughters appealed broadly in the background of war. From *Hotel Monthly* 49 (May 1941): 35.

even though its costs seriously eroded profits.[43] In 1938 the Pennsylvania Hotels Association, whose director and chairman of public relations was Henry Scharf of the Hotel Gettysburg, launched a campaign of printed advertising to stimulate recovery. Techniques included messages on the backs of menus and cards displayed on elevators or slipped between the glass and the tops of bedroom bureaus.[44] Such methods seemed effective.[45] Systematic advice enumerated sixty-four printed advertising tips for "a public relations punch."[46] Scientifically calculated promotion became increasingly serious. In 1939 the author of a book about advertising and promotion for hotels and restaurants wrote, "The more one studies this business of selling hospitality, the more apparent it becomes that it's a business by itself."[47]

About billboards, expert opinion was mixed. In one analyst's estimation, such signs had to be placed at just the right location to get the driver's attention because people drove so fast; also, their effectiveness was not reducible to simple terms because the amount and kind of a hotel's competition made a big difference.[48] Yet, the Associated Hotels of the West undertook a campaign in mid-1940 using billboards as if they were almost a panacea. Radio complemented the roadside signs.[49] The following year, the American Hotel Association started an advertising campaign, National Hotel Week, in cooperation with various service organizations that utilized radio as well as printed material emphasizing hotels' affective appeals, such as its inspiration of improved "social standards" (fig. 31).[50]

Means small and large were also enlisted. Postcards were chief among them. As one of the early voluminous producers, the Detroit Publishing Company, advertised to small members of the lodging trade: "Hotels of importance all use them— views of their own hotels or those of their hotels."[51] The manager of the San Carlos Hotel in Pensacola, Florida, called *Hotel Monthly* readers' attention to an automobile show held in the hotel's lobby in 1934. He restated the hotelier's common claim of reciprocal benefits for local merchants: "Because of the more pleasant surroundings, a larger group of the quality people in town will attend the exhibit. This in turn is of benefit to the hotel for it is a means of attracting local patronage."[52]

The benefits of the automobile trade were mercurial. Spry Main Street hotel managers knew it. Where road conditions were of equal quality, motorists could easily search out the best hotel, as they saw it, scattered throughout those poorly managed. Manager Roy Scott of the Park Hotel in Richland Center, Wisconsin, tied his network of road signs into the area's agricultural economy. Renting the space for 105 signs from local farmers and paying them a dollar to notify him of needed repairs to the signs, he also was sure to buy all his poultry within a thirty-mile radius of the hotel.[53]

Managers begging the question of how to define "modern" habitually took on the latest technology in order to claim their house was modern. Hence, Charles

Baur of the Terre Haute House in Terre Haute, Indiana, was celebrated among his counterparts nationally for introducing a host of machines such as portable electric fans in every room in 1891.[54] He became famous as a manager in the industry's folklore for arranging an elegant service and banquet on five hours' notice, as the *Hotel Monthly* reported it in 1898.[55] The *Hotel Monthly* overtly promoted the latest technologies, editorializing for the telephone to replace the electric-bell system and against one of the most recurrent pests, the bedbug, excerpting the relevant section on "Remedies" from a U.S. Department of Agriculture circular.[56] The trade publication reprinted the *San Francisco Examiner*'s editorial on substituting the new card-index system for the traditional hotel register and commissioned an article by managers of two hotels in Fremont, Ohio, extolling the virtues of the automatic versus the hand-stoked coal boiler.[57] Advertisements for numerous products helped fill each issue: roach control, ovens, coat hooks, cash registers, refrigerators, air conditioners, uniforms, blankets, road signs, clothes hangers, and electronic room and occupancy recorders.[58]

Countervailing machines to perfect managers' evolving systems, managers were advised to rely on human discretion. Here the oscillation between science and art in management swung to the latter. From the Knott chain's house organ in 1934, the *Hotel Monthly* reprinted the article entitled "Technocracy No Substitute for Personality." Later that year it published recommendations entitled "Using Employees' Slack Time to Inspect Rooms."[59] Mine Host's modus operandi never disappeared completely.

Innumerable problems could bedevil managers. Each could be very demanding of time and expertise. Smoking, for example, was very popular with many lodgers and guests during meetings and relaxation throughout the hotel, but others objected to it as unclean and smelly, all the more noxious because it was so widely practiced. It always threatened life because of the fire hazard resulting from the guest who fell asleep smoking and set the surroundings on fire.[60]

Theft gained lots of attention in popular publications. The *Saturday Evening Post* in 1925 carried an article describing the elaborate machinations by which itinerant couples skipped from hotel to hotel without paying their bills. Annually, 2 percent of profits were lost to this and other crimes.[61] Theft of various kinds, including valuables taken from rooms, was the subject of an article in the *Saturday Evening Post* nine years later.[62] Taking small items like paper, envelopes, pens, and ink made up a category known in the trade literature under the humorous name "souvenir hunting," but it was nonetheless a serious concern for managers.[63] Managers resisted in individual ways. For example, the aforementioned Hotel Credit Letter Company's certification of authorized firms whose businesspeople presented checks to be cashed introduced some security for hotels participating in the system.[64]

The whole industry, Main Street hotel operators included, seemed satisfied with the progress they had made by the late 1920s in "mechanical and comfort delivering services," according to an article in the *Hotel Monthly*. [65] A narrative of professionalism then began to emerge concurrently. Mine Host's long-elevated sense of calling and public respect required something more, leaders of the industry began to say. Cleveland's city manager extolled the elements of formal training to the American Hotel Association's critical meeting of 1924. Having ended the indebtedness of its predecessor and wrangling about a constitutional reordering to include an executive council of regionally elected representatives, the juncture seemed auspicious to hear Cleveland's city manager elaborate that "a great modern hotel requires scientifically trained minds. If hotelmen live up to the real and ancient dignity of the *profession,* it must be by the best that can be put into it; the best education, the skill, the standards of the *professional man* [authors' italics]."[66]

Creative work henceforth would be most desirably elevated, according to industry leaders, to training by specialists in schools outside the workplace. In 1922 Cornell established the first school of hotel management.[67] The yen for improved status shared with other "white collar" workers surely added cause for formal training and its concomitant faith in scientific management. Status anxiety for hotel managers was, as Sinclair Lewis sensed in *Work of Art,* overcome by fledgling managers' acquisition of an education for their work.[68] Considerable loss of skilled labor, however, added the immediate demand for a practical remedy because, during World War I, many immigrants who worked in hotels returned to their overseas homes, and stiffened immigration laws blocked replacements from the European hotel trade.[69]

Small-town and small-city managers were comparatively absent at first from the formal education movement. Some, such as Fred Pantlind of the Pantlind Hotel in Grand Rapids, Michigan, and F. Harold Van Orman of the Van Orman chain were members of the early American Hotel Association hierarchy, but neither stood out in the association's commitment to education in colleges. At most, Pantlind spoke favorably of the potential in a hotel management course at Michigan State College seven years after it was first investigated at East Lansing, in 1921. Van Orman preferred trained staff, but in 1934 he revealed that, for some years, he had educated staff at the primary hotel in his chain. Chain owner Edwin Boss held officerships in regional hotel organizations. He preferred to teach his managerial staff and held them responsible to a system known as the "'Boss' way."[70]

Not every potential recruit, of course, could afford formal schooling, and small operators seemed too casual for the sophisticated changes that the editors of *Hotel Monthly,* at least, wanted in the future throughout the whole of the industry—hence, the publication's continued litany of tips to readers, excerpts from other

FIGURE 32. The uppermost two entries depict the unity managers were intended to find between the *Red Book* and hotels. The lowermost entry surely illustrates the *Red Book*'s utility but as well the racial stereotyping of African Americans who were denied hotel ownership and opportunities for hotel management throughout the American hotel industry. From *The Official Hotel Red Book & Directory* (New York: American Hotel Association Directory Corporation, 1930), 154.

relevant publications, and reports on meetings and hotel trade shows readers could not attend.[71]

As a result, Willy's editorship of *Hotel Monthly* meant readers saw repeated assertions exhorting hotel workers to know geography because travelers through their hotels would expect reliable travel information.[72] In many of their entries, allied publications implied that managers should also anticipate the special attitudes and needs of business travelers: orienting to service but not servility because businesspeople do not like fawning hotel workers; specializing in creating a homey ambiance under their supervision because traveling businesspeople miss home; considering the practice adopted by the Raymond Hotel in Williamson, West Virginia, of placing into the commercial traveler's mailbox a brief directory of local services, shops, and industries.[73] Beginning in the late 1920s, information about the size and rates of Main Street and big-city hotels nationwide was published annually in the American Hotel Association's *Hotel Red Book* for easy reference (fig. 32).

For all the residual talk about management as art, preachments to hotel conventioneers and articles alike enumerated the work to be done. By diminishing science in contrast to the coveted artfulness of management, the detractors of science overstated their case, implying that science was mindlessly prescriptive and without interpreted applications. Indeed, at least one proponent of art over science introduced his talk in those terms but proceeded to outline the categories of management a good hotel man should embrace. In the same issue of *Hotel Monthly* in which that talk was published, only two columns below the editors made a brief case for the increasing standardization of hotels—that is, what was identified as a product of scientific management. The manager of the Hotel Fremont in Fremont, Ohio, enunciated eight rules ranging over the tourist court competition, government legislation, staff knowledge about tourist sites, parking, new paint and wallpaper throughout the house, coffee shops versus dining room, kitchen hours, and road signs. Twenty-four years earlier, the *Hotel Monthly* had presented a diagram (fig. 33) showing the manager's central authority in any hotel; control lent itself to increasing standardization if lessons of the next twenty years, that is, until the articles cited above, were not to be lost. In hotel law, uniformity was urged as an implied benefit to management because hotels were deemed so influential in society.[74]

Labor Relations

Scientific management prescribed nothing about recruiting workers by social group. Work assignments had strongly delineated realms for minorities beneath Mine Host's management. Work was highly stratified by gender. As the editors of

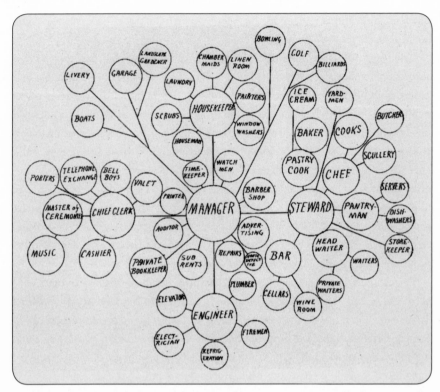

FIGURE 33. Every hotel service is shown accountable to the hotel manager, the supervening authority. From *Hotel Monthly* 12 (Sept. 1904): 32.

the *Hotel Monthly* put it in 1929, "As a general rule, hotels are, at present, largely managed by men. The demand for women workers even in subordinate positions is limited."[75] The Great Depression worsened the situation. At best, a woman might hope to become a head housekeeper, or head a hotel food service. It was in these two areas that most women worked. The latter, as the *Hotel Monthly* noted, was especially an area "instinctively a woman's field." The editors did not believe that the "best future in the hotel field" was as "rivals to men," but rather "in following out those lines which develop those qualities and instincts from home making and hospitality which are women's best gifts to contribute."[76] In 1922 about 56 percent of women working in hotels across the nation did so in housekeeping and 23 percent in kitchen and dining room work. Others worked mainly in hotel laundries or as secretaries, telephone operators, elevator operators, or checkroom girls.[77]

Much hotel work was like what servants did in private households, at least those of affluence. After the Civil War, domestic service had attracted large numbers of

FIGURE 34. At least one hotel in the North, the Hotel Yancey in Grand Island, Nebraska, featured an African-American elevator operator in its postcard advertising. Authors' collection.

African Americans. In the early twentieth century, blacks served as hotel porters, elevator operators, dishwashers, yard men, and the like almost everywhere, but especially across the South (fig. 34). Less frequently, they appeared as waiters and waitresses. By and large, whites were always favored, not only in hiring but in promoting. Widespread was the belief that blacks lacked competence for most jobs. "The colored employee in the South has a grown person's body and consequently a great capacity for work, but a well developed child's mind which is often incapable of developing qualities of judgement, acumen or undirected responsibility," wrote one hotel housekeeper.[78]

Women began to make some gains into the managerial hierarchy. In 1927 a member of the Faculty Club of Ohio State University pleaded for women to be in charge of dining rooms because of their gender-specific skills as homemakers. Employment had preceded recognition. Women had entered managerial roles, in fact, around the turn of the century. The reason was the impracticality of restricting managerial ranks to men if the industry was to expand. The larger hotels made possible by the introduction of elevators, for example, called for larger staffs and enabled women to enter the managerial workforce; the call to arms in World War I furthered the development. Uncommon circumstances left room for unusual talent, as in the case of Juneau, Alaska, where Marie E. Bergmann began her rise in the industry during the gold strikes. This German immigrant started working at a room and boarding house in 1896, moved to manage for her partners the Circle City Hotel a decade later, and, then, in 1913, built and owned the Bergmann Hotel, the city's best at the time. In the often family-managed Main Street hotels, women had long been managers although unproclaimed publicly. Elise, wife of Henry Scharf Sr. of the Hotel Gettysburg, illustrates this: she gained virtually no publicity in the industry despite her centrality in her family's renown Main Street operation. By 1943 the *Hotel Monthly* briefly chronicled the history of women managers and named those prominent at the time. Lewis's widely read *Work of Art* helped inform people of women's important role, for it was the mother in the family-run hotel who started teaching her son about hotel management before he became prominent in the work. Managers were also cautioned not to overlook women in the hotel market. Random evidence from one manager who doubled his hotel's income by directing letters about hotel services to women led one author on a book about hotel promotion to conclude that all women deserved more attention.[79]

African Americans made only limited gains. In 1937, with endorsement by the American Hotel Association and National Restaurant Association, Tuskegee Institute started a three-year curriculum leading to a degree in "Commercial Dietetics." Perhaps with race in mind, if not a sense of obedience to one's employer, the aim of the course was stated, in part, "not to *know more* than their employers, but to fit *in* with their employer's methods."[80] During World War II, some managers reluctantly employed African Americans due to the redirection of white male labor to military service.[81] On the contrary, the Hotel Orlando in Decatur, Illinois, a unit in the Van Orman chain, employed African American waiters in its formal dining room from at least 1934.[82] Where African Americans obtained work, there is little evidence that they worked their way up the chain of command as did whites.[83]

Labor practices distinguished small-town and small-city hotels. The hotel was one of Main Street's largest employers. Even small hotels required a labor force of some size and diverse skills. A hotel was not so much a single business as a cluster of businesses, and each cluster had its own distinctive labor demands. A modern hotel provided transients with meals and overnight lodging and locals with space for community activities. But in terms of business logistics that was only the tip of the iceberg. As the editors of the *Hotel Monthly* argued, "A modern hotel operates a heating plant, perhaps a lighting plant, probably a refrigerating plant, a bakery, a meat cutting establishment, a carpentry shop. It maintains a grocery store. It conducts a public laundry business. It operates a line of busses or of taxis or both. It manages a garage. It furnishes a telephone exchange. It carries on a restaurant business. It runs a beauty shop, a barber shop, a letting shop, a boot stand, a newsstand, a cigar stand, perhaps a gift shop and a florist shop."[84] Hotels, in other words, replicated much of Main Street. A hotel might be thought of as a kind of town within a town, a city within a city.

For a one-hundred-room hotel, the *Hotel Monthly* estimated in 1903, the dining room's labor typically required upwards of thirty people: a steward, a headwaiter, a chef and under-chef, two broiler cooks, two fry cooks, two butchers, a vegetable cook, a pastry cook, a pot washer, four dishwashers, a coffee man, two fruit-pantry workers, a keeper of the silverware, a storeroom manager, and at least eight other helpers variously assigned. Operating a five-hundred-room hotel in the 1920s, not including food service personnel, typically required upwards of 140 people. Necessary, of course, was a manager, an assistant manager, treasurer, and comptroller, all supported in the hotel office by a bookkeeper, ledger clerk, and stenographer. For insurance purposes three watchmen were needed to keep round-the-clock vigilance. Running a fully functional front desk required three room clerks, two assistant clerks, three cashiers, two "write-up" clerks, and a night auditor. Also required were three security people (including a house detective), a superintendent of service, two head bellmen, fifteen bellmen, twelve elevator operators, and three lobby porters. Below the head housekeeper and his or her own assistant, forty-five maids were required, along with six room inspectors, a chief houseman, five housemen, two mending women, and six scrub women. To maintain utilities, a chief engineer and two assistants, two electricians, and two carpenters were needed.[85] Economic hard times had forced the Hotel Tilden-Hall in Bloomington, Illinois, to cut the staff for this 120-room house. During the Great Depression, most hotels reduced services, cut back on repairs, and postponed remodeling but also required many of their workers to take on additional tasks.

The assumption of multiple jobs, of course, has always characterized the nation's smallest hotels. Describing the typical "mom and pop" operation, the *Hotel Monthly* speculated that beyond the husband-and-wife Mine Host,

> His clerks have to be bellboys, porters and quite often chambermaids, besides their regular duties. His cooks have to know how to cut meat, dress poultry and fish, cook all meats, fish, poultry, vegetables, soups, desserts, do all kinds of pastry work, make all salads and breads, do all the buying, take care of all stock, clean and scrub the kitchen, peel their vegetables and sometimes even wash the dishes. His chambermaids have to do all the chamberwork, check the linen to and from the laundry, and in many cases do the laundry. His engineer or janitor has to attend to the boilers, do a lot of repair work in the way of plumbing,

steamfitting, electrical repairing, carpenter work, locksmithing, etc. and he is the yard man.[86]

"Mom and Pop" hotels commonly employed family members and often without wage in part to cut down operating costs. Some parents figured, too, that work in the family business was a good means to inculcate the work ethic and teach their children skills. Myron Weagle in *Work of Art* exemplifies an ultimate success of this school of thought. At the Weagle family's house, Myron's position was "definite and simple: he did everything that no one else wanted to do. . . . He learned in his very bones the insignificant, unromantic, all-important details of hotel-keeping."[87]

Except for management, hotel employment did not pay particularly well. In 1928 a hotel manager might expect to earn upwards of $7,200 a year and desk clerks about $3,000, but maids about $488, and bellmen about $240.[88] But, it all added up. For a five-hundred-room hotel with operating expenses around $280,000, payroll would account for about 40 percent. Other big expenses included light, heat, power, and water (about 14 percent); replacements (about 13 percent); laundry (about 9 percent); and advertising (about 6 percent).[89] Because wages were so low, hotel workers tended to move from job to job looking for advancement if not higher pay. Those moving repeatedly were termed "floaters." Migration chains enabled former friends and acquaintances to follow one another job to job. At the Parkside Hotel at Kewanee, Illinois, the staff's geographical origins were quite diverse. Few came from the town itself. As the *Hotel Monthly* observed, "The auditor, day clerk, day porter, night porter, bell captain, one of the bell boys, the houseman, and pantry girl, all came from the Beardsley, Champaign, Ill. The cashier, two bellboys, second cook, and lunch room waiter from the Plymouth Hotel, Chicago; the night clerk from the Woodworth Hotel, Robinson, Ill.; two waitresses from Hotel Custer, Galesburg, Ill; one from the Graesmere, Chicago; one from Robinson's Chop House, Chicago; and one from the Vendome, Evansville, Ind."[90]

Low wages fostered moves to organize hotel labor but almost exclusively in the nation's big cities. Small towns and cities remained largely unaffected by organized labor until the 1930s, when hotel managers began not only to lay off workers but also to increase their hours and lower their pay as well as to increase their workloads. The *Hotel Monthly* championed various "ways to cut costs." These included considering bellhop tips to be part of their salaries, having the salaries of doormen paid by the taxi companies, and paying housemaids solely on the basis of hours rather than days worked.[91] Not only were hotel employees more receptive in the 1930s to labor organizers but the Roosevelt administration, through its National Recovery Act (NRA) initiative, also required the hotel industry to respect labor organizing.[92] Compelled to accept collective bargaining, the hotel industry railed against the NRA, with the trade journals leading the way. "Our business heretofore almost entirely clear of unionized labor conditions, has been brought to realize that thru the misunderstandings, innocent or promoted, of labor, we are now confronted by the possibility of being controlled by shop communities," warned one commentator.[93]

One way that African Americans played an important labor role in the hotel industry was to serve as strikebreakers where and when unionization did become eminent. Hired in, but then usually let go once regular employees returned to work, blacks only increased the levels of white animosity directed at them from locality to locality. Whereas African Americans struggled against prejudicial treatment in hotel employment, foreign immigrants tended to fare better. Like blacks, immigrant whites were willing, by and large, to accept the low pay scales offered for beginning positions. If difficulties arose, it was because of language inadequacies. Also, many immigrant groups harbored socialist and other left-leaning political tendencies and were, therefore, more amenable to unionization. World War I, however, provided opportunity to "Americanize" workers, not just those in hotels but everywhere in the economy. Passing emphasis was placed on teaching English and requiring employees to take classes in American citizenship. "When all of your employees speak the English language," *Hotel Monthly* readers were told, "they will become more efficient and loyal; will imbibe more of the spirit of America; and you will be better able to realize your ideal—an American hotel—in an American city."[94]

Mine Host and Scientific Management: Part II

Unwanted federal government intervention into the hotel industry, meanwhile, reinforced the trend toward professionalized management when the National Industrial Recovery Act (NIRA) was enacted in 1933. Codes of "fair competition" to stabilize prices and protect wages were stipulated, but the American Hotel Association resisted, suspecting that labor began to be unionized under the act's administrators. Profits recovered when Prohibition ended were immediately lost in compliance with the NIRA Code, complained Horwath and Horwath. Main Street hoteliers felt most acutely pinched between the federal government's demands and their depressed profits in the mid-1930s (fig. 35). The *Hotel Monthly* highlighted the code's formal rejection, which W. G. Nichols, owner of the Hotel Reeves in New Philadelphia, Ohio, directed in the Ohio Hotels Association's southern region. The American Hotel Association's Lucius Boomer, one of the biggest owners, headed a deputation that ameliorated the code in discussions with its administrators.[95]

FIGURE 35. The entire hotel industry's management believed the NIRA codes were unfair. From *Hotel Monthly* 42 (Apr. 1934): 13.

Considerable effort was expended both within hotel companies, especially those that operated multiple properties, and within industry trade organizations such as the American Hotel Association, to systematize hotel work, putting into effect many of the ideas promulgated by industrial time-and-motion analysts. Thoughts on labor were swept along in the move to scientific management. Job descriptions were reformulated, job manuals written, time sheets devised, hiring practices improved, and training programs created, all in an attempt to more fully rationalize hotel work. Hotel work, however, was not so much a science as an art. At bottom, hospitality was what the hotel business was all about, and aspects of Mine Host were valued here and there. Already in the early twentieth century, hotel people were beginning to think of the hotel industry as the hospitality industry.

What every hotel needed to encourage was effective personnel supervision. Employees could not simply be given free reign in meeting the public. As the training manuals emphasized, public relations required constant attention. Nowhere was meeting the public more important than at the registration desk. Desk clerks needed skills akin to those of diplomats. "The clever hotel clerk is well dressed and suave, to be sure," wrote sociologist Norman Hayner, "but first of all he was a diplomat. The government might well insist that future ministers and ambassadors receive some training behind the desk of a leading caravansary. The first lesson for the new greeter is that the guest is always right, and especially so when wrong."[96]

From one training manual we read:

> What are the words, questions, or expressions used by you on the guest's arrival, and on his inquiry for rooms and for rates? ANSWER: Should the guest be a person who has never before stayed at our hotel, I make a quick judgement as to the sort of room he would desire. When we have more rooms with bath than I know we will be able to sell I suggest the priced bath that I think will suit him as follows: "We have a very nice room with a bath at $2.50 that I am sure will please you; it has outside exposure and is well furnished and very comfortable."
> 2. What are the words and expressions used by you in rooming a guest? ANSWER: I greet the arriving guest with a "Good morning, evening, or afternoon," and at the same time start up a conversation that I hinge on himself, his trip, and weather or his car, if he came by automobile. "How far did you drive today? How did you find the roads? Have you selected a garage for your car?"[97]

The front desk, it was argued, was the hotel's "most strategic sales counter."[98]

Perhaps bellboys were next in importance when it came to dealing directly with guests. Sinclair Lewis recognized how off-putting bellboys could be:

> *Bellboys!*
> *They whistle as they carry your bag and look at how shabby it is and*
>   *snicker and point it out to their fellow imps*
> AND
> *Hit your shins with it in the elevator*
> AND

When they have opened your window, on winter days, and slammed it

    shut in August, and put their dirty paw on your towels, they just stand

    there and

IF

You give them less than a quarter they sniff and bang the door.[99]

From a manual for bellboys we read: "After a guest has registered and has decided to go to his room, the clerk will hand you the room-key, with the words: 'Show Mr. ___ to 201' (or whatever the room is.) When taking the key from the clerk, be sure to catch the guest's name—so that you may address him by it later on, if the opportunity presents. Do not start conversations with guests either on the way to the room or inside the room. Be courteous and responsive to anything a guest may say to you, but let it end there."[100]

Part of standardizing hotel work was standardizing employee dress. Not only bellboys but housekeeping maids, waiters and waitresses, and sometimes even room clerks were regularly uniformed. When Sinclair Lewis's Myron Weagle left his parent's hotel to work at the Fandango Inn in a much larger town, he was required to wear a uniform. It caused him some distress: "It was very tight, it had such crampingly tight trousers, and there was a confounded row of little brass buttons to do up and keep done up. In it he felt like a grind-organ monkey."[101] Uniforms helped assure guests that hotel personnel were, in fact, hotel personnel. Perhaps this was most important on the guest-room floors where maids, like the bellboys, had pass keys that gave them entry to the private spaces guests considered their own. So also were manuals written to encourage standardized room preparation, most of them aimed at housekeeping managers. Chapters tended to divide by subject: topics varying from the mundane (how to teach bed making, laundry folding, or furniture polishing) to the ethical (how to keep chambermaids moral).[102] If hotel work could not be completely standardized in the scientific sense as a kind of social engineering, then at least hotel personnel could look the part.

The Changing Challenges

Embracing scientific management was a long-term strategy and did not always suggest tactics to answer comparatively short-term aggravations. Hotel managers in small towns and cities faced an extremely difficult combination of circumstances by the late 1930s. Hotels in receivership either closed, putting an end to Mine Host, or managers quickly learned the systematic techniques to salvage them. The Dunlap in Jacksonville, Illinois, was a study in a 1938 issue of the *Hotel Monthly* about the costs saved from the latest machinery: stokers, new refrigeration equipment, and a laundry. Yet, however more efficient new machinery might render their operations, managers still faced the burdens of social security and real estate payments. Resort hotels were managed the most profitably, but in general, by 1940 profits had improved only among hotels where defense work centered. An advertising campaign to galvanize hotel patronage in the late 1930s failed largely because small hotels could not afford the fifty-cent-per-room assessment to fund it. Some big hotel managers attracted lost patrons by introducing "superservices," as the trade named practices such as circulating ice water and thirty-minute valet service. There is no evidence of their widespread adoption among Main Street managers.[103]

The market during World War II comprised a unique set of circumstances for Main Street managers. Rationing was foremost. Henry Scharf Jr. wrote philosophically in the *Hotel Monthly*, thirteen months after American's entry into the war, that there were some "compensatory features" to gas rationing but reported a decline in car traffic ranging between 50 and 85 percent.[104] However, lost profits were recovered in longer stays by those who did come, and the tourist camps and homes that went out of business proved how essential was the hotel format.[105] Scharf declared that "automobile travel is not a luxury," and small-town hotels remaining open, he had faith, would earn travelers' gratitude and respect.[106] In Peoria, Illinois, the Hotel Jefferson's manager publicized his tactic of advertising cards aboard streetcars and buses to attract customers.[107] Lauris Treadway bemoaned that "my hotels are in no way benefited by war conditions" but stoically described his essential adjustments in management: direct mail, taxiing people from home and railroad stations to his hotels, simplified menus, and elaborate entertainment.[108] Bruce Anderson, owner and manager of hotels in Lansing, Michigan, Bay City, Michigan, and Elkhart, Indiana, outlined his cost-saving measures but, like Treadway, mentioned no advantages for small-town or small-city operation.[109] The *Hotel Monthly* also featured an article entitled "Conservation and Care of Carpet," describing practices in the Hotel Wolford in Danville, Illinois, to demonstrate that meaningful economies were possible in every size of hotel.[110]

Managers turned to problems of unusually high demand in cases of short notice, older equipment, and continuous demand on staff accustomed to short-term, transient lodgers, not residential ones, where the military pressed hotels into maximum use.[111] Of course, resort hotels, which military forces filled, prospered, but prosperous small-town and small-city hotels were still hard pressed for enough workers.[112] Regulated rents also limited profits where the demand for lodging might have otherwise increased them.[113] These were the least of management's concerns.

Main Street managers also readied for the future. Some devised what they believed the best sale prospectus for a hotel that finally went bankrupt. Echoing the call for long-term planning, silenced for a decade in improvised responses, a

businessman with no previous experience as a hotelier admitted the new responsibility was harder than he assumed but foretold that, after the war, new purchasing power should be allocated "in an orderly manner." Scientific management also
gripped those who feared the resumption of the overbuilt market in small towns
and cities. Henry Scharf Jr. advised his Main Street counterparts not to panic over
the possibility that the federal government's pending superhighway program might
siphon business away.[114] He seems not to have foreseen the excitement of new motels along what was eventually named the Interstate.

In the shift to the peacetime economy in the late 1940s, the hotel industry spent
much of its wartime earnings on remodeling.[115] Morale, speed in accomplishing
tasks, and the up-to-date look of the remodeled hotel seemed to justify the undertaking, as the *Hotel Monthly* demonstrated in a series of articles in 1947.[116] The
American Automobile Association contributed reason to the renovation projects
with the new postwar standards it prescribed for a hotel's inclusion in its travel-
bureau data and publications.[117] Trade publications continued to include suppliers'
advertisements of their latest technologies.[118] Popular publications helped the public conceptualize the hotel as a huge machine of interlocking parts whose perfect
workings depended on steps often unseen by patrons.

Prices and wages increased, but occupancy rates fell. Managers returned to advertising campaigns, seeking especially convention-goers and automobile tourists.
It did not work well enough for many hotels, but those on Main Street often received their death blow. Big hotels and chains had the advantages of volume buy-
ing, better financing terms, central staff, extensive advertising, and reference service between individual units in the chain.[119] Talent and size usually went hand in
hand. Lewis's hotel novel characterized the boy who became a great hotel manager
as self-taught but one who had progressed from Main Street through managerial
responsibilities in a succession of larger hotels. *Work of Art* was as much about a
gifted person as about an autodidact in scientific management.

* * *

The evolution of small-town and small-city hotel management—from intuition
guided by response to the obvious, to an attempt at adopting widely validated rules
that would maximize profits and please patrons—brought with it the trappings of
formal education, which beckoned comparatively few managers in Main Street
settings. Rapidly changing geographies of transportation had set the institution
adrift, and for too many hoteliers in small towns and cities, attracting enough transient trade to buoy profits became a rising concern. Declining local populations for
community events took a toll as well. By the 1920s Main Street's hotel managers

could contemplate rationalized procedures and the abandonment of their forerunners' model of Mine Host—trends that had then ballooned to their apogee. The economically depressed 1930s summoned the need, managers thought, for scientific management, but that decade and the war that followed in the first half of the next decade ultimately called up the old model of intelligent response rather than structured forethought as a means to survive, if their hotels could survive at all. No matter how supple, resilient, and optimistic the small-town and small-city hotel manager might be, his or her business's physical plant was too big to relocate for changing travel routes. Thus, Main Street fell from marginal prosperity to antique curiosity with a very small market. Neither artful nor scientific management could effect a different outcome. Geography trumped management in Main Street's hotels.

HOTEL LIFE

As Americans are a people of considerable mobility, it is not surprising that hotels became fully ingrained in American life. The wealthy sustained the grand hotels of the nation's big cities and upscale resorts. By 1900, however, Americans of the middling classes were traveling extensively as well, prime among them the commercial travelers. But Americans also attended conventions in large numbers and otherwise traveled for pleasure. Motoring especially came to generate family-oriented recreational travel, with touring calculated both to the short "getaway" and to the long vacation trip. Local residents, of course, also figured prominently in hotels, although they mainly interacted among themselves at club meetings, banquets, and other social events. The main rationale for the transient hotel was to serve transients. Thus strangers mixing together tended to define what most Americans thought of as "hotel life."

It was generally accepted that the United States led the world in hotel innovation and comfort. As the editors of the *Nation* observed, "Our country might be defined as the land of great hotels, for it is doubtful if anywhere else there has been such lavish expenditure of money and such almost heroic endeavor to minister to the comfort, luxury, or even whim of the passing guest."[1] However, the nation's grand hotels—as elegant as they might be—could also to be quite impersonal. Substantially had hotel management been rationalized against the bottom line. Substantially were hotels conducted strictly as businesses, the host-guest relationship increasingly one of calculated distancing. Bigness had a way of fostering the impersonal. There were simply too many people around in big places to personalize all but a few relationships. Structure and formality prevailed instead. Anonymity grew. Thus, as guest creature comforts increased, hotel guests themselves were left increasingly to their own devices (or vices, as the case might be).

By 1900 many of the newer hotels of New York City and Chicago had guest rooms numbering in the thousands. In them hotel work had become highly specialized with employee work rules strictly codified. Hotel procedure, along with hotel layout, was systematically programmed. Gone were many of the highly personalized host-guest relationships that Americans had known, or thought that they remembered from times past. To the extent that traditional friendliness and personalized attention still remained, it was likely to be found mainly in the nation's smaller hotels in its small towns, or so it was argued. There traditional courtesies still prevailed among neighbors, courtesies that still readily extended to strangers. But even in small towns, and certainly in small cities, life was becoming increasingly impersonal. Hotels there were matching big-city innovations not only with regard to physical plant and technology, but also with regard to business ethics. That was most unfortunate, or so the editors of the Nation editorialized: "It is not in a gorgeous office, in spacious public rooms, nor in complicated system of call bells, formidable bills-of-fare, and superfluous servants that the real comfort of a good hotel resides. It is rather in quiet and respectful service, in fare perfect of its kind, however simple."[2]

The trouble was that many small-town and small-city hotels at the beginning of the twentieth century were languishing. Creatures of the railroad era, they were outdated. Most operated on very narrow profit margins that precluded not only upgrading but even ordinary repair. Service was eroded accordingly. Cutting operating costs, including the disinvesting of buildings, was typical. Whatever a hotel had to offer was what the guest got, a take-it-or-leave-it mentality tending to prevail. In part, however, guests themselves were probably also responsible for how they were treated. Guest indifference, as well as management indifference, prevailed, the editors of the Nation concluded. When it came to hotels, Americans were far "too amiable to find fault, and too busy or indifferent to argue."[3] As a crowd they tended to accept what they got. Social detachment had become all too prevalent.

What was to be done about it? The editors of the Nation were not sure. Perhaps the coming of the automobile would help. "The bicycle," they wrote, "now reaches the remotest corners of the land, and the automobile is to be seen on rural roads, bringing to the smaller inns a class of customers who are reasonably insistent in expressing their wants."[4] Not only were affluent motorists demanding as a class, but they also had the wherewithal to sustain their demands. Motorists represented a potentially lucrative new revenue stream, one that would enable hotel managers not only to upgrade their facilities but play more successfully the role of the host. Was that not something destined to succeed in small towns? Were not small-town Americans still rather open and friendly? Was not the typical small town something like a big extended family? Indeed, automobility did bring renewed custom to small hotels in small places, although hoteliers had to hustle to compete for it. Maybe it did help to be friendly—to extend small-town courtesies. Along with it might come renewed pride in community. Mrs. J. F. Tillman, whose husband managed the Hotel Montgomery in Clarksville, Tennessee, caught the spirit. She parodied a popular poem of day, the most widely quoted lines of which read: "But let me live in a house by the side of the road, / And be a friend to man."[5]

She penned:

> Yes, we live in a house by the side of road,
> Tho the road is now known as Main Street;
> And Main Street's a highway north, south, east or west.
> Echoing sounds of the motors that beat
> Out the rhythm of a nation's ideals,
> Its hopes and its dreams and its gains,
> And no matter how hurried the processions that pass,
> Reflection of each one remains.

And then she continued:

> The traveling man comes with his samples and jokes,
> He lingers to gossip a bit.
> He tells us of Howard, of Frank, or of Joe,
> And how hard his business is hit.
> The Civic Club drifts in to lunch and to talk;
> And ladies to bridge and to tea;
> The townspeople drop by for papers and stamps
> Or to see who the new guests may be.[6]

Commercial Travelers

The excuses to travel on business were varied: interviewing job applicants, assessing new markets, and so on. Certainly, hotels were necessary when changing jobs required a move to a new locality. But the most numerous of business travelers were the salesmen—the *hucksters* or the *drummers* in early twentieth-century

FIGURE 36. Lobby of the Rogerson Hotel, Twin Falls, Idaho. Photo courtesy of the Twin Falls Public Library.

parlance. In 1907 there were some four hundred thousand traveling salespeople in the United States, the vast majority of them men. On average, they paid $2.50 a day for a room, and typically for five or six nights each week for most weeks of the year. Thus nationwide traveling salesmen as a group brought to the hotel industry upwards of a million dollars a day.[7] The typical salesman's life was spent constantly on the go. It was, Forrest Crissey wrote, "a series of quick commercial contacts, a panorama of hustle, a touch-and-go proposition in which he must impress his personality upon the trade with almost the quickness of an 'instantaneous exposure' of a Kodak."[8]

Those who sold in big-city markets, of course, did not need to stay in hotels. They could overnight at home. It was mainly those who sold in small towns and in small cities who were hotel-dependent. In much of rural America, sales territories of sufficient size to support a salesman invariably involved customers widely separated geographically. Most salesmen made do on marginal salaries and/or on limited commissions and were very much budget-minded. Most paid their own expenses. As the new twentieth century dawned, the older hotels of the railroad era suited most traveling salespeople quite satisfactorily, if only for their low rates.

FIGURE 37. Lobby of the Woodworth Hotel, Robinson, Illinois, circa 1900. Photo courtesy of Sue Jones and the Crawford County, Illinois, Historical Society.

Only top salesmen, especially those who worked in a rapidly growing industry, could afford the burgeoning auto era's new hotels.

Fortunate, indeed, were the salespeople who had room, meal, and transportation expenses covered by their employers. An expense account enabled a salesman to rent a sample room and stay in it at night without cost to himself. At Ironton, Ohio, for example, the new 128-room Hotel Marting had ten sample rooms, each measuring sixteen by eighteen feet in size. Each came equipped with several display tables and a fold-down bed (but not a private bath). They rented for $3.50 a night.[9] A sample room enabled a salesman to display a wider array of goods than would otherwise would have been possible, customers tending to come to the hotel to place orders rather than the salesman going to them. This put a hotel's various public amenities at the salesman's disposal in his closing of deals. At the very least, hotel lounges provided writing desks where salespeople might catch up on record keeping or answer correspondence (fig. 36).

A sales territory, wrote William Maxwell in *Collier's,* was "a map containing so many towns and so much possible business." But so also was it "a collection of places with bad hotels and worse railroad connections." Too frequently, Maxwell noted, hotel managers were indifferent to the needs of commercial travelers. Too many of them were "unconscious foes to efficiency on the part of their guests as well as remarkable examples of inefficiency themselves." He concluded, "The bad cooking, untidy housekeeping, and general squalor of the average commercial hotel make if difficult for a commercial traveler to maintain constantly the fervid enthusiasm about his [employer], his goods, and his job,"[10]

Through World War I most salesmen traveled by train. When they were not at leisure in a hotel lobby after business hours, then they lingered there during the business day waiting for train connections (fig. 37). Their sitting around in a hotel's public spaces could be more than a little off-putting to women. So it was with Claire Boltwood, the heroine in Sinclair Lewis's novel *Free Air*. Lewis described her stop at fictional Gopher Prairie's Minniemashie House, the hotel first introduced to readers in *Main Street*: "Claire was conscious of the ugliness of the poison-green walls and brass cuspidors and insurance calendars and bare floor of the office. Conscious of the interesting scientific fact that all air had been replaced by the essence of cigar smoke and cooking cabbage; of the stares of the traveling men lounging in bored lines; and the lack of welcome on the part of the night clerk."[11]

But the automobile, as it stood to change small hotels, also stood to change selling, at least selling "on the road." When a salesman got a car, he found that he could more enthusiastically cover his small-town customers. "Now he consistently visits 72 per cent more towns per day than he did before. . . . He makes 12 per cent more calls a day. His sales have increased . . . [some] 50 percent. His traveling expenses have increased in total amount, but they are somewhat less than formerly, figured as a percentage of sales," or so one journalist surmised. Advantages, he continued, accrued not just to the salesman but, importantly, to his employer. Car travel greatly increased the number of daily calls a sales force could make, diminishing the need to employ so many salesmen. It enabled those salesmen who remained on a payroll to reach even remote customers, those who before had been visited only infrequently, or not at all.[12]

After 1910 the streets around hotels were increasingly filled with Ford coupes, "mud covered and generally travel battered," as the editors of *Hotel Monthly* put it. But alarmingly, at least to hoteliers, those cars enabled salesmen to get home more days each week, potentially cutting into hotel business. Whereas automobiles brought tourists to a town, they also tended to take salesmen away. Hard times during the Great Depression accelerated the decline. By 1935 the number of salesmen traveling nationwide was down to 150,000.[13] On the positive side, improved autos and improved highways enabled salespeople to work out of locations central to their sales territories. Hotels in those locations thus benefitted. No longer did salespeople have to move constantly town to town, changing hotels nightly. They could stay in one place. Observed one hotel manager: "Nothing kills profits for the salesman and the house quite so effectually as being forced to get up at five o'clock in the morning, take a jerk water accommodation train . . . to a couple of small

FIGURE 38. The Traveling Salesman as illustrated by David Robinson. From Don Marquis, "My Memories of the Old-Fashioned Drummer," *American Magazine* 107 (Feb. 1929): 20.

towns and not be able to get back till next day. Great is gasoline!"[14] For many hotels, commercial travelers remained their primary clientele through the Depression. As one hotel manager from La Crosse, Wisconsin, told sociologist Norman Hayner in 1936: "Traveling salesmen make up the bulk of our guests. Their wares vary from silk hose to candy, automobile accessories, meat and Delco lights. Probably the automobile accessories salesmen are the most numerous. The men are usually young, some starting out on their first trips."[15]

It was the stereotype of the older, traditional salesman that long dominated American thinking about hotel life. "The life of the typical traveling man," wrote J. R. Sprague in the *Saturday Evening Post*, "is a carefree, rollicking matter, with a background of big hotels, midnight suppers, taxicabs, song and story." To small-towners, especially, he said, they epitomized big-city sophistication, even if they did sit about in hotel lobbies "to occupy leather chairs and pick their teeth."[16] The drummer "was a brilliant bird of passage ever flitting to and from unknown regions," historian Jefferson Williamson mused. He was for the isolated small town an important connecting link with the great outside world. Did he not habitually visit "such far-away, prodigious, and fabulous centers of the universe as Chicago, St. Louis, and Cincinnati"?[17] Even big-city people considered the breed to be picturesque. The traditional salesman was known, it was said, "for flashy clothes, gay waistcoats, heavy gold watch-chains and rings" (fig. 38).[18]

Salesmen told off-color jokes. They cultivated the image of the ladies' man, or so argued the editors of *Reader's Digest:* "What has happened to the old-time traveling man, his cigar cocked at an angle and his feet cocked higher still, for whose benefit small-town maidens paraded with assumed indifference before the plate-glass front windows of the City Hotel? Or his later and smoother incarnation, with fraternal emblem in buttonhole, a handy bottle or two in his bag, and a line of high-pressure sales talk on his lips?"[19] "Bold, bad, and wickedly dangerous" traveling men thrived in American fiction. Rose Wilder Lane wrote in her novel, *Old Home Town:* "We saw them sometimes through the hotel windows, sitting in the shabby chairs among the brass spittoons; we saw legs sprawled with abandon over chair arms, thumbs in the armholes of resplendent vests, [and] derby hats pushed back on heads. . . . We hurried past modestly, eyelids lowered."[20]

But the traveling salesman was also to be pitied. Robert Tallant's novel, *Southern Territory,* followed the lives of several salesmen across the American South, men who were, according to one reviewer of the book, "devoted to their families at home, nostalgic and lonely while away, yet fatalistically attracted to their careers." The reviewer added, "Lacking inner resources to withstand the dreariness of hotel life, seeking companionship with one another, they drink continuously, becoming maudlin, melancholy, and depressed—hence easy prey for ever present predatory females." The novel, the reviewer said, offered "a compelling picture of a group of innately good-natured, yet boring people, desperately trying to have a 'good time.'"[21] Thus they were the kind of men for whom escaping the monotony of sterile hotel rooms too often led to transgression, followed, as another observer writing in the *Harvard Business Review* phrased it, "by abstinence for a week or so before returning home."[22]

Many were the organizations founded to aid commercial travelers and even improve their morals. The United Commercial Travelers and the Commercial Traveler's Mutual Accident Association of America were prime among them. The former published hotel directories and negotiated with hotels for reduced rates. The latter made accident insurance available at modest cost. Also important was the Gideon Society organized at Janesville, Wisconsin, in 1899, and described by

Newsweek toward the end of World War II as "the oldest interdenominational lay-men's evangelical association in the world." In 1908, the society had placed twenty-five Bibles in the guest rooms of the Superior Hotel at Iron Mountain, Montana. As of the end of July 1945, *Newsweek* reported, total worldwide distribution stood at 2,346,347. The average hotel Bible, the magazine reported, cost the Gideons one dollar to place and could stand, on average, "some fifteen years of thumbing."[23]

Automobile Tourists

Except in resort areas, small-town hotels of the railroad era tended to attract relatively few tourists. Small-city hotels fared better, given that even the smallest of cities tended to have tourist attractions and improved railroad connections. Travel by motor car, of course, put tourists, as well as commercial travelers, beyond the confines of train schedules. Motorists, like salespeople, could better pace themselves in moving across country. Often they found themselves at some hotel's dining room at noon, and, of course, at another hotel's guest room at night, not through planning but merely by chance. Automobile tourists could also be seen picnicking and camping along the nation's roadsides and their cars parked outside the new cabin courts, precursors of the modern motel. Hotels, in other words, were certainly not alone in attracting motorists.

Tourists, just like salesmen, could be stereotyped. There were young couples honeymooning. There were families on vacation, usually middle-aged parents with young children, and, perhaps, a dog. There were retirees. No single tourist type, however, fully stood out. Before World War I, it was the affluent tourist who clearly dominated, some arriving in chauffeur-driven cars. After World War I, however, lowly Fords and Chevrolets mixed with haughty Lincolns and Cadillacs in hotel parking garages. It is interesting to follow the treatment that auto tourists received year to year in hotel industry trade journals.

First mention of an auto tourist in the *Hotel Monthly* came in 1907 in a short article headlined "New Patronage for Country Hotels." The Central Hotel in Goshenville, New York, had benefitted a few years before from a new interurban trolley line, the typical trolley passenger tending to be a "grip man." But unlike salesman before, who had previously spent whole days and overnight in town, he came "in for a meal and off again, or for a lodging with perhaps one meal." As his stay was shorter, his bill was invariably less. But so also the Central Hotel had become a popular place for touring motorists to "refresh and even stay the night." "These automobile people were more uncertain even than the trolley people," claimed Si Smiler, the hotel's manager. He never knew when to expect them or how soon they would "deplete his larder." But their money was "freer than that of any other patronage he had ever before known." It had enabled him to refurbish the hotel's dining room and start up a garage—one that "sold a lot of oil and other things that the chauffeurs must have."[24] He had, in other words, discovered the affluent "carriage trade," the wealthy class of Americans who pioneered motoring for pleasure. Also appearing in 1907 was a short account of Andwar Hotel in Elyria, Ohio. Some fifty years old, the seventy-seven-room hotel had been refurbished, twenty-six of its guest rooms having been given private baths. The manager was "catering quite extensively for automobile trade, and one evening had as many as twenty-one machines lined up in front of his house." Most of his automobile guests came from Cleveland some twenty-eight miles away, he said, orders for "automobile refreshments" being received ahead by telephone.[25]

Ten year later, with lower-priced automobiles available to a majority of Americans, automobile tourists had, indeed, become as numerous as commercial travelers in most small-town and small-city hotels, at least during the vacation season—summer in most localities, but winter also in some states, like California and Florida. Unfortunately, as many articles in the trade journals reported, some hotels were overcharging and otherwise abusing auto tourists. As one hotel manager noted, "The automobile trade is willing to pay the price if they get service, and as in most cases they are traveling for pleasure, it is service they demand first." He added, "But merely because they are willing to pay well for service, they must not in any case be overcharged or be required to pay more than commercial travelers." Indeed, he argued, the future, especially of small-town hotels, might depend on motorist patronage: "The automobile spells progress, and the hotel should certainly get in line with progress."[26]

In 1917 the Bucklen Hotel at Elkhart, Indiana, found itself on the newly marked Lincoln Highway. The hotel's manager reported that his automobile trade accounted for about half the hotel's guests, forty to fifty automobile tourists being "registered overnight on the average." Did he have any trouble, he was asked, with motorists "abusing the house?" No, he replied. "They drive up in fine cars; the car with its baggage, etc., is stalled in a garage; the people come into the hotel with a little suitcase; usually they are quiet and nice and behave, and we take them on faith."[27]

"A great deal of interest is being taken in the modern country hotel," the editors of the *Hotel Monthly* wrote in 1923. It was because "automobile travel has brought about the need for modern conveniences and luxuries of a kind not dreamed of [even] twenty years ago." They continued, "Good roads are responsible for the new requirements. The good road has coaxed the traveler to make long journeys by automobile, both for business and pleasure; and the good country hotel supplements the call of the road and affords comfort in travel, also the opportunity to 'See

America' under the most favorable conditions—to travel without being slave to a train schedule; to find places of rest and refreshment in well ordered hotels away from the big cities."[28]

Motorists had special needs. And hotel managers did well to be alert to them. Every hotel, the *Hotel Monthly* advised in 1924, should furnish its reading room with an atlas, Rand McNally & Co. having just published the first of their annual road atlases. "The walls of the reading room could serve a very useful purpose by being hung with maps showing, in particular, the roads within two or three hundred miles of the hotel; also there should be a map of the city." Additionally, they advised, there should be posted in the reading room daily bulletins giving the condition of local roads: "The hotel that is most generous in giving out information of this kind, gains the friendship of the traveling public, together with much favorable word-of-mouth advertising."[29] An automobile club office located in a hotel was even better.

Most important, hotel managers were encouraged to provide arriving motorists with garage space. Garages represented an important new revenue stream. The Beaumont Hotel in Green Bay, Wisconsin, opened a garage immediately adjacent in a new two-story building, cars being stored on the ground floor. New sample rooms for salespeople were located immediately above. "We make a charge of fifty cents a night for car storage," the hotel's manager reported, "and charge two dollars upward for washing cars. We also keep a mechanic for minor repair work. We also operate eight Red Top cabs, a bus, and baggage wagon; also [we] sell oil and gasoline." Although increasing hotel revenue, the facility also increased expenses. It required both a doorman and extra bellboys at night, especially in the summer months. "We have to keep open now on a 24-hour basis," the manager said, "because of the uncertainty of motor arrivals; and, in the summer time, so many people drive their cars at night for the comfort of the cool night, instead of driving in the hot sun."[30]

With seventy-five guest rooms, a 135-car garage, and a filling station, the Ohio Hotel in Wooster, Ohio, prided itself as "furnishing accommodations for man and car" (fig. 39). Opened in June 1926, the hotel attracted some ten thousand overnight guests in its first eight months of business. Automobile convenience, along with modern guest rooms, did the trick. Each room was, as the manager emphasized, "furnished complete with everything that the better class city hotels furnish—real beds, real mattresses, bed lamps; electric fans are installed in every room regardless of the price." Taking advantage of its new garage, the hotel operated a Buick dealership and sold petroleum products at a gasoline station immediately adjacent.[31]

By 1930, America's network of intercity highways was rapidly maturing, and a new kind of motorway was coming to the fore: the four-lane, divided express

Figure 39. The Ohio Hotel at Wooster, Ohio. From "75-Room Hotel, 135-Car Garage and a Filling Station," *Hotel Monthly* 35 (Mar. 1927): 62.

highway. What would the impact be? The new roads might prove problematical, some thought, especially for hotels located at the centers of cities. On the other hand, the new roads offered opportunity for new rounds of hotel building. "Wide express auto highways will avoid congested areas, making the small hotel located at strategic points on these highways, popular. Such hotels will provide garage and auto facilities of all kinds," speculated the editors of the *Hotel Monthly*. Nonetheless, existing "well-operated" hotels should continue to prosper also, they speculated, particularly if they "specialize in good food and garage service, and have the proper setting and atmosphere." Possibly, the new hotels out on the new roads would be like the old highway inns. Emphasis might even be on old-fashioned hospitality. "We must get away from standardized hotels," they asserted, "and try to bring back the individuality, personality and atmosphere of the old-time Tavern. We must abolish institutional hotel rooms of the bed, dresser and chair type."[32]

The stock-market crash of 1929 and the severe economic downturn that followed curbed new hotel development, whether on the nation's Main Streets or out along its express highways. The nation found itself overbuilt with hotels, especially in small towns and small cities where efforts at emulating the big cities had spawned overinvestment. By 1935 hotel occupancy across the country was down some 60 percent from its 1929 peak. Room rates, accordingly, had declined some 30 percent. However, after only a few years there was once again light on the horizon. Automobility's growing popularity, despite the economic hard times, brought salvation. The American Automobile Association reported a 15-percent increase in auto travel for the first nine months of 1935. Some 37 million tourists had spent an estimated $4 billion, with an estimated $800 million of that going to hotels. And conventions were once again attracting more and more people. Furthermore, the decline in business travel had slowed. But mainly the new optimism lay with tourists traveling by car.[33]

Americans sustained their love affair with the motor car despite the Great Depression. A Chicago business man wrote to the *Hotel Monthly* in 1932, describing his recent trip by car across the Midwest. In small towns everywhere, he and his party "were impressed with the number of automobiles parked on the main and side streets." They could not imagine that there was a depression, what with the "exposition of wealth" evident: "We found in many places great difficulty in securing a parking space. We could drive around for blocks and often could not conveniently reach the hotel door to park long enough to find out what accommodations were available."[34]

Conventions

Conventions brought hotels fully to life. "To appreciate the importance of conventions to hotels," wrote G. K. Dahl, "one needs only to be present when a delegation of lawyers, doctors, nurses, or business men arrives—and transforms what seemed like a deserted village into a thriving, populous community." Once again money flowed: "from room rentals down to tips for the shine boys in the washrooms." Business flourished in the coffee shop, and "the silken rope" once again controlled the influx into the dining room and cocktail bar.[35] Through the 1920s, most Americans traveled to conventions mainly by rail, chartered trains booked at special rates being especially popular in that regard. Convention travel by car, however, was greatly on the increase.

Wide-awake hotel managers were always cognizant of their bottom line. They knew what their weekly, monthly, and seasonal occupancy levels needed to be in order to stay above the break-even point—the point below which accumulated expenses (taxes, payroll obligations, food bills, and bond payments, for example) could not be met. At most city hotels, the normal flow of transients was simply insufficient to meet operating costs, let alone meet debt retirement, capital improvement, and other costs. "Conventions overcome this difficulty by supplying guests in *wholesale lots*—supplying them, moreover, according to schedule, so that the incoming groups are large when transient guest business is small, and vice versa," G. K. Dahl advised.[36] Convention business boomed nationally, twice as many conventions (approximately 8,500) being scheduled in 1930 as in 1920. About half of them were state-level or regional gatherings, a large proportion of them, therefore, conducted in small cities. It was, however, the big national and international meetings that had increased the most, fourfold in fact. Most of these conventions were held in but a handful of cities. Chicago, for its centrality both in the nation's railroad network and its highway network, led the field.[37] In 1934, 9.7 million people attended some 18,000 conferences and conventions in the United States.[38]

Who was the typical conventioneer? Perhaps, he was a member of a fraternal organization: a Mason, an Odd Fellow, or an Elk. Maybe he was a member of a service club like the Rotary or the Kiwanis. Maybe she was a member of a patriotic organization like the Daughters of the American Revolution. He or she might be a delegate to a political convention, to a trade organization convention (like that of the American Hotel Association), or to a labor union convention (like that of the Hotel and Restaurant Employees Union).

By the 1950s conventioneers had come to outnumber other kinds of guests in both big-city and small-city hotels. Who it was that typically attended conventions was no longer quite the mystery. According to Donald Lundberg,

> Mr. Average Guest was a 35-year-old businessman attending a convention or a conference. With him goes [the] "two-suiter" and the ubiquitous briefcase, symbol of considered importance. He arrives at the hotel on Mondays, leaves late Thursday or early Friday.... He has his shoes shined, and calls on valet service to have his clothes pressed and laundry done at least once during his hotel stay. His diet is good but lacks imagination. For breakfasts it's juice, bacon and eggs and for lunch he has a meat entrée with potato and vegetables, tossed green salad for vitamins, ice cream and coffee. Supper time finds the Average Guest sitting down to soup, roast beef, which, of course, is medium rare, and that all-American must for dessert, apple pie.[39]

African Americans

Through the 1950s, hotel interests, if not Americans generally, thought of the typical hotel guest not only as male but as white. Before the Civil War, wealthy white Americans had employed black caterers, patronized black restaurants, and stayed in black-owned hotels and resorts as a mark of status. With the rise of Jim Crow, however, attitudes changed. Not only did entrepreneurial opportunity in the food and lodging industries evaporate for blacks, but they were also increasingly denied hotel employment, especially in managerial positions. So also were African Americans barred as hotel guests, resulting in the rise nationwide of a subset of hotels, mostly black owned but almost always black operated, that catered exclusively to African Americans.[40] Guidebooks—for example, *The Negro Travelers' Green Book*—listed them, along with the boarding houses, tourist homes, and motels that also accepted blacks.[41] When African Americans were employed in mainstream hotels, it was usually in menial, low-paying jobs. Of course, the Civil Rights Movement of the 1960s opened up the nation's hotels to black patronage and set the stage for blacks moving up the managerial ladder in hotel employment. However, it also brought decline to most of the nation's *Green Book* hotels, most black travelers opting for what most perceived as the far better hotel accommodations of hotels previously denied them.[42]

Hotels run by blacks for blacks were restricted mainly to the large cities, or to small cities with large African American populations. For example, Mansfield, Ohio, a factory town, had two.[43] Relatively few were located in small towns, there simply being insufficient numbers of African Americans traveling to support them. In small towns, as in the cities also, black- operated boarding houses and tourist homes might be used or, perhaps more commonly, a private home sought for overnighting. Simple inquiry in the black part of town told visitors who to contact. In general, most African Americans tended to travel between big cities, thus avoiding having to look for overnight accommodations in small towns in between. Alfred Edgar Smith noted that most black motorists were, in fact, "interurbanists."[44] Thus, unlike white tourists, they had less time to tarry along their routes to explore and to savor. Constantly did they rush on toward the cities, "hemmed in" as they were by lack of lodging options. Many, if not most, of the black-owned and black-operated hotels were poorly outfitted. Jim Crow, in fostering a monopoly over a limited clientele (a clientele generally lacking in affluence), tended to discourage hotel improvement from locality to locality.

Women

Women—that is, unescorted women—tended to receive less than enthusiastic welcome at hotels, at least up through World War I. "A lady, unescorted," wrote Jefferson Williamson, "may sometimes be refused admission to a hotel by a plea of lack of rooms or some evasion of that kind. It is well, therefore, for the 'lone woman,' especially if young, to write or telegraph in advance; or, better yet, to take a note of introduction."[45] The intent behind the discrimination, of course, was to keep women of "loose morals" away. Even as late as World War II, industry trade journals were still publishing articles with such titles as "Do Hotels Want Women Guests?"[46] In 1953 one journalist headlined his article "The Forgotten Guest." "What ever became of the 'Floor for Women'?" he asked. Prior to World War II, many large hotels had reserved for unescorted women at least one floor where they might receive special treatment, including a concierge to cater to their needs. "Today more traveling dollars are being spent by women than ever before," the journalist noted. "But few hotels are making an effort to cater to them. Listening to traveling women executives one could get the impression that many hotels are about as keen on having women guests as they are about admitting pets."[47]

Initially, separate floors for unescorted women, as well as separate hotel entrances, lounges, and dining rooms, existed not so much to pamper as to segregate. Despite their secondary status, however, the influence that women had on hotel life in America was significant. They might come escorted by fathers and husbands, or chaperoned as part of a large group, but once they arrived they did tend to make demands—demands that impacted not only the quality of hotel services but also hotel layout and design. The nation's grand hotels were especially made, in the words of historian Carolyn Brucken, "to accentuate the presence of women and put them on display."[48] And most mothers and wives wanted to be displayed at their best. At the very least, observed historian Jefferson Williamson, women as guests kept hotels more "spruced up" than otherwise: "Mine Host was quick to perceive that women were more fastidious in the matter of general cleanliness, more conscious of any deference paid to their tastes and convenience, and more responsive to the little things that might please them." Williamson further observed, "During the motor-touring season, the number of women guests is around fifty per cent. How to make hotels more attractive to women and how to give them more and more special service is a stock subject at hotel conventions and is frequently discussed in hotel trade journals."[49]

It was almost always the man who took the lead at the hotel register when accompanied by a wife or a daughter. In that and in many other ways, women, when "escorted," found themselves kept outside normal hotel routines. Once women did begin to travel alone, they found it necessary to learn the many ins and outs of hotel life, and articles to instruct them appeared in popular magazines. "Once you have a general knowledge of the situation," one article began, "you will understand how to meet successfully such problems as arriving, registering, tipping, ordering meals, entertaining, and all the many phases of daily hotel life."[50]

Hotels could be difficult even for working women. That was especially true of women who traveled to sell. "You must have nerve enough to stand unperturbed at the foot of a line of road men all intent on hogging the best sample rooms," Emma Danforth advised in *Woman's Home Companion*. One had to be alert to details:

"When you register, leave your baggage claim-checks with the room clerk for the head-porter. Never patronize the local truckman at the depot. The hotel head porter has a rake-off on all baggage transportation, so don't get 'in Dutch' with him, for he is the best friend you can have in the entire corps of hotel employees." Above all, it was necessary for women to keep up appearances. A woman did not want to be stereotyped negatively—which, of course, was a woman's main problem all along. "Don't take much stock in this 'freedom of the road' stuff," Danforth wrote, "but 'Stop, Look, and Listen,' and guard your reputation very closely." Even the oldest and best-behaved women were often misjudged, she warned: "So if you're young, unsophisticated, *and* pretty, watch your step, and avoid being too friendly with chance acquaintants, [even of] your *own* sex."[51]

Complaints and Problems

Expressions of displeasure shot both ways. Guests, at least on occasion, complained about hotel facilities and services, and hotel employees complained about guest behavior. Studies aimed at understanding guest complaints were legion. The hotel business was, after all, mainly about hospitality, and guests needed to be, if anything, kept content. The successful hotelier, it was repeated over and over again, needed to anticipate guest displeasure, thus to avoid unpleasantness. What was it that might irritate guests? The list was long. Room rates and food prices were frequently thought too high. Importantly, employees were thought too impersonal and even "high-hat." Noise was especially troublesome. In the cities, even in the small ones, there always seemed to be taxi horns sounding or newspaper boys calling out headlines on streets outside. Early in the morning, trash men seemingly everywhere threw garbage cans around with abandon. Inside it seemed like there were always maids talking, vacuum cleaners running, loud partying going on, phones ringing, or doors slamming. There were beds that were uncomfortable, plumbing that wouldn't work, lighting that was inadequate, or ventilation that was lacking. Room service never seemed fast enough. Then there were the truly petty things. As one guest in one hotel complained, "I don't like the trouser hangers that have a bar at the bottom. I like to hang mine by the cuffs."[52] It was not just in the poorest of hotels that bedbugs and other vermin were problems.

It was generally agreed that men tended not to complain as much as women, at least when they traveled alone. But when accompanied by their wives they more often did. "This is largely because the wife being in the hotel more than her husband in the course of the day, and knowing more about the details of good housekeeping, may notice things that would escape her husband's attention," one writer speculated. "Then she tells him about them—perhaps in an if-you're-a-real-man-you'll-have-this-remedied tone—and he feels duty bound to go to the desk and enlighten the clerk."[53]

Tipping was a constant headache, not just knowing when to tip and how much, but realizing fully that the hospitality one was enjoying hinged substantially on doing it right. As sociologist Norman Hayner observed, "The traveler may rest assured . . . that whatever the bellboy, waiter or maid is thinking about, the tip plays a role in that thinking." That was because wages were usually so low that employees were much dependent on tips to make a decent living. "By means of more or less subtle gestures," Hayner wrote, "he lets the guest know his attitude."[54] Hotel personnel, of course, played the constant game of sizing up the potential for guest largess. The salesman who dressed well and was "always spotless and smiling" was invariably a good tipper."[55]

Numerous were the editorials and articles that castigated the difficult hotel guest. Perhaps, at the top of the typical hotel manager's list was the souvenir hunter. Losses to theft or pilfering were part of every hotel's expense sheet—from the taking of towels and other linen in guest rooms to the taking of silverware and salt and pepper shakers in the dining room. In this regard, men seemed to outdo women, but whoever was at fault, the souvenirs taken were usually minor: the carnation from the lobby flower bouquet or the odd hanger from the guest-room closet. "Some people clean out a writing desk of everything it contains: paper, envelopes, penholders, extra pens, telegraph blanks, laundry lists, blotter—even the ink bottle itself! They take all the soap from the bathroom. Sometimes they take the glass tumblers," journalist Allison Gray wrote in *American Magazine*.[56]

All hotels suffered from wear and tear in the normal course of doing business and, accordingly, rooms had to be periodically redecorated. Walls had to be repainted and furniture reupholstered, for example. But some guests were especially hard on hotel furnishings. As Sinclair Lewis observed in his novel *Work of Art*:

> *Guests!*
> *They burn cigarette holes in the bedspread, the carpets, the chair arms.*
> *They leave the water, the costly hot water, running in the bowl*
> *For hours.*
> *They sit on edges of beds and ruin the mattresses.*
> *They cut the towels with safety-razor blades.*
> *They use the towels to clean mud off their shoes.*
> *They use same to wipe off mascara when they are females of the species.*[57]

Most problematical were the "deadbeats," those guests who left without paying their bills. Their behavior was rarely inadvertent or spontaneous. It was usually fully criminal in intent and execution. Forgery was a problem when it came to passing checks. Most hotels were plagued by room burglaries. Often it was a matter of hotel guests victimizing other guests. "A host of professional crooks travel about the country, living at the best hotels and preying upon the unsuspecting public. Bandits, burglars, blackmailers, forgers, confidence men, white slavers, dope sellers and bootleggers are included in the tribe of nomadic parasites," the *Hotel World* editorialized.[58] Hotel detectives helped identify and apprehend criminals, but few small-town and small-city hotels were large enough to afford a detective. Desk clerks, bellboys, and porters alone manned the front lines of hotel defense.

Actors traveling with theatrical groups and athletes traveling with sports teams tended to be troublesome. Stranded actors were notorious for not paying up. Not infrequently was a hotel's trunk room filled with baggage being held against an actor's or actress's unpaid bills. Thespians, it was said, were a hard lot to handle. "They were the only class of travelers who carried cats, dogs, birds, and other pets about the country with them," one author noted. "They slept most of the day, so that chambermaids had to work late cleaning their rooms; and they held parties in their rooms after a show until break of day, keeping other guests awake and burning up the hotel's costly gas and electricity. Worst of all, they were chronic abusers of the hotel's property, doing much washing and cooking in their rooms and not caring a rap what happened to the furniture and bedding."[59] Baseball players seemed to be an especially difficult lot. Many hotels forbade them to wear spiked shoes, as they were wont to do in coming and going to ball games. Even then they had a way of trampling about on carpets and over painted floors with great indifference. "The average ball player knows very little about hotel life or how to conduct himself in a dining-room," one hotel clerk reported. "I've seen them play catch at the table with hard boiled eggs and salt cellars."[60]

Despite a management's efforts at personalizing hotel hospitality, most hotels, especially those in big cities, were becoming, so it was recognized, more impersonal year by year. This was especially true where employee behavior had been highly systematized through coded work rules. But small hotels, even those in small towns, were hardly immune, especially where cost cutting reduced personnel and, accordingly, hotel services. Souvenir hunting and abuse of hotel property were more likely when a guest's relationship with his or her host was impersonal. In twentieth-century hotels, as in American society generally (and especially in the nation's big cities), social status had become increasingly a matter of outward appearances. People knew little about one another except by what they saw in ephemeral circumstances. People were not expected to really know one another. Indeed, meeting strangers in hotels was something to be valued for its anonymity. In hotels, people could behave in untoward ways and, having done so, largely escape responsibility for their actions. "Released from the bonds of restraint operative in smaller and more intimate circles," sociologist Norman Hayner argued, "the individual tends to act in accordance with his impulses rather than after the pattern of the ideals and standards of his group."[61]

The hotel, in other words, was an excellent place to take a "moral holiday," not just to let down one's guard but to deliberately violate behavioral codes. During Prohibition, bellboys could be relied upon to connect guests with bootleggers. They could be relied upon to direct guests to gamblers and to prostitutes. Then there was the problem of unmarried couples seeking places for "incognito and irregular sex relations," as Norman Hayner put it. "This is more or less taken for granted by the managers," he concluded, "and, unless too obvious, is ignored."[62] Indeed, hotel life was expected to have something of a pathological side. The hotel was, after all, a place where social mores could be pushed. But free play of impulses was something that emerged whenever and wherever transiency and impermanence pervaded. Hotels were not the only places. Hayner feared, however, that in hotels such behavior was becoming "overly symptomatic." Hotel life, for its increasingly impersonal and transient aspects, stood fully symbolic of what modern life, especially in urban places, was rapidly becoming. But hotels were leading the way. "The detachment, freedom, loneliness and release from restraints that mark hotel population," he wrote, "are only to a lesser degree characteristic of modern life as a whole."[63]

* * *

The owners and managers of hotels might be successful business people, but the hotel business—that of catering to or being hospitable to strangers—tended not to carry the prestige that other occupational endeavors enjoyed, especially in small towns. Certainly the hotelier did not enjoy the status accorded the banker, the lawyer, the doctor, or even the merchant. Hotel life, for not being home life, carried a certain stigma. It had very much to do with the untoward aspects of life which, unlike in private homes, were less hidden to public view. To the extent, of course, that a hotel catered to locals (who usually behaved) and not just to transients (who could be counted on to misbehave), the social stigma that attached to running a hotel might be overlooked. When hoteliers proved to be successful entrepreneurs by creating, for example, hotel chains spread across large regions, or when they displayed important civic leadership by providing, for example, important public venues for community interaction, their reputations soared. The latter was what small-town and small-city hotels owners and managers increasingly came to emphasize. But when motoring brought tourists (husbands with wives and, especially, fathers and mothers with children), then collectively hotelier reputations soared even more. Motoring did not just bring new custom to small-town and small-city hotels but also enhanced reputation through increased family orientation.

FOOD AND DRINK

Lodging was the hotel's primary *raison d'etre,* the hotel business being built around the renting of overnight guest rooms. But that did not mean that renting guest rooms was necessarily a hotel's most important source of revenue. Indeed, through the early twentieth century, especially in small-town and small-city hotels, income from food and drink usually equaled, if it did not exceed, what room rents generated. When calculated as a return on investment, a hotel's food and drink venues almost always proved the more profitable. Every hotel had a formal dining room. And most hotels had a banquet room, or at the very least a large event room that could be set up for banquets. Before Prohibition, virtually every hotel had a bar, although it might be dubbed a "men's grill" in offering a limited food menu as well as drink. With the coming of Prohibition, however, most hotels replaced their bars with "coffee shops." There, it was hoped, the serving of light meals, ice-cream desserts, and, of course, coffee, would recoup lost bar revenue. After Prohibition's repeal, bars quickly reappeared as "cocktail lounges."

Dining Rooms

Everywhere were the public spaces of American hotels intended to be formal. Early in the twentieth century guests were expected not only to be civil but to look civil—civility being a matter both of one's behavior and of one's appearance. Dress codes put men in jackets with ties, if not suits, and women in skirts or dresses. So also were women expected to arrive in hats and gloves and come, of course, escorted by a male companion or as part of a group. A facade of gentry acceptability was important to maintain. It was a facade that even the most outrageously behaved of commercial travelers—the more obnoxious of traveling salesmen—could not stretch with complete impunity. It was a facade largely male, almost exclusively white, and of relative affluence, if not of pretentious wealth. African Americans, as well as others looked upon as somehow "foreign," tended to be denied access to hotel public spaces, at least as guests. Nowhere, perhaps, were social codes privileging to white males more strictly enforced than in hotel dining rooms. There the tables were set with fine linen, china, and silverware, and the wait staff finely uniformed. Room decor was always in some way fashionable, often through allusion to European aristocracy. In many hotels, especially in the smallest of towns, finery was actually quite minimal but, nonetheless, fully communicative as to tastefulness, if not stylishness.

Except for the banquet room, and sometimes the lobby, the dining room was typically a hotel's largest and most highly decorated public space. Just how big ought it to be? How many diners, in other words, ought it to seat? It depended, of course, on the number of guest rooms or, more specifically, the number of beds that a hotel had. But the relationship between beds and table settings was not a simple one, although rules of thumb were widely adopted. If the house operated on the "American Plan" (where meals were included in the price of the room), then one table setting was required for each bed, except where guests were fed at two or more separate meal hours. Then only half or one-third that number were needed. If the house operated on the "European Plan" (where meals were bought separately with guests themselves choosing what and when to eat), then one table setting per room was usually adequate. Adequacy, of course, was also a function of whether a hotel operated other restaurant venues—a coffee shop, for example. C. Stanley Taylor thought that a 100-room commercial hotel needed the following: an 80- to 100-seat dining room, a 40- to 60-seat lunchroom, a banquet hall with seating capacity for at least 250 guests, several small private dining rooms, and a soda fountain, one either operated by the hotel or contained in a rental space.[1]

Through World War I, almost all small-town hotels, and quite a few of those in small cities as well, operated on the American Plan. It was a custom that originated with the coaching inns of the early nineteenth century. A reporter for the *Hotel Monthly*, traveling in Illinois, stopped at Hennepin's Cecil House. Before sitting down to dinner, he was shown "the room where Abraham Lincoln once slept." Then with other guests he was placed at one of several long tables. "There was no printed bill-of-fare, but the dishes were cooked and served family style, just as appealing as if served in the swell hotels in the big cities," he said.[2] Charming as the

FIGURE 40. Dining room, Hotel Shepard, Union Grove, Wisconsin. From "He Serves Dinner 'til the 'Vittles' Run Out," *Hotel Monthly* 44 (Oct. 1936): 26.

scene was, it was also clearly anachronistic. Novelist Theodore Dreiser found himself stopped for the night in a small Pennsylvania town. Of breakfast the next morning he wrote: "In a little while we were called to breakfast in a lovely, homely dining room such as country hotels sometimes boast—a dining room of an indescribable artlessness and crudity. It was so haphazard, so slung together of old yellow factory made furniture, chromos, lithographs, flychasers, five jar castors, ironstone 'china,' and heaven knows what else, that it was delightful. It was clean, yes; and sweet withal—very—just like so many of our honest, frank, kindly psalm singing Methodists and Baptists are."[3] In such hotels, hosts tended to flit constantly from dining room to front desk in covering multiple tasks, trying to stay up on things at their charming best, even on occasion in shirt sleeves (fig. 40).

The American Plan system might suit the very small hotel, especially in towns where few eateries existed beyond the hotel. The number of guests expected at meals and just how much they might eat were usually easily calculated, and food in just the right amount prepared and served. But in larger hotels such calculations were difficult. Too often was food wasted, either not taken by guests or, if taken, not eaten. Cost cutting through the elimination of waste was the prime argument for adopting the European Plan. Ottumwa, Iowa's Ballingall Hotel switched to the European Plan in 1904, the editors of the *Hotel Monthly* offering the following appraisal: "Mr. Ballingall's hotel is become one of the first in the Central West to cure the hog habit by operating so that the diner pays for what he orders only, and, for this reason, orders only just as much as he feels he can eat. Consequently there is very little waste of good food."[4] So also did the Barrett House of Logansport, Indiana make the switch, its manager reporting: "Since adopting European Plan our issues from store room have been from 25 to 35 per cent less [and] our receipts are more." Luckily relatively few guests opted to eat outside his hotel. "I figure," he continued, "that if we rent a room for a dollar and the patron spends only 25 cents in our diningroom for breakfast, we make as much as under the old 'wasteful breakfast' regime."[5]

But not every hotel manager was so sure. They included Edwin Boss, outspoken operator of a small midwestern hotel chain. The managers of his hotels, located mainly in small Iowa cities, found themselves competing vigorously with outside restaurants and losing ground continuously in the process. As he put it, "Our good friend Mr. Guest evidently liked eating where and when he pleased, in fact he liked the new liberty so well that about a third of our guests forgot that we were running a dining room at all."[6] In the 1920s, many hotels actually offered both meal plans, allowing guests to choose between them. During eight months of the year, the manager of the Lafayette Hotel in Clinton, Iowa, observed, "about 30 per cent of our business comes to our doors in automobiles, [people who] invariably prefer the American plan, especially for families. They like to go into a hotel and know what it is going to cost them to have service and food for the times they are planning to stay."[7]

Employees in hotel dining rooms, as hotel employees generally, were usually very low paid and thus heavily reliant on tips. Many hotel managers, however, considered tips to be potential hotel revenue, income that was diverted and thus lost. Under the American plan, it was said, tips were earned mainly at the expense of management, employees considering the tip to be a kind of incentive to supply guests with more food, even when it was not wanted. When hotel dining rooms converted to the European plan, employees had reason to improve the quality of their service instead. As one hotel manager wrote, "The European hotel proprietor has got the best of it over his brother of the American plan in this matter, as the tip given in the European hotel is given for service, and not as a bribe, as in a great many cases in the American plan hotels."[8]

Except in the smallest hotels, where managers tended to direct dining room operations, food service was usually overseen by a dining-room steward. He or she

FIGURE 41. An attentive dining-room wait staff, uniformed and eager. From advertisement for the Angelica Jacket Co., St. Louis, Missouri, *Hotel Monthly* 29 (July 1921): 111.

had charge of setting the menu day to day, ordering the appropriate supplies for the kitchen, and organizing kitchen procedure. But they also took an active role in greeting and seating dining-room patrons and, in general, sought to assure their satisfaction. "The steward," wrote John Tellman in *The Practical Hotel Steward,* "has charge of the back part of the house, attends to the marketing, sees that the help are all in their places of duty, that the meals are on time, superintends the preparation of the bills of fare, is particularly careful that economy is observed in all branches of his department, and sees to it that his expense account does not exceed the fixed limit for the class of house in which he is working."[9]

Theodore Nathan, in his book *Hotel Promotion,* offered a lengthy checklist for assessing whether hotel stewards were up to snuff. Heading his list were the following concerns: Is there a head waiter, captain, or hostess on hand to greet you as you enter? In what manner are you greeted and led to a place? When you object to the table to which you are first shown, is your objection met courteously and sympathetically? Are the headwaiters, waiters or waitresses, bus boys, and other employees well groomed? Are their uniforms clean? Are the tables properly set? Are there ash trays and matches? Are the service plates and all other dishes clean and without scratches and chips? Are the napkins fresh, properly folded, and unfrayed? Is the silverware polished?[10] In other words, was the steward fully attentive (fig. 41)?

FIGURE 42. Dining room, Florence Hotel, Missoula, Montana. From "The Florence Motel of Missoula," *Hotel Monthly* 49 (Aug. 1941): 22.

At the Stoddard Hotel in La Crosse, Wisconsin, the dining room measured some forty-one by sixty-one feet, with an eighteen-foot ceiling. It was a room "unmarred by pillar or post." "All around is a deep wainscoting of mahogany," the *Hotel Monthly* reported in 1904. "The walls are of a light olive shade, delicately frescoed; the ceiling is beamed; the floor is of colored tile in unique patterns. At the far end is a musician's gallery. Windows of stained glass, picturing grape vines, extend along one entire side, and at the base of each window is a wide ledge for jardinaires. Light draperies of rich material dress the windows. Illumination is by hanging clusters of round globes. The tables are two, three, and four seat; each has candelabra."[11]

The Lowell Inn at Stillwater, Minnesota was Colonial Revival in style, both inside and out. The dining room the *Hotel Monthly* described as "pure Colonia." It was provided with accordion partitions so that it could be made into two or three rooms as needed. "The floor is ceramic tile in 9-inch squares of black and white, laid alternately. The walls are papered and hung with appropriate prints. The table cloths are green and amber; the glassware and sugars amber; chinaware . . . willow pattern, in ivory and green. The chandeliers are crystal, these copied from Mount Vernon and with amber bulbs."[12]

The Florence Hotel in Missoula, Montana opened in 1942 and was rendered both outside and inside in Art Deco style, the dining room being "carried out in a modern adaptation of Grecian treatment." The far end of the room was covered with mirrors, thus to make the room appear larger. The two side walls contained false windows recessed and lit from behind so as to suggest natural light. The floor was of oak laid out in a mosaic pattern. As with hotel dining rooms generally, the room was intended not only to impress by size but also by decor (fig. 42).[13]

Through World War I, especially in small-town America, the noontime meal remained the principal meal of the day. But from the 1920s on, what had been supper increasingly replaced it. Whenever it was served, it was invariably formed around a "meat and potatoes" core, hotel food invariably made "hearty" for male appetites. At the Hotel Schuler in Marshall, Michigan, grilled beef tenderloin—covered with mushrooms sautéed in butter and served with a starter, a salad, baked potato, vegetable, dessert, and coffee—was the dining room's biggest seller. Priced at a dollar in 1941, the hotel was filling about one thousand orders a month.[14] Chicken was included on every hotel dining room menu, given its ready availability in every locality. Invariably it was fried and served with mashed potatoes and gravy.

In the cities the favoring of the evening meal in hotels came earlier, a function, no doubt, of the very brief lunch breaks imposed on office workers, store clerks, and even their managers. City hotels, those in small cities included, came to provide food of greater sophistication, as to both type and manner of preparation. In August 1929, at the Hotel Graham in Bloomington, Indiana, a typical menu featured broiled tenderloin or sirloin steak and fried spring chicken with cream gravy; but also available was baked white fish with Tartar sauce and either baked ham or roast beef with potato salad. Side vegetables included potato hash "en cream," corn on the cob, and sliced tomatoes. For dessert there was peach pie, Dutch apple pie, Neapolitan pudding with vanilla sauce, and various flavors of ice cream. Prices ranged from one dollar to a dollar and a half for a set meal.[15]

Hotel outfitting companies offered a variety of services. Their architects and interior designers might help plan a hotel. But mainly they served to supply hotel equipment and furnishings. Or hotels could order directly from manufacturers without recourse to jobbers or suppliers. The hotel steward was especially canvassed by salesmen selling chinaware from Syracuse, New York, or silverware from Waterbury, Connecticut. It is surprising how many companies with principal product lines other-directed chose to expand into one or another hotel line. Colt's Patent Fire Arms Manufacturing Company of Hartford, for example, produced a line of dishwashing machines.

Banquet Rooms

Banquet rooms were designed to host large sit-down dinners and other events such as formal dances. Rarely were they as elegantly decorated and furnished as hotel dining rooms, although by their size they could be quite impressive. At the Hotel Lancaster in Lancaster, Ohio, completed in 1940, the banquet room opened off the back side of the lobby. It flanked the kitchen on one side; a combined dining room and coffee shop lay adjacent to the kitchen on the other. "There are two ceiling chandeliers of silver and indirect wall fixtures. Five large windows, facing the north, are draped and curtained. The room is air conditioned," observed the *Hotel Monthly*. Folding tables and chairs were stored in a small room adjacent, all hotel banquet rooms being necessarily outfitted for quick set up and take down. "Chairs are attractively designed," it was reported, "some of them straight chairs and others wood folding chairs. . . . Tray stands of the folding variety, made of tubular chrome steel, are used. This room is carpeted to the walls, but when the carpet is removed it reveals a parquet floor which is ideal for dances."[16]

Local social organizations, including service clubs and political groups, were important users of hotel banquet rooms. But hotels themselves also frequently sponsored many events, making them appear as if community organized. In the 1920s testimonial dinners became quite popular, dubbed by *Business Week* as one of the hotel industry's "gentler rackets." Proposing to honor some local luminary at a sit-down dinner, the hotel manager (or sales manager) approached a sponsoring organization, supplied that organization with the names of prospective guests, organized an after-dinner program, and then facilitated the sale of tickets to the event, all the while keeping discreetly in the background, thus to make it appear that the occasion had been organized through "voluntary action by the great man's admirers." Even the depression years of the 1930s failed to dampen enthusiasm for such events, although profits were somewhat diminished. "Formerly the going rate was $7.50 to $10.00 a plate," *Business Week* reported. "Now $5 is about the top. Promoters clear from $2 to $1.50 on each ticket sold."[17]

Kitchens

Of course, the kitchen, along with its storerooms and other auxiliary spaces, stood at the heart of every hotel's food service. At the Hotel Vicksburg in Vicksburg, Mississippi, the kitchen was located just off the lobby at the back of the building, large windows supplying abundant natural light off an alley (fig. 43). The kitchen was separated from the dining room by a "serving room" where plates were finalized and which also acted as a "noise deadener" for diners.[18] In most hotels, waiters and waitresses experienced extremes of light and dark as they came through the swinging doors that separated the kitchen, usually painted white and brightly lit, from a darkened dining room kept romantically dim.

FIGURE 43. Kitchen, Hotel Vicksburg, Vicksburg, Mississippi. From "A Modern Fireproof Hotel Built for the Needs of an Average Small City," *Hotel Monthly* 37 (Nov. 1929): 59.

At the Hotel Otsego in Jackson, Michigan, the kitchen floor and the walls, at least to a height of five feet, were of cement, thus making the room reasonably "roach-proof" (fig. 44). Several stoves and a broiler were located along one wall along with a pudding steamer, vegetable steamer, soup kettle, and roaster. In front of these ran a set of tables for plate preparation, each equipped with plate warmers. To one side was the dishwashing department through which the wait staff could access the hotel bar. Along the opposite wall, doors gave access to smaller rooms containing bakery, scullery, and pantry. Also located there was entry to the hotel's freight elevator.[19]

Kitchen layout needed to expedite flow of food from storeroom, refrigerator, and freezer chest through all the necessary steps of cooking and plate preparation to the service counter where waiters and waitresses submitted food orders and eventually took loaded food trays away. Activity was best kept in full view to facilitate the head chef's oversight and that of respective department supervisors.[20] Various supply companies not only equipped hotel kitchens but also provided designs to maximize kitchen efficiency (fig. 45). Just how big a kitchen ought to be was related to the number of meals to be served per hour, especially at peak hours. As a rule of thumb, a dining room of 125 seats required 1,750 square feet and its kitchen at least 750 square feet. These were spaces large enough to handle some 190 meals per hour, assuming 1–1½ meals per seat per hour.[21]

Refrigeration was an especially important concern. Meat, vegetables, and dairy products required cooling. Most innovation in the hotel industry tended to come

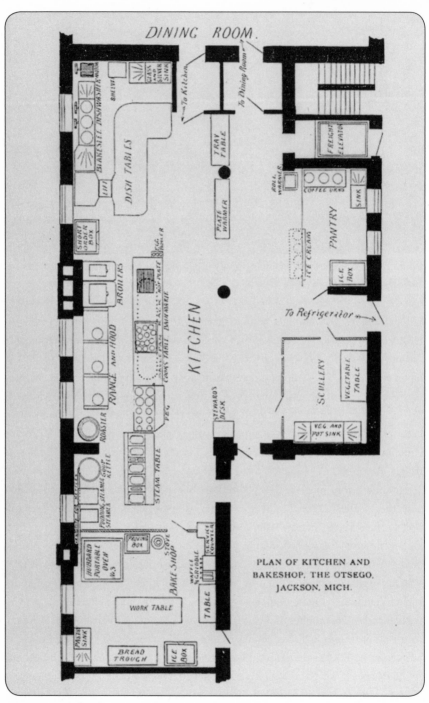

FIGURE 44. Kitchen layout, Hotel Otsego, Jackson, Michigan. From "The Otsego of Jackson, Michigan," *Hotel Monthly* 12 (June 1904): 31.

FIGURE 45. Advertisement for the Duparquet, Huot, and Moneuse Company. From *Hotel Monthly* 36 (May 1924): 95.

FIGURE 46. Men's café and bar, Leland Hotel, Springfield, Illinois. From "The Leland of Springfield, Illinois," *Hotel Monthly* 20 (June 1912): 45.

from the top down (from large big-city hotels down to the smaller hotels of small cities and towns), but improved refrigeration, in fact, ran the other way. The Terre Haute House in Terre Haute, Indiana was the industry leader. Jacob Baur pioneered the use of carbonic gas as a refrigerant for soda fountains, founding the Liquid Carbonic Company in the process. His brother Charles, manager of the Terre Haute House, adapted the new technology to hotel-kitchen use, Liquid Carbonic vigorously promoting his innovation nationwide. The Terre Haute House was one of the first hotels in the United States to install an electric dishwashing machine, an important laborsaving device.[22]

Hotel Bars

The hotel bar was an important profit center. It was often where management worked the hardest to personalize hotel life, in part by making it less formal than other areas of a hotel. Fortunate was the hotel with a charismatic bartender, one who could "hold court," thus to draw in commercial travelers, among others, as regular hotel guests. The hotel bartender became, Sinclair Lewis wrote in *Work of Art*, "the confidant of traveling princes and admirals, of thirsty authors and scientists, of apprentice drummers and of anxious insurance salesmen who wanted to know the rich men in town, of tired surgeons and swivel-eyed newspapermen, of crooks and yeggs and panhandlers, of pompous merchants and mufti-cloaked clergymen from distant towns." It was the bartender's privilege "to know them better than did their own brothers, as the magic of alcohol opened their wicked hearts and made them say what they really thought to the one confessor near at hand." Bartenders heard everybody's troubles. And they always "knew the best churches, the best fishing-tackle shops, and the best prostitutes in town."[23]

At the Leland Hotel in Springfield, Illinois, the Hotel Monthly reported, the room that attracted the most attention for its novel decorative scheme was the men's café or bar: "This room is 29 by 40 feet, an old English creation, the finish is brick and oak, the floor of red tile, and back of the bar a large painting of the Maxfield Parrish type, picturing a typical scene in an old English tavern" (fig. 46). Bars were not only places to drink but also to smoke, the odor of pipe and cigar smoke fully permeating the upholstery and rugs of most hotel bars accordingly. For customers who desired to eat as well as drink, food was usually available from a hotel's kitchen.

Prohibition spread across the United States, jumping from locality to locality, through the first two decades of the twentieth century. Only in 1921 was national prohibition established, making the sale of alcoholic beverages illegal everywhere. When a town switched from wet to dry, local hotels lost an important source of income. Not only were bar customers lost but, in most instances, dining-room business declined as well. With hotel profits thus diminished, hotel upgrading was usually put on hold, and, as well, even everyday maintenance delayed. "In the present transition stage from wet to dry, our little towns in the east," wrote W. B. Cleaves, manager of the Sherwood Hotel in Greene, New York, "do not yet appreciate the fact that if a hotel is to be maintained in a manner to be acceptable to the traveling public, it must have a generous support for the table from citizens; but seem to feel that the hotelkeeper ought to get along somehow with half his former income cut off. Result: many dying communities."[24]

Coffee Shops

With national prohibition established, the editors of the Hotel Monthly argued for different tactics when it came to promoting hotel food service. The effort had, theretofore, been to capitalize the "vices of life." This had to be replaced by capitalization of the "graces," they said.[25] That is, an effort had to be made to substitute a "home and club atmosphere" for what hotel dining rooms, but especially hotel bars, had previously been: male-dominated spaces where too often wayward

FIGURE 47. Coffee shop, Baxter Hotel, Bozeman, Montana. From "Hotel Baxter of Bozeman, Montana," *Hotel Monthly* 39 (Feb. 1931): 66.

behavior was conveniently blinked at. Not just women but whole families now had to be attracted and made to feel comfortable. The solution was the hotel coffee shop. Sometimes called a lunchroom, coffee shops were organized around lunch counters laid out very much like the soda fountains then becoming popular at drug stores. Patrons sat on stools placed in front of a counter from which they could readily watch food preparation, or, alternatively, they sat at tables or booths arranged elsewhere in the room. At the Baxter Hotel in Bozeman, Montana, the coffee shop dealt in "food, delicacies, soda fountain refreshments, candy and smokes." It was entered both directly from the street outside and through a pair of French doors from the hotel lobby. "The architecture of this shop is a modern treatment of English medieval of the Norman Period," reported the *Hotel Monthly,* "with its beams and brackets supported by grotesques. Brown predominates, with a generous application of stencils and penciling in gold, red and green." The room, some twenty-nine by fifty-three feet in size, accommodated fifty-two customers in booths, twenty-four at tables, and fifteen at the counter (fig. 47).

At the decades-old Hotel Powers in Fargo, North Dakota, a coffee shop was opened in 1937. Modern architectural allusions were made both inside and out. Inside, the restaurant was simplistically styled. Booths, tables, and chairs were given rounded edges and left largely unornamented. The walls, ceiling, and floor were also kept plain. New materials were used throughout: Formica for the table tops

FIGURE 48. Coffee shop, Hotel Powers, Fargo, North Dakota. From "A Modern Coffee Shop for Hotel in 30,000 Town," *Hotel Monthly* 45 (Oct. 1937): 19.

and plastic for upholstering, for example. A new front window, which enabled pedestrians outside to easily look in, was designed with distinctive streamlined curvature. Ornamentation throughout the room was mainly in the form of metal strips, but very sparingly used (fig. 48). Careful attention was given the room's layout: the flow of patrons coming and going and that of waiters and waitresses waiting on tables separated as much as possible. Work stations were "so lined up that the path of the waitress is progressive and there is not reason for backtracking."[26]

Outside, at least at the sidewalk level, a new veneer of Vitrolite was placed, and the streamlined coffee shop window reinforced with a banded aluminum surround. Above the door a large neon sign, which read quite simply "Coffee Shop," projected out over the sidewalk (fig. 49). Reaching out to the street, as it did, the restaurant attracted business from beyond the hotel throughout the day. "The terrific difficulty with old types of coffee shops," the hotel's manager explained, "was that they had high peak loads at meal hours, followed by very unprofitable periods of operation in-between meals. In our new room the in-between, unprofitable periods are made profitable by the sale of soda fountain items."[27]

FIGURE 49. Street entrance to the coffee shop, Powers Hotel, Fargo, North Dakota. From "A Modern Coffee Shop for Hotel in 30,000 Town," *Hotel Monthly* 45 (Oct. 1937): 20.

Cocktail Lounges

Repeal of Prohibition brought back the hotel bar but not in its traditional form. During Prohibition, in so-called speakeasies, for example, Americans had become addicted to the novelty of mixed drinks. Enter, therefore, the hotel cocktail lounge of the 1930s. There informality and homey socializing could mix with what had become modern adult sophistication: the cocktail. Very quickly most hotel cocktail lounges began to prosper, especially in the nation's cities both big and small. Hotel managers found that, as before Prohibition, serving alcoholic drinks returned more revenue per dollar invested than any other hotel activity.[28] And when conducted in good taste, the new bars could reflect a kind of glamour across an entire hotel property, something important to making the nation's increasingly dated hotels at least seem up to date.

Many Americans, having forgone drinking in public for decades, had to be re-educated in the ways of the bar. Hotel cocktail lounges, many with nightclub functions, were popularized in many a Hollywood movie in the 1930s, Americans enabled to learn by merely watching. Bartenders, however, represented the most important promotional front line. They kept patrons hip. What, for example, ought

FIGURE 50. Cocktail lounge, Hotel Lancaster, Lancaster, Ohio. Source: "Ohio's New 75-Room Hotel Lancaster," *Hotel Monthly* 48 (July 1940): 11.

one consume seasonally? "Beer is a summer drink," advised Theodore Nathan in his book *Hotel Promotion,* "and, although not a big profit item, it does deserve promotion during hot weather. So should the Collins family, juleps, and highballs." "In colder weather," he continued, "your more substantial potions, such as old-fashioneds, hot rum punches, sherry and port, Alexanders and Martinis, will be preferred."[29] In hotel dining rooms, stewards, for their part, promoted informative wine lists, recommending specific wines with specific meats, for example. Wine cellars needed to include a number of very expensive vintages, thus to give a dining room credibility. Customers needed help, it was argued, if, as a lost art, drinking was to be artistically restored to the nation.

As cocktail lounges needed to look fashionable to be fashionable, architects and interior designers well into the 1950s inclined their clients toward one or another form of modernism—from Art Deco to streamline modern to what came to be a bland kind of generic modernism fully stripped down to bare essentials. Cocktail lounge design at the new Hotel Lancaster in Lancaster, Ohio, followed closely 1930s modern styling that had been adopted for the building as a whole, only with much greater emphasis on detailing (fig. 50). "Opening off the lobby is the door to the cocktail lounge—a highly decorative room making use of glass mirrors, brass and a number of modern building materials," the editors of the *Hotel Monthly* reported.[30] Combined in a space adjacent was the hotel's dining room and coffee shop where, as in the cocktail lounge, informality rather than formality was also programmed to reign.

* * *

For transients overnighting, hotel dining rooms, coffee shops, and bars offered convenience. Increasingly demanded, however, was convenience mixed with informality. After World War II, more and more patronage came from women traveling alone and from family groups. Whether in a dining room, a coffee shop, or a bar, hotels found themselves catering not only to wider tastes but to more discriminating tastes. Until the 1950s, the luxury of "eating out" for pleasure was not something most Americans did with regularity except when traveling or, perhaps, on Sundays after church. In the 1950s, however, restaurants proliferated across the United States, and eating out became quite popular indeed. Most of the new restaurants were specialized as to market segment: kind of food, theme of decor, price of food, level of auto convenience, and so on. Whether "fast food" eaten handheld, or food consumed in leisurely sit-down circumstances, the exotica of ethnically based menus was popularized: Italian, Mexican, and Chinese, for example.[31] Hotel dining rooms were poorly equipped to compete, for the most part remaining generalists in a specialists' world. The typical hotel chef remained a jack-of-all-trades and master of none, making fewer and fewer customers happy. Whereas neighborhood taverns might orient to a distinctive ethnic, occupational, or income group, hotel bars, by and large, could not. Thus, both dining rooms and bars began to atrophy in hotels. Today they are gone from most of the nation's hostelries, especially the motels.

CHANGING WITH THE TIMES

Americans put into play a highly contingent set of conditions with unusual transformations of the built landscape beginning in the late nineteenth century. The boom of prosperity and materialism—along with the headlong rush to build up the West, space only sparsely settled since the national acquisitions in the first half of the nineteenth century—helped engender a period of unbridled optimism. Faith in technology, overestimated materialism and pragmatism, the belief that everyone could become wealthy, and the enjoyment of consumer goods produced towns and cities that were at first small but grew larger, ideally, over time. Railroads connected these centers of settlement in a national network, which enabled further thoughts of expansion. Constant and precipitant growth, however, engendered rapid obsolescence and abandonment. Periodic economic doldrums or, in the 1890s, panic interrupted but never brought into question the values effecting the growth of Main Streets nationwide, much less halt their growth.

Even as automobility reinforced the Main Streets of larger towns (and, of course, the cities) during the 1910s and 1920s, it greatly depressed retailing in the nation's villages and hamlets. The rise of motoring meant that customers were no longer bound to trade mainly in a nearby locality. Able to provide wider ranges of goods and services—and at lower prices, given a larger scale of business—Main Street merchants in the bigger places continued to thrive, though they were largely oblivious to the fact that motoring convenience was about

FIGURE 51. The Stoddart Hotel, Marshalltown, Iowa, in 1930. Authors' collection.

to render traditional Main Street business districts substantially obsolete. Only the disruptions of the Great Depression and World War II delayed the coming of peripheral shopping districts spread along highway roadsides, with stores set in parking-lot surrounds either standing alone or linked together in shopping centers. Not just automobile accessibility but automobile convenience, if not automobile orientation, lay on the horizon. The full dawning of the new day after World War II curbed Main Street optimism.

While unbridled optimism reigned during and after the late nineteenth century, the fact that it was limited to the middle and upper classes was clearly manifested in small-town and small-city hotels. From the grandeur of their facades to their private rooms for travelers, these places of conspicuous display were key settings to exhibit and reinforce the assumed virtues of material wealth. Hotel-room treatments were made up to date as much as profit permitted. Pressing ever forward in the name of improvement, the landscape outside these interior domiciles of temporary occupancy reflected the same business interests steeped in materialism and luxuriant in the latest technology: paved streets (wood block brick, gravel, or brick), street lights, telephone wires, railroads, streetcars, and, finally, automobiles and trucks. Not only were there new buildings constructed expressly as hotels but also older buildings converted to this purpose—such as the Stoddart Hotel in Marshalltown, Iowa (fig. 51), which was rendered from a private house through a series of additions. Such construction and renovation were material evidence of the excitement in the field of Main Street hotels.[1] How Main Street hotels adjusted to changing circumstances discloses a great deal about them. Au courant renovation inside and out and competition with the nascent tourist court and motel, the lodging type more convenient to automobilists and their casual manners, transformed Main Street hotels in their frenetic decline during the late twentieth century.

Renovation

In such a consumer-oriented business as the hotel trade, renovation constantly redefined the successful operator's agenda, or it troubled the unsuccessful operator's agenda either because he was unaware of it or could not afford it. Renovation required attention to every aspect of the hotel's physical plant, what every patron saw or felt whether they stayed overnight or passed time in the hotel's public places. Main Street hoteliers faced the same renovation problems as did those classed as urban leaders. The latter, however, could better afford the most up-to-date technologies because of their larger scale of economy. Main Street hotels fell behind because they were small—a general rule of hotel economics.[2]

The required renovation was obvious in many cases. The Hotel Livingston, built in Dwight, Illinois, to house patients and their families during alcoholic rehabilitation at the adjacent Keeley Institute, was a fireproof replacement of the forerunner that had burned in 1902. The owner, Leslie A. Keeley, knew some of his patients and their families could be counted on to lodge from three weeks to a month.[3] Although owners everywhere were cautioned not to take "fireproof" to mean the hotel could not catch fire but, instead, to understand that, in the insurance industry's vocabulary, something could remain after a fire, "fireproof" entered travelers' vocabulary by the turn of the nineteenth century.[4] In this same way, as part of a culture of rising expectations, owners tried to anticipate travelers' tastes. No explanation was required for the *Hotel Monthly* in 1915 to brag about the "remodeled, redecorated, and refurnished" Hotel Hildreth in Charles City, Iowa: "The picture speaks for itself; the luxurious furniture, polished wood wainscot . . ."[5] In 1921, the General Lewis Hotel at Lewisburg, West Virginia, was changed, not by remodeling the interior décor but by adding to the building, furnishing guest rooms with colonial furniture and changing most rooms to include a bath.[6]

Owners and operators on Main Street, sensing increased profits, deferred renovation no longer than necessary. Three railroads converging at Salina, Kansas, brought travelers to the Lauer, but the owner waited until he could lease to a capable manager before he "almost entirely rebuilt" the hotel.[7] A would-be lessee explained in glowing terms to the *Hotel Monthly* about his prospect that, for every

FIGURE 52. In 1941, the Hotel Gardner, Fargo, North Dakota, executed a "modernizing treatment" of its lobby, in the words of the *Hotel Monthly*. Gone were the overstuffed sofas and potted plants in favor of an almost stark simplicity. From "How the Powers Boys Plan Their Work, and Work Their Plan," *Hotel Monthly* 49 (Nov. 1941): 16.

dollar spent on renovation, twelve or fifteen cents will be earned, and he could expect a "reasonable profit" for himself if fifty thousand dollars came in annually. He dealt selectively with renovation, seeing no need to provide a bath in every room because he found "automobile parties are glad to get two connecting rooms with one bath" but insisted on new furniture throughout the house.[8] He spoke anonymously, perhaps because he did not want to ruin his chances to become the lessee. In listing remodeled hotels, the trade publications brought implicit pressure to renovate.[9] According to the *Hotel Monthly* in 1923, a model owner was like the one in Poughkeepsie, New York, who told his local Rotary, "Every year brings new ideas that must be installed for the comfort and convenience of the guest."[10] Materials manufacturers and supply houses persistently worked to convince hotel men by advertising and showing their products.[11] Automobiles also enabled change because, as Edwin Boss affirmed, hoteliers could easily drive to see what the competition was changing and what it looked like when finished.[12]

During the Depression of the 1930s, hotel operators took advantage of the comparatively lower costs of labor and materials to update hotels dissuaded from it in the 1920s because of prohibitive costs. Not much occurred in the most depressed economy, that of the early 1930s; one owner who did so was celebrated for modernizing in the emphatic terms "at this particular time" (fig. 52).[13] *Business Week* reported in 1937, however, that with the economy in recovery, hotel men were spending $136 million on improvements and applied the word "modernization" to keep in step with the word's general adoption in those years.[14] Main Street hoteliers were among them.

Renovations included many changes throughout hotels. An end to Prohibition put bars back into legal use, and General Kincaid, president of the American Hotels Corporation, which included Main Street hotels, set a pattern for cocktail bars because they were, with room rental, the biggest profit makers. A redesigned coffee shop could attract profits in times between meals, it was discovered.[15]

The automobile continued stimulating change. Although bigger hotels converted many of their upper floors into apartments, they were a temporary expedient.[16] In the vanguard of adapting to automotive revenue, the Nelson House in Poughkeepsie, New York, had by 1923 built an adjacent six-level garage with slopped ramps between levels. Neither repairs nor parts were available in the garage, but gasoline and oil were (fig. 53).[17] This was merely the latest change that had kept the Nelson House open since 1876. Relatively small but profitable accommodations to the automobile trade were possible, even in the early 1930s, at a "very old hotel," as labeled in the *Hotel Monthly*, by the addition immediately off the entrance of "a rest room for ladies, a dainty affair, appreciated by motorists in particular." As a side benefit, patronage increased in the dining room.[18]

Edwin Boss drew the most praise among the Main Street hotel renovators in the *Hotel Monthly* in the late 1930s because he undertook costly systemic renovations. "Refacing" was Boss's most visually powerful renovation technique. He employed an architectural firm in Des Moines, Iowa, to adhere an entirely new exterior in the latest styles to a number of the hotels in his chain. The *Hotel Monthly* published tributes showing "before" and "after" photographs (fig. 54).[19] Boss learned from experience that automobiles permitted their drivers and passengers to select their overnight lodging. The automobile quickened competition and facilitated how owners took on novel technologies to stay profitable. A Boss competitor concluded, "The exterior of the hotel, we discovered, is just as important—in fact, more so— than the interior, because unless the outside is attractive you can't even attract the guest in the first place."[20] O. A. Clark, who owned several hotels in Iowa, had driven out to see Boss's first face-lifted hotel and returned to remodel his similarly.[21] Boss also led Main Street chain owners in hiring professional designers for interior renovations throughout their network. Paul Dorris was taken on for Boss hotels, and he argued in 1941 for change most in each hotel's public spaces. For example, dining rooms and coffee shops with "massive hangings, high ceilings, Ionic columns and

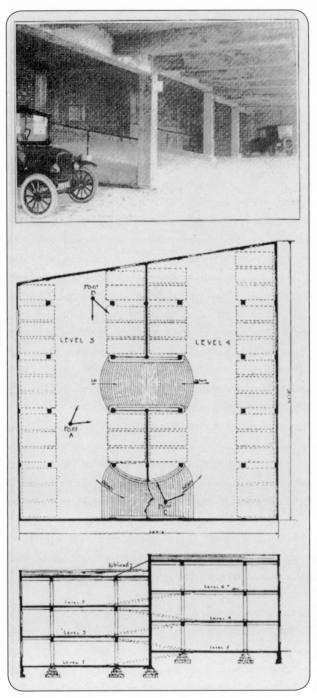

FIGURE 53. A photograph and diagrams of the innovative Main Street hotel garage at Poughkeepsie, New York. From "A Country Hotel that Caters to Man and Car," *Hotel Monthly* 31 (Aug. 1923): 49.

HOTEL ANTHES, FORT MADISON, IOWA
As it appeared before being resurfaced.

HOTEL ANTHES, FORT MADISON, IOWA

FIGURE 54. The Hotel Anthes in Fort Madison, Iowa, before (above) it was "face lifted" and afterward (below). From "Refacing Hotel Anthes, Fort Madison, Iowa," *Hotel Monthly* 45 (Jan. 1937): 13.

FIGURE 55. Renovated lobby of the Hotel Burlington. From "How Obsolescence is Being De-feated in a 200-Room Hotel," *Hotel Monthly* 55 (Aug. 1947): 22.

pilasters here and there, with perhaps Gothic openings" might be impressive, he reasoned, but lacked the look of home that contemporary travelers wanted.[22]

The confluence of numerous problems for Main Street hotels in the fifteen years following the end of World War II virtually drove them into extinction by the early 1960s. Competition from motels more luxurious than their spartan tourist-camp and tourist-court forerunners, limited parking space, resistance to tipping, and physical obsolescence left Main Street hotels "hurting," in the assessment of one analyst in 1959.[23] During the waning days of World War II, deferred wartime maintenance and modernization induced considerable renovation, which was charged against the future and made it seem that profits had returned after a fifteen-year decline.[24] The American Hotel Association also encouraged these calculations.[25]

Main Street hotel operators faced no other prospect for the resumption of business than systematic renovation unless they converted their businesses, demolished their hotels, or simply permitted them to slide into dereliction and abandonment. The *Hotel Monthly* publicized the renovation work of a few brave stalwarts in a series of articles in 1947. The Hotel Burlington, which had opened in 1911 in

Burlington, Iowa, and had an annex added about twelve years later, was in the limelight again in 1947 for its substantially renovated interior. The *Hotel Monthly* elaborated most on the "streamlined" lobby's revolutionary appearance, as if that would clinch readers' thinking about whether to renovate (fig. 55). It would be good for another thirty-six years, the *Hotel Monthly* predicted; in fact, the Burlington Hotel's last occupant vacated the building thirty-seven years later.[26]

Among Main Street hotels revitalized through their extensive renovation, several other examples merited the industry's attention in the postwar crisis. One was the Hotel Glen View on the county courthouse square in Mt. Carroll, Illinois. Its owners judiciously reworked the sixty-year-old hotel to introduce new features (iron beds but with new mattresses) and yet retain those older features that were comfortable (furniture). Foremost, however, was cleanliness, even above renovation. Laurus Treadway's chain was showcased for how lighting and furnishings could enhance the chain's "latest colonial warmth."[27]

Another example of the atypical small-town and small-city renovations was displayed on the *Hotel Monthly*'s pages in 1947 about the Kewanee Hotel, in Kewanee, Illinois. A hotel built with community funding in 1916 but allowed to degrade without a maintenance program until 1931, when an individual owner invested $100,000 and added to the hotel, the Kewanee required substantial renovation within fifteen years to remain competitive.[28] The renovation was outlined in the trade publication. "But all the gloss and smart furnishings could not counter changing trends in the U.S. hospitality field," wrote the Kewanee's two historians.[29] The Kewanee Hotel remained open until the 1990s under reduced income and lacking its former luster.[30]

The Changing Hotel Room

The hotel room, for its reserve of privacy, including later for making one's toilet, deserves attention among the various rooms in an institution known as much for public space. The hotel room's very thorough documentation in the trade literature also permits a thorough examination of how Main Street hotel owners and managers renovated to stay in business.

On the subject of the hotel room for private space, the hotel bathroom gained the trade's focus for a history, whereas the other aspects of the room can be assembled from random descriptions throughout the trade literature. In a brief article in 1941, the *Hotel Monthly*'s editors treated the bathroom as a subject of increasing refinement over the years. The first luxurious baths were thought perhaps to have been installed in 1831 into the Tremont House in Boston, but it was not until Ellsworth Statler's famous slogan "every room with bath," meaning a shower or bath in each

FIGURE 56. This comedic postcard, postmarked 1910, illustrates how generally lodgers found the shared bathroom to be vexatious. Authors' collection.

room of the hotel he opened in Buffalo in 1907, that lodgers could count on bathing in their room. The Victoria Hotel had preceded the Statler in offering this luxury in 1888, but after Statler's installation in a transient hotel, public demand for it spread rapidly.[31] Main Street hotels lagged behind for about a decade before this feature came to be common in remodeled hotels and in the rash of community hotels built in the 1920s.

Various provisions were made before Statler's arrangement. The bowl and pitcher, so common that an era of hotel history was named for them, were routinely offered in combination with a bath; later, a bath and shower alternative was offered for common use by lodgers in different rooms, with the accompanying inconveniences (fig. 56). For example, the model Hotel McKinley in Canton, Ohio, offered hot and cold running water in every room in 1904, but 70 of the 110 rooms were serviced by common baths.[32] The *Hotel Monthly* in 1906 portrayed the Branham House in Union City, Indiana, as a representative Main Street hotel with four of its fifty rooms having private baths; bowl and pitcher were offered in all other rooms, which a single common bath served. Referring to their inconvenience, the *Hotel Monthly* noted that hot and cold running water was available to lodgers at all times at both ends of each hall.[33] Ten years later, when the Parkside Hotel (later known as the Kewanee Hotel and treated in the foregoing "Renovation" section) opened, it boasted that all bedrooms had a private toilet and lavatory, more than half had a bath tub, and several had a shower.[34] An expert to the Kansas-Missouri-Oklahoma Association of hotel men counseled in 1920 that questions regarding the number of rooms with tub bath or shower should best be determined by local circumstances and the "class of patronage" served; however, if one could afford the added expense and demand existed, he advised, they could earn more profit from a room with a bath than one without it. Public demand for a private bath was rising, the association's advisor concluded. Scharf remodeled the Hotel Gettysburg to provide a common bath but one that could be closed in sections to accommodate large parties traveling by automobile.[35] Owners commonly preferred showers over tubs by the early 1920s.[36] Some Main Street hotels ranked as exemplary although they did not convert all their guest rooms to ones with private baths until the rash of remodeling after World War II.[37] Many small-town and small-city hotels in the mainstream had already converted their guest rooms without baths to storage because they could be rented only when they were the last rooms available.[38]

Room size differed depending on the hotelier's anticipated market. In St. Charles, Illinois, the Hotel Baker was a resort hotel catering mostly to motoring and interurban arrivals.[39] Its rooms were spacious by contrast with most Main Street hotels, not to mention appointed in spectacular fashions.[40] Typical guest rooms, as the *Hotel Monthly* categorized them in the Hotel Hayes, which opened in 1926

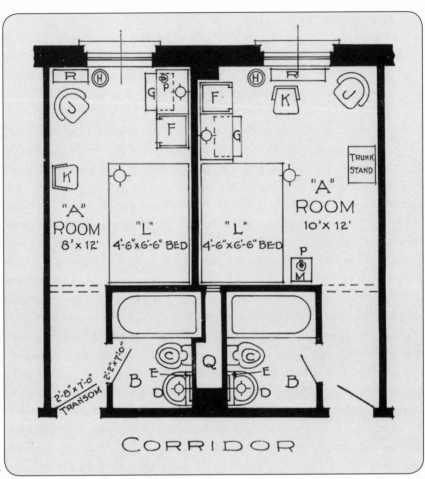

FIGURE 57. Two idealized floor plans presented in the *Hotel Monthly* in 1917. From "Practical Hotel Construction," *Hotel Monthly* 25 (Aug. 1917): 55.

in Jackson, Michigan, ranged from nine feet six inches by fifteen feet to fourteen by sixteen feet.[41] This hotel was a community-financed establishment characteristic of the type nationally. Advice given in 1917 to the Northwestern Hotel Men's Commission recognized the widespread tendency to adhere to Statler's strategy to rent "a room and bath for a dollar and a half" dictated smaller rather than larger rooms but said the former could be self-defeating. It was possible to lose money by making rooms too small just to charge a cheap rate. Confining by contemporary standards, the adviser in 1917 calculated the costs and profits of a room ten feet by twelve feet (fig. 57).[42] The original-size rooms in the Hotel Bothwell in Sedalia, Missouri, required an explanation on the hotel's Web site seventy-eight years later.

Although "smaller than today's standards," it said, the rooms were amply compensated in their furnishings.[43] Few anticipated passing many waking hours in such Main Street hotel rooms. Throughout town, the lobby, the dining room, the coffee shop, and the lounge were the transient guests' places and their extensions beyond Main Street hotels. The vocabulary of room design reserved "spaciousness" for locations downstairs from the guest rooms and their public traffic.[44] Light-colored rooms and wide hallways were intended to compensate for the cramped dormitory quarters, but hoteliers regularly underscored the available light from outside.[45] The Hotel Marting in Ironton, Ohio, publicized its "extra large" windows; in Gadsden, Alabama, the Hotel Reich publicized that every room had two or more windows,[46] and in other hotels, courtyards that supplied ample ambient light were common for "inside" rooms.[47] As late as 1942, owners of the Northern Hotel in Billings, Montana, exulted that the exceptionally large, seven-foot-wide windows allowed "plenty of daylight in all the rooms."[48]

What was the ambiance of the guest room over the arc of time during which Main Street hotels prospered? Sinclair Lewis's *Work of Art* included a description of the rooms for single occupancy in the fictionalized American Hotel of 1897, characterized as a "vigorously modern hotel." In Lewis's portrayal (quoted at length in our introduction), each room contained a wooden bed with worn varnish, a straight chair, a strip of carpet, and a gas lamp emitting dim light. In addition, a "slop jar" on a simulated-marble linoleum strip, a bar of soap, a threadbare towel, and a distinctive odor arising from the whole completed the picture.[49]

In the *Hotel Monthly,* a state-of-the-art room in 1929 at the Benwalt Hotel in Philadelphia, Mississippi, was described as

about 10' by 14'. It is equipped with Simmons metal furniture, the beds having the Beautyrest mattress and Ace spring, slip covered. There is a dresser, writing desk and chair, Windsor chair, telephone stand, trunk stand, costumer and waste basket. Every room has [an] Emerson wall fan. The two windows are shaded and screened and are draped with brightly printed cretonne. The furnishings are in different color schemes, as a cool green shade, a black lacquer with red trim, a blue shade and an imitation mahogany. In all cases the drapes are selected to provide a harmonious combination. The rooms also have an upholstered lounge chair made by the Kroeller Manufacturing Company of Naperville, Ill. The floors are carpeted over Ozite. Beds are fitted with the Play-O-Lite attachable lamp. A feature that makes the rooms particularly livable is the use of three pictures—two large ones and one small one.[50]

FIGURE 58. A representative room in the Boss chain, circa 1940. Courtesy of John Patrick Reilly.

Descriptions in the trade literature of the 1920s were rather placid, underwriting the replication of a bedroom like those at home, and nothing exceptional.[51] Taste and refinement reflective of a people's lifestyle and gay colors to yield cheerfulness and brightness: these were sample generalizations.[52]

In the 1930s a shift to the word "modern" and a break from the ordinary domestic setting distinguished the decade's publicized Main Street hotel rooms. Instead of colonial furniture, the furniture was given to simpler lines often sporting metal appliqués or was all metal. "Homeyness" was reiterated in one description, but the purpose was to buoy profits in the depressed economy of 1934.[53] The emphasis on installing every latest fashion only belied the claim that the effect would replicate home. A *Country Life* columnist in 1931 feared no contradiction that "the average person is more comfortable in a large hotel than he is at home."[54] It seems no less safe to estimate, given the smaller budgets of Main Street hotels, that they may have approximated the conditions of home. The "sudden big swing to modern styles in decoration for hotels generally," *Hotel Management* editorialized in 1936, could be attributed to four advantages: simple contours without "over-elaborate ornamentation" made it enduring, not something of which one was easily tired; the bland style made a good background for other guest room features such as textiles and wall coverings; its lack of intricate details made it "practical" and easy to maintain; and rooms seemed more spacious. A room fashioned in this aesthetic was not the average guest room, *Hotel Management* insisted.[55] One designer defined "modern" as simply the "furniture of the day" and "of no particular period."[56] In 1940 a room at the forefront of small hotel design in the Hotel Lancaster in Lancaster, Ohio, called for plenty of lighting, colorful drapes, two upholstered arm chairs, box-spring mattresses, chrome luggage rack, smoke stand, and glass-top table, dresser, and writing desk (fig. 58).[57]

While Main Street's hoteliers confronted the reality of business moving away from downtown and onto highway venues, the most advanced designers conceived expensive packaged designs. Carson, Pirie, Scott and Company and the Simmons Company, both of Chicago, offered, respectively, a double-bedroom package for $532 and $659, or $599 in quantities of fifty or more. Conceptions inflated beyond "modern"—meaning now something along the lines of "The Room of Tomorrow" offered in 1960—beckoned hotel operators to rooms measuring twenty-seven by seventeen feet maximum with eight-foot-high ceilings; in this new thinking, rectangular closets and bathrooms were replaced with ones entered on a "zig-zag" corridor. The bathroom floor was wedge shaped.[58] Such aerodynamically inspired motifs were substantially of the same origins as the up-to-date rooms of the 1930s, but there is no evidence small hotels could implement these latest versions.

Four technologies that found their way into the guest rooms on Main Street had less to do with the look of the room than with the lodgers' comfort and convenience: radios, televisions, fans, and air-conditioners. These devices helped make the lodger's stay more fully enjoyable, transforming it so that the private experience in the room complemented the public one in the spaces downstairs. The Drake of Chicago was reported in 1925 to be one of the first hotels to offer lodgers a radio rental.[59] Radios with headphones minus an extra fee were available in every room of the Hotel Maytag in Newton, Iowa, in 1927.[60] Edwin Boss's chain was still charging a twenty-five-cent fee in 1941, considering it cheap for the lodger and a source of good revenue for the chain.[61] Based on the dates for advertisements for televisions in Main Street guest rooms, it appears the earliest installments likely occurred in the early to middle 1950s.[62] Similarly, fans, although manufactured since the 1880s, seem to have entered common hotel rooms by the 1930s; however, they were routinely absent in illustrations of the latest remodelings of the decade.[63] According to common accounts, the first hotel to be fully air conditioned appeared in either 1927 or 1934.[64] But, as is typical in disagreements over "firsts," an even earlier date for air conditioning—1907—was also claimed for the St. Regis in New York City.[65] In 1935 the manager of the Treadway Inn system's unit in St. Clair, Michigan, was still trying to reckon whether the added patronage was worth the added cost of the air conditioning he installed, even as *Hotel Monthly* was encouraging its consideration among small-town and small-city hotel operators.[66] Advertisements of guest rooms with their own air-conditioning units appeared in the late 1950s.[67]

Mass-manufactured furnishings, such as towels and bedding, completed the accouterments of the evolving standardized hotel, whether it was on Main Street or in the big city. Judging by articles in the *Hotel Monthly* about leaders in the small-town and small-city market, it appears these elements came concurrently with the big-city operators.[68] Albert Pick and Company in Chicago specialized in hotel supplies, virtually dominating the field by the 1910s.[69]

Hotel versus Motel

Renovations and room changes on Main Street, after all, were strategies to keep current with competitors. Nothing more hobbled their future, however, than the startling accommodations made for travelers by the emerging "Roadside Touring Competition," as one hotel man called it.[70]

The first of these competitors to crop up were not motels but tourist camps and tourist homes. The latter were private homes, some in towns and some on farms, whose families opened rooms that included bathing facilities and provided meals. Camps and homes were especially prevalent in and around small towns and cities, making them most troublesome to Main Street operators. Free municipal tourist camps were only competitive through the mid-1930s when they began to wane for various reasons, including the reluctance to compete against local hotels; however, commercial ones continued, often altered to providing indoor lodging.[71]

Main Street hoteliers' responses ran a wide emotional gamut. Some believed the roadside lodging alternative would not survive. As early as 1922, one hotel man held that tourist camps were a thing of the past.[72] Editor John Willy of the *Hotel Monthly* never believed they were threatening because the class of people who patronized them was not inclined to go to hotels.[73] The manager of Hotel California in El Centro, California, at first thought when the competitors appeared that travelers would soon tire of them; he believed that the new format was but a fad.[74] In Rutledge, Tennessee, the manager of the Rutledge Inn suspected his seven-year-old hotel's rates were simply assumed to be too expensive, athough travelers seldom checked and just drove on by.[75] Some seemed confused about why the roadside challenged Main Street lodging but felt assured that all the personal attention hotels offered—their hallmark—would triumph over competition, if only hotel operators paid attention to format.[76] Here the code of Mine Host thrived amid the growing faith in scientific management. Burdened with the prospect that roadside lodging would not have to comply with the National Recovery Act's code for hotels, the president of the American Hotel Association angrily stereotyped the roadside as "guerilla competition."[77] A year later, in 1935, an analyst before the annual convention of the American Hotel Association dismissed the persistent tourist camps, saying their owners comprised "all classes of people and organizations . . . and so on down to convicts, and even one convict now in the Maryland state penitentiary."[78]

Rational responses simultaneously produced a host of piecemeal accommodations attuned to automobile travelers. The Hotel Pathfinder in Fremont, Nebraska, set up an information booth on the highway at the edge of town where "the *informality* [authors' italics] of the roadside stand, the ease with which it can be reached, and the chance for the prospective guest to talk with the representative of the hotel on neutral ground, free from the possibility of embarrassment in the lobby" were strategically persuasive to many passersby.[79] Convenient parking was understood as something hotels had to learn from the roadside lodgings, and Main Street hotel men were not especially quick to respond to the consequences of the automobile's improvisational capacities. The owner of the Beaumont Hotel in Green Bay, Wisconsin, was uncommonly adaptive when he realized that the predictability of arrivals had become far less possible than it had been when people arrived by railroads run on timetables. "We have to keep open now on a 24-hour basis, and, in the summer time, so many people drive their cars at night for the comfort of the cool night," he said. This receptive owner built an adjacent two-story garage for storage, car washing, and light repairs.[80]

Some problems could not be fixed. Much lower rates made roadside lodging a more attractive option for automobile travelers. That was an essence of the American Hotel Association's complaint about unfair competition in 1933. One reporter on Main Street hotels, for example, learned in 1933 that the competition in Sault Ste. Marie, Michigan, charged between fifty and seventy five cents, having dropped rates in the Depression from one dollar. Hotels could not match these rates.[81] In 1931 transient hotels averaged $3.50 per room.[82] Sinclair Lewis pointed out in *Work of Art* that people no longer entertained as much in hotels because travelers' interests turned to experiences along the road; hotels were less a destination than a support.[83] Consequently, travelers were willing to be put up in less than the palatial habitat hotels felt was their claim.[84]

During the era of elated "community hotel" overproduction, and then during the Main Street hotel crisis, the opportunities arising from Americans' love of motoring stimulated a few hotel men to conceive and build a novel form of accommodations that combined the traits of both hotel and highway lodging. The *Hotel Monthly* editors encouraged hotel managers to open a "tourist camp annex," claiming to have seen the attractions of informality to travelers as far back as twenty

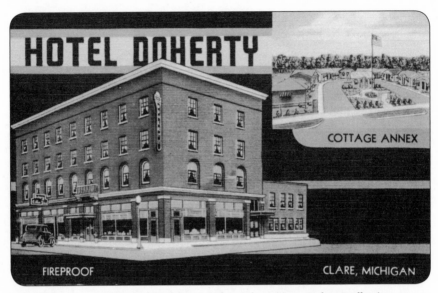

FIGURE 59. A postcard view of the Doherty lodging alternatives. Authors' collection.

years earlier in the profits hotels earned in their lunchrooms and coffee shops as opposed to their formal dining rooms. Hotelier Colonel Fred Bartholomew, originally of the Frederick Hotel in Grand Forks, North Dakota, expected to open the Arlington Inn at Santa Barbara, California, in 1931. It would combine easy access off Cabrillo Boulevard with hotel-like amenities: guest rooms with either bath or shower and a large dining room that would eliminate the need for lodgers to go in search of food outside the house. The Philson family, characterized by *Hotel Monthly* in 1934 as fresh entrants into the hotel trade, opened the White Star Hotel in Jennerstown, Pennsylvania; this operation featured a regal revival-style building at the intersection of the Lincoln Highway and Route 219. It included elegant landscaping, a parlor, a tearoom, a lobby, and guest rooms. It replaced a traditional hotel that the family owned before it burned four years earlier. John Brunner of El Centro, California—proudly claiming a hotel operator's knowledge that travelers expected special treatment, not the indifferent services customary at cabin camps—opened Las Palmas Court Hotel with forty rooms and an adjoining garage for each. It generally filled up before Brunner's hotel downtown; thus, he directed the overflow to the downtown hotel.[85] The new sustained the old.

Fred Doherty of the Hotel Doherty in Claire, Michigan, opened a cottage court of ten units immediately alongside his hotel (fig. 59). Hoping to mantle the units with the assumed higher respectability of hotels, Doherty named the adjacent unit an "annex." His version capitalized on hotel-oriented elitism mixed with the new-fashioned implementation of cabins, diverging from Brunner's more consistent appeal of the former. In 1930 owners of hotels in Manchester, New Hampshire, and Portland, Maine, started the "Danish Village," a romanticized setting of tourist cabins eight miles south of the latter hotel.[86] These were creations of Main Street hoteliers.

A sufficient part of the transient market wanted combinations of class, understood as high quality, and convenience to foster several variations on the hotel-motel theme by people new to the lodging business. One travel writer acknowledged that trailers were no substitute because they were uncomfortable and troublesome, however much money seemed to be saved by traveling in them.[87] Most hotels earned disapproval because of their poor services and food as well as deficient parking provisions and guest rooms,[88] and hotel men like Edwin Boss insisted his counterparts should get back to the "comfort, convenience, and cleanliness" that he believed distinguished good hotels from the average tourist courts.[89] Even with the admission of a category labeled the "deluxe tourist court," hotel operators continued lauding the superiority of their mode when it was run properly.[90] However, businesses new to the hotel industry melded the old and the new in ways appealing to the market. The Pierce Petroleum Company, headquartered in St. Louis, developed a series of hotels that were situated on key highways with services in one of the units far beyond hotels, namely, a hospital with operating table and nurse on call. The company projected a chain coast to coast, but the company sold out before it was built.[91] Although this scheme was short-lived, put out of business by the Great Depression after Sinclair purchased the initial units, the hybrid of hotel-motel endured.

Hotel men started to make their peace with the interloper roadside entrepreneurs in the early 1940s. The manager of the Hotel Cherokee in Cleveland, Tennessee, called for cooperation with tourist courts regarding rates and accommodations, and noted Main Street hotels remained competitive if they offered special group rates, free parking, good food at reasonable rates, and high standards of comfort and convenience.[92] In 1942 the manager of the Hotel Auditorium in Cleveland proposed that motels be invited into membership in the American Hotel Association.[93] After World War II class and convenience yielded a hybrid venue whose name embodied the amiable union and combined appeals of the two venues: "motor hotel." Significantly, in 1953, *Hotel Management* added this phrase its title page: "Includes Motor Hotel Operations."[94] TraveLodge from San Diego in 1946 and Holiday Inn from Memphis in 1952 had led the way. Holiday Inn began inside the city, proliferating on highway locations later, but TraveLodge brought the minimal services of the prewar motels to the downtown, where hotels had once reigned supreme.[95] In 1959 the Downtowner Corporation began in Memphis siphoning customers from the city's premier hotel, the Peabody, but added some units in small cities, hiring a young hotelier from Paris, Tennessee, to start its second motor hotel. Don T. Baker took this assignment knowing a strong future no longer lay on Main Street and committed to the Downtowner's construction of a big-city chain.[96]

Hotels struggled in the last half of the twentieth century. Motel rivals gained advantage from the 1954 federal income tax code provision of accelerated depreciation and mushroomed along exits from the nation's interstate-highway system that had begun in 1956.[97] Unadapted hotels were strongly advised to look at the motel format. A student in the Cornell hotel management program, Robert P. Bryant, published an article in *Hotel Management* in 1947 tellingly subtitled, "The Only Way in Which to Beat This Fast-Growing Form of Competition Is To Build Bigger, Better Motels Ourselves."[98] Main Street hotels languished. Few could afford to build the adapted venues of class and convenience architects designed. The big-city Sheraton chain was one of the rare exceptions.[99] The large hotels that had implemented scientific management remained solvent by the early 1970s.[100] Even these suffered after a brief span of growth in the 1960s. Examples abound of the huge toll taken among the Main Street hotels. The model Main Street hotelier Henry Scharf of the Hotel Gettysburg had recognized the threat of the "obsolescence factor," as he called it, installing the latest technologies for over forty years, but was forced to close in 1964. The Holiday Inn opened a year before, and other factors too preyed on the hotel's vitality.[101] Less publicized, the Monon Hotel in Crawfordsville, Indiana, typified many of its kind: reportedly a "handsome little hotel" when it opened in 1927, it closed fifty years later and was condemned by the city.[102] Recession, higher gas prices, traffic flows that shifted off Main Street, and higher operating costs were bad for small-town and small-city hotels. Planners envisioned a new day in locations near airports and in suburbs.[103]

As Main Street hotels went, so did Main Street itself. These bellwethers of small-town and small-city economies fared no differently than their host environments. Within each small town and city, they followed a pattern like that of the Main Street grocery store versus the outlying supermarket, or the line of downtown stores specializing in particular products versus the shopping malls outside of the old city center. The stronger each was and the stronger the whole, the better the chances of survival when they faced the challenges presented by rivals both in their own towns and in larger towns beyond. Perhaps the hotel function was the most important of all Main Street activities. Hotels attracted people from away and thus emphasized a business district with money from beyond the community. As the hotels prospered, so did Main Street. As Main Street prospered, so did the hotels.

* * *

Change is a natural consequence of any line of business in a culture valorizing innovation. Throughout the twentieth century, circumstances ultimately beyond the hotel industry buffeted hotel men, who responded with varying degrees of success in their adoption of technologies, and ultimately their business venue itself. Born themselves of the change when the hotel industry took root in the smallest markets, the entrepreneurs, managers, and staffs of Main Street hotels only briefly profited until the Great Depression of the 1930s. Thereafter, many could no longer afford to realize the faith of unbridled optimism with its constant material demands, or they remained assured in holding to what they had achieved—all with the consequence that surrounding circumstances did change and issued their demise. A few pressed on but in the process so substantially altered their operations that they remained barely recognizable in their original format.

EPILOGUE

We sketch here recent times among the nation's Main Street hotels. Our aim is not a definitive review of current happenings. Rather, drawing on a few examples, we want merely to illustrate how old hotel buildings have been put to new uses. We also consider examples of attempted reuse that failed. The Main Street hotel's halcyon days certainly were a matter of historic record as the twentieth century came to a close. Most Main Street hotels were well past their prime so far as accommodating transients was concerned and, of course, their functioning as community centers. This does not mean that most hotels stood vacant merely waiting for the wrecking ball or that most had already been razed. Indeed, many had successfully taken on new functions, flexibly reused to meet new demands. Hence we do not arrive here at a conclusion. The story we tell is still very much unfolding. Instead, we end by delineating current trends, with description based on our own personal observations along America's Main Streets, attention to local newspaper reporting, and interviews with people who are today variously involved with resuscitating old hotel properties.

Generative as well as responsive to small towns and small cities from their inception, the ever-adaptive hotel has certainly experienced its ups and downs during the past half-century. Most remain serviceable in some capacity. Despite various alarms today about being an "endangered species," they remain at least as alive as their locales allow. Categorization provides a general framework for appreciating the various directions that Main Street hotels have taken over recent decades. First, and perhaps most encouraging, are those hotels that have been fully renovated and are effectively serving

FIGURE 60. Advertisment for the Hotel Greystone, Bedford, Indiana. From *The Official Red Book and Directory* (New York: American Hotel Association Directory Co., 1950), 307.

a contemporary clientele, whether as a transient hotel, a conference center, a residence for the elderly, an office building, or some combination of the above. Others, of course, languish, awaiting reuse in various stages of disinvestment. Some stand vacant. A portion, perhaps the smallest portion, have been demolished as either beyond repair or unsuited for contemporary use. Many hotels, as we have outlined, were built during 1910s, a decade that began with great optimism. In the 1920s that optimism returned, in part stimulated through capital and energy pent up during World War I. Spawned was a period of vigorous economic growth, at least in the nation's cities and larger towns. As before the war, economic expansion was substantially sustained by the coming of the automobile, an exciting new technology. Automobility fostered new hotel development, the early twentieth century standing, accordingly, as a kind of golden age for the hotel industry. There were, of course, older hotels that survived from the railroad era, hotels that, once renovated and/or enlarged, also came to depend upon the custom of affluent automobilists.

With the Great Depression of the 1930s, and growing competition from the nation's new motels, small-town and small-city hotels of every vintage tended to languish, beginning what for many became a long period of decline. Perhaps, we are correct to consider that those remaining today are, indeed, plucky survivors. The Greystone Hotel of Bedford, Indiana, however, was not one of the lucky ones. Completed in 1923, the hotel was fully intended as a community showplace, being veneered in the town's principal product: limestone (fig. 60). The hotel was built not just to provide overnight accommodations for transients but to act as a community

FIGURE 61. The Hotel Greystone in decline. View through the front door, 1994. Authors' photograph.

center for Bedford, the center of Indiana's limestone belt. The hotel was very much a landmark symbolizing community pride. What obsolescence did not accomplish, a fire in the 1980s did, gutting several floors of the hotel. Derelict for over a decade, the building, perhaps beyond saving, was razed (fig. 61). Saving America's Main Street hotels would seem to be the latest phase in the hotel story we tell herein, something part of an even larger excitement: the preservation of America's Main Streets per se. The Greystone, however, did not benefit from the nation's current embrace of historic preservation values. Its demise was premature.

Private business interests as well as not-for-profit community organizations have and are contributing to the recycling of old hotel buildings from locality to locality. In virtually every instance, key individuals rise to spark activities, individuals knowledgeable as to a town's past but also insightful as to current investment possibilities, their insights very much future oriented as well. However, smart entrepreneurship over the last half-century, unlike that of the 1910s and 1920s, has entailed considerable government intervention, and at every level: local, state, and federal. Whereas investor syndicates once organized around the initiatives by a local chamber of commerce or other booster group, today they organize, as often as not, through preservation-minded organizations. They seek not to build anew but to save what is. Importantly, however, private initiative today very much depends on governmental largess. Especially important is the levering of investment capital through the federal Tax Reform Act of 1986, legislation that allows use of federal income tax credits for rehabilitating commercial structures appropriately designated on the National Register of Historic Places. Tax credits serve as a kind of "carrot"—one held out before a new generation of investors.

Nearly everywhere there are people willing to preserve old things, including things at the scale of architecture. When usefulness seemingly lapses, there are those who, as if by instinct, prefer to find new functionality, very much in preference to discard. It is a sentiment that spans the generations, exciting, as it does, both young and old.[1] Not everyone, however, remembers or thinks of the past fondly. Many withhold affection from old things and from old ways of doing and being. They, or people like them, may have been neglected or mistreated in the past. Fondness for things related in memory may be hard to come by. One cannot expect everyone to become an ardent preservationist.[2] But sentiment—fond sentiment, most particularly—has been a most forceful agent in promoting preservation, including the preservation of old hotel buildings. A hotel is a construct of social imagination. It is not merely a kind of business enterprise. Hotels by their very presence can either grant or deny a sense of community as well as a sense of personal well-being. That is what makes the present preservation-minded era so important. Much, of course, depends upon a hotel's physical condition and, as well, its economic viability, either actual or potential. Preservation, irrespective of sustaining sentiment, does not operate in a vacuum.

When Main Street hotels first opened, or when funds for their building were initially subscribed, residents in most places boasted of their locality having come of age. Similar pride is elicited today when hotels now dated are renovated or financed for renovation. On the other hand, most people feel embarrassed when a hotel in a community sits run-down and only marginally viable, or even boarded up and derelict. Such circumstances speak not just of the failure of a property owner or of a business person, but of a community to prevent and then correct an embarrassment. Old hotel buildings are difficult to ignore. The typical Main Street hotel for its size (usually one of a community's largest structures), for its location (usually at a highly visible location), and for its function (in the past, at present, or potentially for the future) usually looms large in the public mind. Old hotels have place-defining qualities as landmarks one way or another.

The General Morgan Inn at Greeneville, Tennessee

Many small-town and small-city hotels remain very much community enterprises across the American South. The General Morgan (now both a hotel and conference center) sits in a picturesque valley town situated in the eastern mountains of Tennessee, the successful public outcome of four separate hotel buildings privately developed over time and located immediately adjacent to one another. The De Woody Tavern dates from the early 1790s. Known as the Bell Tavern in the early nineteenth century, it was advertised as "A Public House at the Sign of the Bell in Greeneville." It was here that an informant shouted out to Union Troops the whereabouts of Confederate general John Hunt Morgan, who was immediately shot—a tale every child schooled locally knows. Other buildings followed the arrival of the railroad in the 1850s, all eventually connected at the second story to form a single hostelry. One of these sections, the Grand Hotel built by the Bromley family, became the town's leading hotel in the 1920s and remained for decades the center of Greeneville social life. The entire complex, upgraded following World War II, suffered disinvestment as Greeneville's downtown changed, retailers accelerating their departure for peripheral highway shopping centers after 1960. Additionally, the two Bromley family members instrumental in actually running the hotel died in 1964. Although the hotel's guest rooms were closed, the coffee shop remained open, a kind of dying ember.[3] When in 1981 former customers and friends of the family came to a special dinner to bid the hotel "farewell," it was widely believed that an era in the town's history, and not just in the hotel's history, had closed.[4]

The hotel's demise, however, fostered much public debate. Some wanted to raze the complex for a parking lot, reasoning that a lack of parking downtown was what had pushed business out to the suburbs. Additional parking, it was argued, would energize what business there was left and attract new. The town's building inspector, however, refused a permit for demolition.[5] A local bank took the property in 1981, business interests in the city sensing that hotel renewal could be the means by which revival of the whole downtown might be sparked. In 1983 an investor syndicate formed, sending a grant application to the National Trust for Historic Preservation's Main Street Program, a trust initiative that originated in the 1970s to help spark downtown renewal in America's small towns and cities. Greeneville became the first of five communities in Tennessee ultimately targeted for funding. Greeneville's project was organized under the promotional name "Morgan Square," the bank donating the ex-Bromley property to it. Although carrying strong historical "patina" (it was to most locals "run down"), the complex was, nonetheless, still attractive to the eye, everyone in Greeneville knowing it by sight. Indeed, local attachment to the complex would provide an important foundation for commercial success.[6]

Gregg Jones, copublisher of the *Greeneville Sun*, helped lead the preservation cause in Greeneville between 1986 and 1997. Through patient development the hotel complex slowly came back to life as a fulcrum for Greeneville's downtown revitalization, each important step dutifully reported in the *Sun*.[7] Had the hotel complex not been renovated, or so the newspaper editorialized, it would have seriously jeopardized, through negative spillover effect, nearby buildings, if not the whole of downtown.[8] Several members of the Morgan Square Board formed a partnership to reopen the hotel and run it for a period of ten years, the board, in turn, providing them a modest start-up grant. In turn, the partners assumed responsibility for all back taxes and for continuing insurance costs. They agreed to stabilize the building and, importantly, hire and oversee a developer to restore the property. Thus was born the Olde Town Development Corporation, an organization that would not only see the hotel complex revitalized but also several other buildings nearby. A hotel-management company, which would actually run the hotel, was then given equity interest in the project, necessitating creation of Morgan Square, Incorporated, Olde Town Development selling its interest to that entity.[9] Not everything went smoothly, however: the management firm's promise to direct tour buses to the hotel fell through when it, in turn, was acquired by another company.[10]

Nonetheless, in the fall of 1996 hope shone brightly. Of the $15 million package finally arranged for renovation, funds had come from a variety of sources: (1) Greeneville City bonds; (2) a grant from the Tennessee Valley Authority; (3) loans from a consortium of six local banks; (4) loans and contributions from both individuals and various businesses in the community; and (5) money from the State of Tennessee, much of it coming via the 1991 federal Intermodal Surface Transportation Efficiency Act (ISTEA). Designed to improve travel safety, diminish transport congestion, and protect the environment, ISTEA was aimed, in part, at redressing the nation's overdependence on the automobile, a circumstance that had undermined many if not most of America's traditional small-town and small-city business districts—including Greeneville's. On September 18, 1996, the Morgan Inn and Conference Center held a grand opening, with employment in downtown Greeneville having doubled overnight. Opened with the hotel were several restaurants, a community art center, and a suite of offices. The entire Morgan Square venture would yield an additional $275,000 in local tax revenues its first year.[11]

In 2000 the hotel portion of the property was sold to the Morgan Inn Corporation headed by local businessman Scott Niswonger.[12] Its holdings, including all hotel fixtures, furnishings, and equipment, were then valued at some $7.5 million. Niswonger also purchased several adjacent properties as well and leased the conference center. Not only a businessman but also a dedicated philanthropist, Niswonger, perhaps more than any other individual, continues today to spearhead Greeneville's revitalization. Although the hotel's restaurant and banquet facilities have thrived, overnight room rentals have not met expectations.[13] Commercial travelers and conferees have proven very supportive. The need now is to focus more on tourists, especially automobile tourists.[14]

The Hotel Bothwell at Sedalia, Missouri

Small-town and small-city hotel renewal thrives in the Midwest also. Opened in 1928 to provide Sedalia, a small industrial city in central Missouri, with quality hotel accommodations, the Hotel Bothwell languished, as did the Morgan at Greeneville, with the opening of new motels at the city's edge, and shift of downtown retailing there as well. Incorporated by the Community Hotel Company, a publically held corporation, the Bothwell—named for John H. Bothwell, its primary advocate and financial benefactor—was sold to the Boss Hotel Chain in 1953.[15] Remodeling at that time brought mixed results. After the hotel was old again, steps were taken to convert it into an assisted-living facility, shifting hotel occupancy over several years from transients to permanent residents. In 1968 these residents occupied some 60 percent of the hotel's rooms.[16]

Doyle D. Furnell, born to a family drawn originally to Sedalia by railroad work, was a bellhop at the Bothwell in the late 1940s. He went on to become a successful real estate developer. His son, David, recalled how his father loved the building. It was, his father thought, what Sedalia was all about: "I remember him saying as far back as the mid-1980s that if this property ever came up for sale, we would try to buy it and fix it back up."[17] In 1998, when the Furnell Company, operator of over fifty assisted-living facilities for seniors across Missouri, did indeed purchase the building, clear-eyed monetary considerations rather than personal sentiment dominated. What was really purchased was the care-facility license so that a totally new facility for the elderly might be built nearby.[18] What was intended for the old building was nothing short of full renovation, returning it to the transient hotel that it had been but also with a few rental apartments remaining. Returning fine dining to the community (there being only chain restaurants in Sedalia at the time) was an important concern. The hotel dining room, along with its kitchen, was totally refit and the hotel's ninety guest rooms reconfigured into forty-eight, building rejuvenation being partly financed by Sedalia's Downtown Redevelopment Agency.[19] Besides the reworking of the guest rooms—complete with new plumbing and air conditioning—the hotel's lobby, its lounges, and its ballroom were also totally refurnished.[20] Touches such as the lobby's mosaic tile floor, the ballroom's original French doors, and the large neon sign atop the hotel were retained. Where missing, moldings throughout the hotel's public spaces were replicated, as the Furnells wanted to capitalize on what they considered the building's ambience as a "historic site." They wanted guests to feel that they were "stepping back in time."[21]

Historic allure would, they thought, offset the hotel's disadvantageous downtown location, then as now well off the city's marked highways. The hotel joined a Web-based reservation service that specialized in "boutique" hotels.[22] The Furnells very much thought their hotel property key to downtown Sedalia's eventual rejuvenation.[23] The hotel, along with adjacent stores and office buildings, constitutes one of the Midwest's finest surviving early-twentieth-century residual streetscapes. Those other buildings have been at least partially rehabilitated since the Bothwell's reopening.[24] As in Greeneville, Tennessee, commercial travelers rather than tourists mainly patronize the revitalized hotel today (some 60 percent of guests). Automobile tourists have been slow in coming. Locals in search of food and drink represent another important revenue source.[25] History repeats itself in the sense that the Hotel Bothwell and downtown Sedalia mutually benefit one another in a kind of symbiosis as reciprocal beneficiaries. And, at least to a limited extent, the hotel continues to serve as a focus of community. However, service clubs that once met at the hotel have yet to return.

The Stonewall Jackson Hotel at Staunton, Virginia

Since 2002, the Stonewall Jackson has benefitted extensively from a city economic development program. As in Sedalia, however, the hotel's renovation also enjoys the strong personal commitment of a private businessman, Allen Persinger, and, as well, of a development company, Armana/Hoffler Holdings. Following its opening in 1924, motorists and railroad travelers in the Shenandoah Valley found the Stonewall Jackson premier among the region's hotels. In 1968, after customers had been drained off to highway motels nearby, the Persinger family purchased the building, refitting it for a new customer base, which again, as in Sedalia, comprised elderly residents requiring minimum assistance. They always hoped, however, that one day the hotel would resume its original status as a transient hotel.[26] Allen Persinger, who moved into the hotel penthouse at age fourteen, had especially developed a deep personal attachment.[27] The hotel went into a long decline. In the 1980s an attempted partnership with the city to rehabilitate the hotel as part of the Radisson hotel chain failed due to soaring interest rates at the time.[28]

Actual renovation began in 2003, a grant for planning assistance having come from the Virginia Department of Housing and Community Development.[29] The building's residents, in a sense, were essentially bound in place. They were mainly low-income people without automobiles. However, they could walk to shopping in the city's downtown, and many walked to jobs there as well.[30] Many residents simply could not afford to live elsewhere.[31] Nonetheless, the building was very much in physical decline, its utilities obsolete. Management's ability to sustain the status quo, given the building's marginal profitability, was seriously in doubt. A mix of affection and worry about the future weighed on residents when they were ultimately asked to leave. "I like it here," said one, "but I guess change is inevitable. I'll miss the people—the people that run it, the people that own it, and my friends that live here."[32]

The large neon sign atop the building, similar to the one on the Bothwell at Sedalia, was, like the building itself, an important icon of place. The National Register of Historic Places agreed, requiring the sign's preservation as a condition for listing the building, thus making it eligible for renovation tax incentives.[33] The "bottom line" turned out to be those tax credits, two million dollars worth. That was what drew investors in.[34] However, National Register administrators had also insisted that a town house adjacent to the hotel be included in the project. To do so, however, would have jeopardized adding a conference-center addition. Thus, city officials applied political pressure that resulted in an overturning of that requirement. The conference center went forward.[35] Importantly, the center rendered the project admissible for additional federal tax credits under the Tax Reform Act of 1986.[36] Indeed, the mulitistory addition has proven critical to the project's success.[37] Besides meeting facilities it contains a fitness center, swimming pool, additional guest rooms, and, importantly, a parking garage.[38] The hotel reopened in 2005, renamed the Stonewall Jackson Hotel and Conference Center. The hotel has not only had a positive impact on business downtown but has also benefitted business at a distance. Motels peripheral to the city, for example, have benefitted from conference overflow.[39]

The Frederick Martin Hotel at Moorhead, Minnesota

Long considered by locals to be one of the nation's finest small hotels, the Frederick Martin was, nonetheless, unable to keep abreast of fad and fashion. It was closed twice before being converted to offices.[40]

Construction of the hotel (named in honor of the newborn son of one of its initial investors) began in 1948, only to be halted the next year when funds ran out and a liquor license could not be obtained. Also at work was investors' distaste for their builder, a Minneapolis contractor who, eventually taking ownership of the project, completed the hotel and ran it for its first twelve years.[41] A linchpin on the city's main thoroughfare, the "FM," as it became endeared to local residents, boasted a reputation for especially fine cuisine. The hotel's manager, it is said, was promoted in the local press like a movie star.[42]

The hotel's "golden years" were brief. Closed for several years, the hotel was acquired in 1961 by the Kahler hotel chain based in Rochester, Minnesota. A decade later it was sold again, this time to another local investor group.[43] This was a period when hotels, and motel properties also, regularly changed ownership, usually on regular eight- to ten-year cycles, an effect of the 1954 revision of the federal tax code. The tax code remained a built-in mechanism for commercial-property turnover well into the late 1980s. It allowed an investment's equity value to be sheltered over its early life by the investor taking accelerated depreciation allowances. But after eight to ten years, when amortization payments became greater than depreciation charges, it made sense for an investor to sell his property to take a long-term capital gain. Then he or she could reinvest in another property and repeat the process.[44] Accordingly, ownership of both hotel and motel buildings not only turned over frequently, with investors, in a sense, "trading" properties with one another repeatedly. Encouraged over the life of an investment was property disinvestment, property owners not only resisting upgrading but even ordinary repair. Accelerated, therefore, was the decline of many a Main Street hotel.

Unprofitable, the Frederick Martin eventually reverted to a local bank. Then, after standing empty once again, it was sold to a local developer who, despairing of the hotel function, converted the building to condominium offices.[45] It has not been operated as a hotel since. In 2002, a proposal to refit the building as a hotel and conference center, through a municipal bond-issue initiative, failed at the polls.[46] Instead a local telecommunications company and a marketing firm (one specializing in e-mail and direct-mail sales), refit various portions of the building for their own use.[47]

Randolph Stefanson, a principal in various of the FM's rounds of resuscitation over the years, believes the building is well suited to its present business use. The nature of its construction "made it ideal for conversion to office and commercial space," he remembers. "The building has a clean, uncluttered and modern design. Frankly, it resembles an office building more than a hotel."[48] Several factors underscored the FM's conversion, but prime among them, perhaps, was the hotel's unfortunate location adjacent to a well-used railroad main line. Frequent train traffic had made it difficult for guests to sleep at night. It had become a common complaint. Also, much of downtown Morehead's retailing, as in Sedalia and Staunton, had shifted to the suburbs. Additionally, most travelers through the area preferred to stay in nearby Fargo, a much larger city immediately across the Red River in adjacent North Dakota. An office building is what the FM will likely remain.

The New Southern Hotel at Jackson, Tennessee

The product of a local partnership and the Albert Pick Company (then a hotel supplier, hotel developer, and operator of a hotel chain), the New Southern opened in

Figure 62. The New Southern Hotel, Jackson, Tennessee, 1928. From C. Stanley Taylor and Vincent R. Bliss, eds., *Hotel Planning and Outfitting: Commercial, Residential, Recreational* (Chicago: Albert Pick–Barth Co., 1928), 14.

1928 following the demolition of an older hotel at the site (fig. 62). Jackson prospered as an important railroad center, entrepot for West Tennessee farm products, cotton-milling center, and seat of Madison County. Located on the courthouse square, the new hotel was an instant success with transients moving through the city, whether by rail or by car, and remained the city's leading venue for social events until it closed in 1970.[49]

Morris Crocker, who bought the property in 1964, operated only portions of the building as a hotel, converting the lower floors into offices. In 1978 he dedicated the remainder of the hotel to elderly housing. Crocker eventually created a chain of retirement homes, using grants from the U.S. Department of Housing and Urban Development (HUD). Although sympathetic to Jackson's revitalization plans for

FIGURE 63. Top: Reconstituting interior moldings, New Southern Apartments, Jackson, Tennessee, 2004. Courtesy of Hal Crocker of Crocker Construction Co.

FIGURE 64. Bottom: Restoring the hotel mezzanine, New Southern Apartments, Jackson, Tennessee, 2006. Courtesy of Hal Crocker of Crocker Construction Co.

FIGURE 65. Top: Refurbished mezzanine, New Southern Apartments, Jackson, Tennessee, 2006. Courtesy of Hal Crocker of Crocker Construction Co.

FIGURE 66. Bottom: Refurbished lobby viewed from mezzanine, New Southern Apartments, Jackson, Tennessee, 2006. Courtesy of Hal Crocker of Crocker Construction Co.

the city's downtown, Crocker's business decisions were just that—business initiatives. Full family involvement was part of the picture. His father owned the building. His wife managed the property. A son's construction company handled what little remodeling there was. Tax implications, however, inclined the family toward fully renovating the building once HUD reclassified it as a "troubled property."[50] Since running an apartment building required specialized expertise, the Crockers decided to take on a partner, an apartment management firm. Federal income tax credits for historic structures available under the provisions of the Tax Reform Act of 1986, and administered through the Tennessee Historical Commission, generated funding for cosmetic improvements (figs. 63–66). Then a tornado struck Jackson on May 5, 2003, devastating the city's downtown, and badly damaging the New Southern. A HUD agent on the site following the storm advised that the building be torn down. However, the Crockers pressed on, insurance compensation enabling a complete refurbishment of the building.[51]

Renamed the New Southern Apartments, the building stands laudable both as a historic preservation victory and as a business proposition. The commercial spaces on the building's ground floor are rented, the County Assessor's Office being located on the former hotel mezzanine. Apartments are filled and have a healthy waiting list. As at Staunton, residents, most of them on limited incomes, enjoy not only relatively low rents, but housing that is safe and well located, especially for those without cars. Most enjoy living in Jackson's downtown, many very much for sentimental reasons. However, Hal Crocker avoids words like "sentimental" and "romantic," although he admits to engaging in hotel restoration and adaptive reuse (he has since restored the much older Neely House Hotel near downtown Jackson) because he enjoys the work so much.[52]

The Wolford Hotel at Danville, Illinois

Substantial demand for rentals by elderly residents of Danville, coupled with municipal government incentives, persuaded the Capital Associates, a Chicago investment firm, to take on the Wolford Hotel. For Danville, however, it was a rather difficult road getting there. The hotel had opened in 1926 without any public involvement, its nine stories towering at the edge of downtown, a major landmark. It was common to hear: "I'll meet you at the Wolford."[53] A local radio station operated in the basement beginning in 1938, and the local United Fund headquartered its annual fund-raising campaigns off the mezzanine.[54] The hotel closed in 1975 after years of fruitless wrangling between its longtime owner and state and local fire and health authorities over unaddressed code violations.[55] One potential purchaser proposed refurbishing the hotel completely—not just the guest rooms, but the retail shops, professional offices, and, of course, the large dining room. The Danville City Council moved to use city bonds to subsidize same, thinking that a refurbished hotel substantially advanced downtown revitalization. But when bonding restrictions were imposed by a change in state law, the initiative collapsed. Then the City Council agreed to purchase the hotel, cover the back taxes owed, and sell the building to a not-for-profit organization formed to renovate the property. But that initiative also fell through when an application for HUD funding was rejected.[56] Rumored that political cleavage between Chicago and downstate Illinois was at fault, Danville's application likely lacked polish.[57]

It was then that the Capitol Associates, owner of a small motel chain, and also owner of a downtown hotel in Rock Island, Illinois, took ownership of the Wolford. With a successful bid for funds, channeled through the State of Illinois's Housing Development Agency in 1979, HUD agreed to subsidize rents for a refurbished hotel's low-income tenants.[58] Many of the 112 tenants initially housed turned out to be former hotel employees. They remembered when the hotel symbolized the city's high life. For city planners, however, the view was forward and not back in time. The Wolford's reopening in 1981 seemed to signify a new beginning for Danville's much diminished downtown, a promotional brochure being distributed to celebrate.[59]

The Casa Munras Garden Hotel at Monterey, California

Historic preservation initiatives have saved hotel buildings in many small towns and small cities across the United States, initiatives highly reminiscent of how enlightened community self-interest helped finance and build Main Street hotels in the first place. Preservationists seem especially attracted to the unique in architecture and to the very old, especially those hotels that predate the automobile era. Such was the case with Monterey's Casa Munras Garden Hotel, the core of property being the 1824 abode hacienda of a Spanish colonial official, Don Estaban Munras. It was occupied by his descendants until 1941. Soon after, concerned citizens took an option on the property, thus blocking pending demolition and fear that the property would succumb to a gas station or possibly a parking lot.[60] The city had been the capital of Spanish-held and then Mexican-held Alta California. In 1846 it became California's first state capital. A 1941 plan for a city park on the Munras site—a park that would celebrate the city's past—came to naught. That year, however, the property did come under the sympathetic ownership of P. J. Dougherty, the city's postmaster and a former mayor.[61] Dougherty built a fifty-two-unit motel on the grounds, making it Monterey's first large motel. But he also fitted out the old house with a lounge, bar, and dance floor on its first floor and sleeping rooms upstairs. The whole gained general approval notwithstanding its garish neon sign placed on the roof of the house.[62]

In later years, Dougherty's son, Jack, undertook several aggressive remodelings, including the addition of an outdoor swimming pool and a restaurant with dining room and coffee shop. An account in 1955 ranked the property "the most extensive motel-hotel business in the area." The complex contained 130 guest rooms.[63] Various service clubs (Lions, Exchange, Serra, Soroptimists, and 20/30) met weekly at the hotel. It employed a hundred people when sold in 1965 to a hotel corporation with holdings both in California and New York.[64] Some of the core building's ornamentation was stripped away during a 1972 renovation, somewhat compromising its historic look. Considerably relandscaped in 1979, however, some the property's historic ambience was returned, the grounds being highly reminiscent of the flower garden the last Munras occupants had maintained. In 1996 the property was reportedly the largest parcel privately held in downtown Monterery. More a finely crafted series of physical adjustments in response to a changing marketplace than an archeologically correct historic site, Casa Munras as palimpsest demonstrates functional resiliency.[65]

The Marshall Hotel at Marshall, Texas

Marshall, Texas, boasts a colorful regional history: first Texas town with telegraph service, location of a firebrand Confederate newspaper, home of the state's first (and last) Confederate governor, and early railhead for the Texas and Pacific Railroad. The railroad long maintained its principal shops in the city. The city was also an important cotton depot for eastern Texas, the central hub of an important oil field, and home to a booming ceramics industry (Marshall once calling itself the "Pottery Capital of the World"). The Marshall Hotel was opened in 1930 by the Perkins Brothers Company. Nine stories tall, it was located immediately southeast of the courthouse, an impressive and highly visible structure. Among its many amenities was a roof garden placed adjacent to the hotel's banquet hall and ballroom on the building's top floor. According to an architectural firm's description, "Residents and guests enter the fifteen foot tall balcony pavilion through seven-foot tall brass doors into the soaring Grand Lounge with sixteen-foot tall plaster columns and a massive Venetian crystal chandelier suspended from the coffered ceiling."[66]

Developer Jerry Cargill, a Marshall native and Dallas businessman, bought the hotel in the 1990s from the not-for-profit Marshall Downtown Development Corporation.[67] Conceived as a community project, Cargill welcomed, in his words, "as

FIGURE 67. Atrium of the Windsor Hotel, Garden City, Kansas, 2006. Courtesy of the Kansas State Historical Society, Topeka, KS.

many people as possible," thus "to contribute what they could." That gave members of the community, he thought, a sense of ownership—"something they can be proud of."[68] The Marshall Hotel reopened as both a transient and as a residential hotel in 2003. Jerry Cargill and his wife dedicated a vacant half-acre of land on the west side of the hotel to a wildflower garden, dedicating it to Lady Bird Johnson, who had grown up in Marshall.[69]

The Windsor Hotel at Garden City, Kansas

The Windsor Hotel offers an excellent example of how purist preservation instincts have saved a building from demise. Unfortunately, preservation impulses have not as yet fostered meaningful redevelopment. Today, the only occupant in the building is a civic group, the Garden City Downtown Vision, charged not only with saving the building but with revitalizing downtown also. But even in a large metropolis, much less in a small Great Plains city, would a hotel building like the Windsor stand out, both as an object of curiosity and as a clear historic resource. One architectural historian has called it "a sprawling fortress," embodying "a spirit of elegance." Locals dub it the "Waldorf of the Prairies."[70] The hotel's large interior court, three stories high and roofed over by a skylight, is especially to be commended (fig. 67). The building was built in the late nineteenth century for a local businessman (an ex-buffalo hunter) in a florid Renaissance Revival style. It was a building easily dismissed as gauche by twentieth-century modernists. However, it remained a one-of-kind building and, certainly for Kansas, a unique structure. It was once considered, with its 125 rooms and large public spaces, the finest hotel between Kansas City and Denver. Its fortunes spiked and declined in cycles until finally in 1977 it closed, being judged unsafe by municipal officials. Failure to meet contemporary building and fire codes is, of course, a problem that older buildings universally face.[71]

Like a gem in plain view, the Windsor had been under the watchful eye of various preservation groups for some twenty years, being long included on the Kansas Preservation Alliance's "Most Endangered List." Listed in 1972 on the National Register of Historic Places, the Windsor was, of course, eligible for federal income tax credits for rehabilitation. The local Finney County Preservation Alliance commissioned a rehabilitation assessment, finding the building not only relatively sound but also potentially a very important tourist draw as a historic landmark. "The hotel is seen as a cultural anchor locally and a key piece to the fabric of the downtown," the report concluded.[72] Written up in the *Garden City Telegram,* the hotel was praised for its distinctiveness. It was vital, the article said, to preserve such important icons of place.[73] But was the building actually too unique to attract a developer? With its atrium, could the building be brought up to code? Was Garden City sufficiently large enough to profitably sustain meaningful reuse? The building needed a benefactor.

The Hotel Pattee at Perry, Iowa

Build it (or remodel it) and they will come. Such was the philosophy that seemingly underwrote a benefactor's renovation of the Hotel Pattee. Although once hailed as a "poster child" for small-town hotel renovation, the property closed at the end of 2006 and remains closed at this writing. Extraordinary care and attention was lavished on the Pattee. Accordingly, it is assumed that its closing will only be temporary. The Pattee became a "boutique hotel" targeted at affluent travelers looking for a special lodging experience. The decor of each of its forty rooms celebrates some aspect of Iowa history, especially as it has played out in Perry. Roberta Green Ahmanson, a graduate of Perry High School and wife of a philanthropist in religious causes, bought and refurbished the hotel, directing its furnishing and decorating personally—very much as a labor of love. The hotel's public spaces follow "Prairie Style" edicts, at least of the Max Parrish tradition, if not the Wrightian tradition. The very fact that Roberta Ahmanson successfully infused her project with regional sentiment only makes the hotel's closing all the more heartfelt. The hotel had become the bellwether of the town's health and vitality. If it does not attract another investor it would be a great loss, expressed one local businessman: "Part of our identity will be gone."[74] When and if the Pattee reopens, continued participation in the National Trust for Historic Preservation's "Historic Hotels of America" program will help. To date, however, most of that program's listings, begun in 1989, are either large big-city hotels or grand resort hotels. The historically significant hotels of Main Street America, like the Pattee, have been slow to be included.

The Terre Haute House at Terre Haute, Indiana

Not all the elegant Main Street hotels that ought to have been "saved" have been saved. Many have fallen victim to sheer indifference. Decades after closure, substantial neglect, and numerous failed attempts to fund renovation, the Terre Haute House, long the largest and tallest building in the Indiana city of the same name, was demolished to make way for a new motor inn. The "Crossroads of America" will never be the same. The building that truly anchored that downtown intersection is gone. Once symbolic of Terre Haute's embrace of the urbane and the cosmopolitan, the hotel is no more. The motel building that has replaced it will certainly carry on as a place for visitors to overnight. But a true community resource has been lost.

The Terre Haute House replaced a succession of preceding hotel buildings. Chauncey Rose, one of nineteenth-century Terre Haute's leading business entrepreneurs, bought land at the edge of the town in the late 1830s to build the Prairie House. That hotel, renamed the Terre Haute House, thrived after railroads arrived in the city, several of them financed by Rose. What was once the edge of town, however, quickly became the very center of the city's business district. In 1884 Charles Baur bought the hotel and launched his string of technological innovations so important to the evolving hotel industry nationwide. Ranked as obsolete when a rival hotel was built to the "Statler formula" (a bathroom for every guest room),

FIGURE 68. The vacant Terre Haute House, Terre Haute, Indiana, 1990. Much of early twentieth-century downtown Terre Haute had already been stripped away for parking lots. The few new buildings constructed were (as on the lower left) fully automobile-convenient, being clones of what Americans were then building in city suburbs. Authors' photograph.

the Terre Haute House was remodeled in 1914. In 1925, however, it was razed and replaced with the fourteen-story, Italian Renaissance building recently torn down (figs. 1 and 68).[75]

The hotel's vitality had waned as retailing relocated to the city's suburbs, a process delayed in Terre Haute by the city's depressed economy but, nonetheless, largely complete by 1990. For decades rebirth seemed to beckon. In 1988 a developer, forging an agreement with the Radisson hotel chain, agreed to renovate and reopen the hotel, but financing failed to materialize. In 1993 the city engineered an agreement, including tax and other subsidies, whereby a developer might be enticed to purchase the building, one of the city's wealthier families having long owned it. Ten years later, when a developer indeed came forward, the building was deemed too deteriorated for renovation to be feasible. Most city residents probably welcomed the building's demolition, so long had it been an eyesore and a civic embarrassment.[76] Unfortunately, no benefactor ever stepped forward.

What choices had been considered? The merits of a landmark renovated in accordance with a preservation ethnic had won some local support. Overwhelmingly, however, letters on the editorial page of the city's newspaper over time had called for action—any action.[77] At the time of the building's demise, at least one letter writer charged malfeasance, especially by the city. Why had various potential de-

FIGURE 69. Sign for new motor inn under construction on Terre Haute House site, Terre Haute, Indiana, 2006. Authors' photograph.

velopers willing to restore the building not been aggressively encouraged? Was it lack of imagination, not lack of money? Was it connected vested interest, not community welfare, that prevailed? Why had the building's landmark status not been forcefully asserted? Why had its community value been ignored?[78]

What did demolition cost the citizens of Terre Haute? Although both U.S. 40 and U.S. 41 have moved to other streets in downtown, a historical plaque still declares its intersection to be "The Crossroads of America." That phrase is now applied elsewhere, including nearby Indianapolis, Terre Haute having lost something of its place in the American scheme of things. With a "cookie-cutter" design taken largely from the current plan books of a large lodging chain, the new building only replicates some traditional hotel functions. This motel-like structure does not serve the city as a community center in that it lacks necessary public spaces. The new building hardly symbolizes local community save, perhaps, insofar as it is new. True, the community was almost desperate for something new (or renewed) on the site (fig. 69).[79] Yet today the place looms very much as "Anywhere USA." Building after building over the decades have been lost in downtown Terre Haute, the Terre Haute House the biggest loss of all. Today, downtown Terre Haute looks more like a commercial strip than a city downtown. It is a downtown very much "suburbanized" (fig. 70). Very much gone are the density and the crowdedness, and thus the vibrant street life that once made the city's main street, Wabash Avenue, so vibrant. What one sees are new buildings largely isolated in parking-lot surrounds, every

FIGURE 70. Hilton Garden Inn, Terre Haute, Indiana, 2008. Authors' photograph.

one of them bland and totally predictable. In the 1950s John Jakle's father, a native of Terre Haute, could walk along Wabash Avenue and encounter people he knew even though he had not been a resident of the city for decades. Were he alive today, he would be hard pressed to even recognize many a building.

* * *

In a sense, automobile use turned American towns, but especially its cities, inside out. Many commercial activities that had once been centrally located downtown followed the American flight to the suburbs, especially that of affluent white Americans heading for suburban subdivisions. New things, motels for example, were mainly located out along the new commercial strips. Motels were more fully automobile-convenient, being provided with sweeping driveways, entrances shielded by large porte-cocheres, and parking lots immediately adjacent. Some incorporated dining room and conference facilities just like traditional hotels, but most were merely places of overnight accommodation. Transiency was everything. Community was given little thought. By the 1990s new motels were invariably called "inns" (a shortening of the term "motor inn").

In most small towns and small cities, traditional hotels downtown suffered. With business declining in the face of increased motel competition, reinvestment in old hotel buildings was difficult. In most localities, the best that could be accomplished was to either target a new kind of resident or new kind of building use. Might not a more affluent traveler be attracted—one in search of and willing to pay for a novel lodging experience?[80] Or might not a new kind of resident be served—less affluent senior citizens, for example? Might not a hotel building be totally repackaged for reuse—reoriented as an office building, for example? Elderly housing, as it has turned out, has proven to be the avenue most taken, given the sorts of governmental subsidies, including tax credits, available to developers over past decades.

A hotel renewed to provide both overnight lodging for transients and to attract conferees for meetings through the facilities of a conference center is, perhaps, a locality's best option. Thus a revitalized building can continue to serve (or serve once again) as a kind of local community center as well as a transient hotel. The critical roles that hotel dining rooms and banquet rooms (as well as smaller public spaces) once played in sustaining locality-based community can potentially play out again but with even more in the way of public space available. It is one thing for a landmark building to survive as an icon of community. It is quite another for it to survive with its traditional social functions sustained. Where today one finds small-town and small-city downtowns truly alive and prospering in the United States, one usually finds new uses, but also traditional activities, filling old as well as new buildings. And, as often as not, an old hotel buildings asserts itself in a vital scheme of things.

The nation's Main Street hotels built during the early automobile era were for the most part solidly built. They were built not just as business propositions but as social centers—both functions intended to be long-term. They were promoted enthusiastically. Perhaps, in retrospect, too much money was lavished on many of them. How quickly times changed. The Great Depression reduced most of them to marginal profitability. Travel by automobile, the major rationale for their being, actually made them functionally obsolete. And yet structurally most of them have persisted. Main Street hotels were built in a time of boundless optimism, especially in the years just after World War I. Even the smallest places thought it feasible to embrace early automobility in reviving themselves at their traditional centers. Substantially, it was a matter of civic pride.

The new "stranger's paths," with their "other-directed houses" more auto-oriented, became, on the other hand, more ephemeral year by year. Motels have hardly proven as durable as the nation's traditional hotels. Things out along the nation's highways have, for the most part, not been built to last. Nor were they ever intended to be icons of community. They were meant solely to be business ventures, largely for the short run. It is doubtful whether their passing will be much regretted. Not so with America's Main Street hotels. Or so we wonder.

NOTES

Preface

1. J[ohn]. B[rinckerhoff]. Jackson, "The Stranger's Path," *Landscape* 7 (Spring/ Summer 1957): 11–15.

2. J[ohn]. B[rinckerhoff]. Jackson, "Other-Directed Houses," *Landscape* 6 (Winter 1956–1957): 29–35.

3. Ibid., 29.

4. See John A. Jakle and Keith A. Sculle, *The Gas Station in America* (Baltimore: Johns Hopkins Univ. Press, 1994); John A. Jakle, Keith A. Sculle, and Jefferson S. Rogers, *The Motel in America* (Baltimore: Johns Hopkins Univ. Press, 1996); and John A. Jakle and Keith A. Sculle, *Fast Food: Roadside Restaurants in the Automobile Age* (Baltimore: Johns Hopkins Univ. Press, 1999).

5. See John A. Jakle and Keith A. Sculle, *Signs in America's Auto Age: Signatures of Landscape and Place* (Iowa City: Univ. of Iowa Press, 2004); and John A. Jakle and Keith A. Sculle, *Lots of Parking: Land Use in a Car Culture* (Charlottesville: Univ. of Virginia Press, 2004).

6. John A. Jakle and Keith A. Sculle, *Motoring: The Highway Experience in America* (Athens: Univ. of Georgia Press, 2008).

7. J[ohn]. B[rinckerhoff]. Jackson, "The Almost Perfect Town," *Landscape* 2 (Autumn 1952): 2–8.

Acknowledgments

1. [John Willy], "We Celebrate 38th Anniversary," *Hotel Monthly* 38 (Sept. 1930): 33.

2. Ibid.

Introduction

1. We found the back issues of one trade journal, the *Hotel Monthly,* especially useful for its historical insights. First issued in 1893, the magazine provides for our entire period of interest feature articles (concerning literally every aspect of hotel planning, management, and promotion), news briefs, hospitality industry statistics, and extensive advertising, especially for hotel suppliers. Other trade journals of note published over various decades include the *Hotel Bulletin,* the *Hotel Gazette, Hotel Management,* and *Hotel World.* A credible sampling of popular magazine articles is cited chapter to chapter.

2. Examples include [C. Stanley Taylor and Vincent R. Bliss, eds.], *Hotel Planning and Outfitting: Commercial, Residential, Recreational* (Chicago: Albert Pick-Barth Companies, 1928); Randolph William Sexton, *American Apartment Houses, Hotels, and Apartment Hotels of Today* (New York: Architectural Book Publishing Co., 1929); American Institute of Architects, *The Hotel Building* (New York: American Hotel Association, 1947); and Henry End, *Hotels and Motor Hotels* (New York: Whitney Library of Design, 1963).

3. Examples include Mary Bresnan, *The Practical Hotel Housekeeper* (Chicago: Hotel Monthly, 1900); Lucius M. Boomer, *Hotel Management: Principles and Practice* (New York: Harper & Brothers, 1925); John Dismukes Green, *The Back of the House* (New York: Gehring Pub. Co., 1925); and Joseph Oliver Dahl, *The Efficient Room Clerk's Manual* (Stamford, CT: J. O. Dahl, 1939).

4. Overview books include Jefferson Williamson, *The American Hotel: An Anecdotal History* (New York: Alfred A. Knopf, 1930); Norman S. Hayner, *Hotel Life* (Chapel Hill: Univ. of North Carolina Press, 1936); Richard Oliver, *America's Grand Resort Hotels* (New York: Pantheon Books, 1979); Catherine Donzel, Alexis Gregory, and Marc Walter, *Grand American Hotels* (New York: Vendome Press, 1989); and Elaine Denby, *Grand Hotels: An Architectural and Social History* (London: Reaktion Books, 1998). Recently published is A. K. Sandoval-Strausz, *Hotel: An American History* (New Haven: Yale Univ. Press, 2007). Recent Ph.D. dissertations include Molly Winger Berger, "The Modern Hotel in America," Case Western Reserve Univ., 1997; and Lisa Pfueller Davidson, "Consumption and Efficiency in the 'City Within a City': Commercial Hotel Architecture and the Emergence of Modern American Culture, 1890–1930," George Washington Univ., 2003. Worthy of mention also is a 2005 special-issue volume of the *Journal of Decorative and Propaganda Arts* (Issue 25: *The American Hotel*), guest-edited by Molly W. Berger. The Waldorf-Astoria Hotel in New York City is, perhaps, the most studied of all American hostelries. See Edward Hungerford, *The Story of the Waldorf-Astoria* (New York: Knickerbocker Press, 1925); Henry B. Lent, *The Waldorf-Astoria: A Brief Chronicle of a Unique Institution Now Entering Its Fifth Decade* (New York: Currier, 1934); and Albin Pasteur Dearing, *The Elegant Inn: The Waldorf-Astoria Hotel, 1893–1929* (Secaucus, NJ: Lyle Stuart, 1986). Biographies of leading hoteliers include Rufus Jarman, *A Bed for the Night: The Story of the Wheeling Bellboy, E. M. Statler and His Remarkable Hotels* (New York: Harper & Row, 1952); Whitney Bolton, *The Silver Spade: The Conrad Hilton Story* (New York: Farrar, Straus & Young, 1954); and Harl Adams Dalstrom, *Eugene C. Eppley: His Life and Legacy* (Lincoln, NE: Johnsen Pub. Co., 1969). Books on important hotel chains include Susan R. Braden, *The Architecture of Leisure: The Resort Hotels of Henry Flagler and Henry Plant* (Gainesville: Univ. Press of Florida, 2002); and Paul L. Ingram, *The Rise of Hotel Chains in the United States, 1896–1980* (New York: Garland, 1996).

5. Quoted in Williamson, *The American Hotel*, 294.

6. See William A. Hayes, "An Economic Analysis of the American Hotel Industry," *Catholic University of America Studies in Economics*, Abstract Series, Vol. 4 (1952): 5.

7. Anonymous letter to the editor, *Hotel Monthly* 28 (Mar. 1920): 19.

8. A. K. Sandoval-Strausz, "A Public House for a New Republic: The Architecture of Accommodation and the American State, 1789–1809," in *Constructing Image, Identity, and Place: Perspectives in Vernacular Architecture, IX,* ed. Alison K. Hoagland and Kenneth A. Breisch, 68 (Knoxville: Univ. of Tennessee Press, 2003); Williamson, *The American Hotel*, 300.

9. Williamson, *The American Hotel*, 10.

10. See Brian McGinty, *A Connoisseur's Guide to Historic American Hotels* (Harrisburg: Stackpole Books, 1978), 13–17.

11. Ibid., 20–21.

12. Catherine Cocks, *Doing the Town: The Rise of Urban Tourism in the United States, 1850–1915* (Berkeley: Univ. of California Press, 2001), 72.

13. Ibid., 74–75.

14. See Daniel J. Boorstin, *The Americans: The National Experience* (New York: Random House, 1965), 146.

15. Doris Elizabeth Kind, "The First-Class Hotel and the Age of the Common Man," *Journal of Southern History* 23 (May 1957): 177.

16. Cocks, *Doing the Town,* 81.

17. John Willy, "The Word Hotel," *Hotel Monthly* 30 (Oct. 1922): 40.

18. See John Lloyd Thomas, "Workingmen's Hotels," *Municipal Affairs* 3 (Mar. 1899): 73–94.

19. See John A. Herbst, "Historic Houses," in *History Museums in the United States: A Critical Assessment,* ed. Warren Leon and Roy Rosenzweig, 105 (Urbana: Univ. of Illinois Press, 1989).

20. "NRA's Definition of Hotel," *Hotel Monthly* 41 (Dec. 1933): 40.

21. U.S. Bureau of the Census, Department of Commerce, *Fifteenth Census of the United States, Census of Hotels, 1930* (Washington, DC: U.S. Government Printing Office, 1931).

22. Harper E. Carraine, *Census of Business: Hotels* (Washington, DC: Department of Commerce and Bureau of the Census, 1937), iv.

23. See Karl B. Raitz and John Paul Jones, III, "The City Hotel as Landscape Artifact and Community Symbol," *Journal of Cultural Geography* 9 (Fall/Winter 1988): 16–36.

24. "Historic Nachusa Tavern, Dixon, Ill.," *Hotel Monthly* 26 (June 1918): 63.

25. "Stage Coach Taverns for Motor Stages," *Hotel Monthly* 33 (Apr. 1925): 72.

26. Dianne Newell, "The Short-lived Phenomenon of Railroad Station Hotels," *Historic Preservation* 26 (July–Sept. 1974): 31–36.

27. See "Interesting Journeys to Country Hotels," *Hotel Monthly* 23 (Aug. 1915): 83–85.

28. Edward Hungerford, "The Coming of the Hotel," *Harper's Weekly,* Jan. 11, 1913, 8.

29. Daniel P. Ritchey, "Economics of the Hotel Project," *Architectural Forum* 39 (Nov. 1923): 219.

30. "James K. Polk Hotel of Murfreesboro, Tenn.," *Hotel Monthly* 42 (Aug. 1933): 19.

31. H. L. Stevens, "Construction Problems Discussed at Convention," *Hotel Monthly* 28 (Jan. 1920): 50.

32. Lewis Atherton, *Main Street on the Middle Border* (Bloomington: Indiana Univ. Press, 1954), 59–60.

33. Martha Haskell Clark, "Saving the Country Hotel," *Country Life* 30 (Aug. 1916): 52.

34. Sinclair Lewis, *Work of Art* (Garden City, NY: Doubleday, Doran & Co., 1935), 6–7.

35. [Willy], "We Celebrate 38th Anniversary," 33–34.

36. "Shears Salad With Epigram Dressing: Good for Mental Digestion," *Hotel Monthly* 33 (May 1925): 49.

37. Williamson, *The American Hotel,* 294.

38. Hayes, "An Economic Analysis," 9.

39. Suzanne Keller, *Community: Pursuing the Dream. Living the Reality* (Princeton, NJ: Princeton Univ. Press, 2003), 4.

40. Claude S. Fischer, *Networks and Places: Social Relations in the Urban Setting* (New York: Free Press, 1977), 12.

41. Park Dixon Goist, *From Main Street to State Street: Town, City, and Community in America* (Port Washington, NY: Kennikat Press, 1977), 13.

1. Laying Out the House

1. Sinclair Lewis, *Main Street* (1920; reprint, New York: New American Library, 1961), 37.

2. Theodore Dreiser, *Hoosier Holiday* (New York: John Lane, 1916), 130.

3. See Jakle, Sculle, and Rogers, *The Motel in America.*

4. "The Braham of Union City, Indiana," *Hotel Monthly* 14 (Jan. 1906): 26.

5. "One Hundred Dollars Offered for the Best Set of Plans for a 50-Room Country Hotel, Conforming to Specifications," *Hotel Monthly* 20 (Oct. 1912): 27.

6. "New 50-Room Hotel in Arkansas Town of 7,500 Population," *Hotel Monthly* 22 (Oct. 1914): 80–83.

7. "One Hundred Dollars," 27.

8. Ibid.

9. "The Russell-Lamson of Waterloo, Iowa," *Hotel Monthly* 22 (Dec. 1914): 48–49.

10. "New 50-Room Hotel," 81.

11. Taylor and Bliss, *Hotel Planning and Outfitting*, 13.

12. Ibid, 16.

13. C. Stanley Taylor, "The Practical Approach to the New Hotel's Building Problem," *Hotel Management* 10 (Dec. 1926): 401.

14. "The Relation Between Hotel Builder and Architect," *Hotel Monthly* 25 (July 1917): 62.

15. "The Altamont of Hazleton, Pennsylvania," *Hotel Monthly* 32 (Sept. 1924): 35.

16. Ibid.

17. "The Urbana-Lincoln Hotel of Urbana, Illinois," *Hotel Monthly* 32 (Apr. 1924): 74.

18. Ibid., 74–75.

19. "A Modern Fireproof Hotel Built for the Needs of the Average Small City," *Hotel Monthly* 37 (Nov. 1929): 55.

20. "Hotel Julien-Dubuque of Dubuque, Iowa," *Hotel Monthly* 24 (Feb. 1916): 62.

21. "The Hotel Bothwell of Sedalia, Missouri," *Hotel Monthly* 35 (Aug. 1927): 29.

22. "A Modern Fireproof Hotel," 55.

23. "Hotel Ashtabula of Ashtabula, Ohio," *Hotel Monthly* 28 (Nov. 1920): 33.

24. "The Fowler of Lafayette, Indiana," *Hotel Monthly* 23 (May 1915): 56.

25. "The Lincoln Hotel of Danville, Illinois," *Hotel Monthly* 33 (May 1925): 39.

26. "Hotel Tallcorn of Marshalltown, Iowa, Newest of the Eppley Chain," *Hotel Monthly* 37 (Jan. 1929): 59.

27. "Hotel Hayes of Jackson, Michigan, 200 Rooms," *Hotel Monthly* 35 (Mar. 1927): 39.

28. "The Lincoln Hotel of Danville, Illinois," 41.

29. Ibid.

2. The Business of Starting a Main Street Hotel

1. Lewis, *Main Street,* 398.

2. "Hotel Ashtabula of Ashtabula, Ohio," 32.

3. "Hotel Keeping In Small Town," *Hotel Monthly* 29 (Nov. 1921): 36.

4. "The Hotel Farragut of Knoxville, Tenn.," *Hotel Monthly* 27 (Mar. 1919): 48.

5. "Other Hotels of Mason City, Iowa," *Hotel Monthly* 30 (July 1922): 28.

6. "The Hotel Wyanoke of Farmville, Virginia," *Hotel Monthly* 33 (Aug. 1925): 34.

7. For example, see "The Parkside Hotel of Kewanee, Illinois," *Hotel Monthly* 24 (Nov. 1912): 68; "The Fowler of Lafayette, Indiana," 60; and "The Lewis-Clark Hotel of Lewiston, Idaho," *The Hotel Monthly* 31 (Feb. 1923): 41.

8. Taylor and Bliss, *Hotel Planning and Outfitting,* 16, 30.

9. For example, see "Michigan's Hotel Training School," *Hotel Monthly* 36 (Dec. 1928): 39; and "Hotel Chandler of Decatur, Georgia," *Hotel Monthly* 36 (Aug. 1928): 26 [26–30].

10. J. K. W., "Ohio Hotel Association Holds 33rd Annual," *Hotel Monthly* 39 (Jan. 1927): 42.

11. For an exception, see "The Hotel Reich of Gadsden, Ala.," *Hotel Monthly* 38 (June 1930): 34.

12. "How Obsolescence is Being Defeated in a 200-Room Hotel," *Hotel Monthly* 55 (Sept. 1947): 34.

13. Jeffrey A. Charles, *Service Clubs in American Society: Rotary, Kiwanis, and Lions* (Urbana: Univ. of Illinois Press, 1993), 72.

14. In the rich scholarly literature on the early twentieth century, see especially Robert Wuthnow, *Loose Connections: Joining Together in America's Fragmented Communities* (Cambridge: Harvard Univ. Press, 1998), 9–13, 33–37; Charles, *Service Clubs in American Society,* 9–75; and Atherton, *Main Street on the Middle Border,* 245–353.

15. Thorstein Veblen, "The Country Town," *The Freeman* (July 11, 1923): 418.

16. Timothy R. Mahoney, "The Small City in American History," *Indiana Magazine of History* 99 (Dec. 2003): 311, 327.

17. "Application for Registration[,] New Mexico State Register of Cultural Properties," SR 1541, Hidalgo Hotel, sec. 12, 1 (Dept. of Cultural Affairs, New Mexico Historic Preservation Division, Santa Fe, NM).

18. "Hotel Hidalgo Throws Open It's [*sic*] Doors As One of the Finest in the Southwest," *Lordsburg [NM] Liberal,* Nov. 30, 1928, sec. two, 1.

19. For an example of these steps in Paducah, Kentucky, see Barron White, *I Remember Paducah When . . .* (Paducah, KY: McClanahan House, 2000), for a locally

distinguished family razing their ancestral home for the Irving Cobb Hotel in 1929 (p. 80) and public sentiment for removal of the Oxford Hotel in 1966 (p. 32).

20. John Troesser, "Hotel Wars in Seguin in 1916," *TexasEscapes.com,* http://www.texasescapes.com/FEATURES/rooms_with_a_past/Hotel_wars_Seguin_Texas.htm (accessed May 7, 2007).

21. For example, see "Hotel Tallcorn of Marshalltown, Iowa," 52.

22. Regarding some of these, see David Warren Howell, "The School of Hotel Administration at Cornell University, 1921–1961: A History," Ph.D. diss., State Univ. of New York at Buffalo, Vol. I, 1994, 373–74.

23. Williamson, *The American Hotel,* 15; Howell, "The School of Hotel Administration at Cornell," 64.

24. Ruth Dunkar, "Adventures of a Small-Town Hotel Keeper," *American Magazine* 99 (Mar. 1925): 54.

25. Donald S. Lamm, *The First One Hundred Years: A History of the City of Sedalia, Missouri, 1860–1960* ([Sedalia, MO]: Sedalia, Missouri Centennial History Committee, 1963), 73.

26. "Early Plans Have New Hotel Erected in City," *Sedalia Democrat,* June 9, 1927, 2.

27. Becky Carr Imhauser, *All Along Ohio Street: Sedalia, MO: 1856–1970* (Marceline, MO: Walsworth Publishing Company, 2006), 211–12.

28. William B. Claycomb, Becky Carr Imhauser, and Rose M. Nolen, *Bothwell Regional Health Center* (Sedalia, MO: Inter-state Printing, 2005), 34–36; and Imhauser, *All Along Ohio Street,* 211–12.

29. "Early Plans Have New Hotel Erected in City," 2.

30. "The Hotel Bothwell of Sedalia, Missouri," 28.

31. "Hotel Cherokee, 72 Rooms, Cleveland, Tennessee," *Hotel Monthly* 36 (May 1928): 70; William R. Snell, *Cleveland the Beautiful: A History of Cleveland, Tennessee, 1842–1931* (Nashville: Williams Printing Co., 1986), 336, 346; "Penn-Wells Hotel Has Been In Business for 50 Years," *Wellsboro Gazette,* Dec. 22, 1976, 8.

32. Berger, "The Modern Hotel in America," 249–79.

33. J. K.W., "Hotel Eldridge, Lawrence, Kansas," *Hotel Monthly* 38 (Sept. 1930): 40.

34. Keith A. Sculle, "The Woodworth Hotel: An Emblem of Robinson's Civic Growth," *Historic Illinois* 28: 4 (Dec. 2005): 4–5.

35. David Lee, "Stringing Hotels Seems a Game to This Three-Company President," *Minneapolis Tribune,* June 8, 1958, sec. F, 9.

36. Lloyd W. Sveen, "FM Hotel was Catalyst for Moorhead Improvements," *Fargo Forum,* Sept. 3, 1961, C-7.

37. Ibid.

38. R. Stephen Sennott, "Roadside Luxury: Urban Hotels and Modern Streets along the Dixie Highway," in *Looking Beyond the Highway: Dixie Roads and Culture,* ed. Claudette Stager and Martha Carver, 120 (Knoxville: Univ. of Tennessee Press, 2006); "National Hotel Show Week in New York," *Hotel Monthly* 35 (Dec. 1927): 55; "Hotel Leased," *Roseburg [OR] Evening News,* Apr. 4, 1913, 1; "Umpqua Hotel," *Roseburg [OR] Evening News,* June 24, 1913, 1; "Hotel to Open," *Roseburg [OR] Evening News,* June, 27, 1913, 1; "The Hotel Bothwell of Sedalia, Missouri," 28; Imhauser, *Along Ohio Street,*

211–12; Martha Gray Hagedorn, "Eldridge House Hotel, National Register nomination form, Sept. 1982," sec. 8, 1 (Kansas State Historical Society, Topeka, KS); untitled item, *Hotel Monthly* 26 (Sept. 1918): 61; "Boom-Time Financing Explains Sad Plight of Hotel Business," *Business Week* (July 1931), 18–19.

39. "Practical Hotel Construction," *Hotel Monthly* 25 (Aug. 1917): 52.

40. Ibid., 53.

41. "Novel Features in Hotel Lease," *Hotel Monthly* 28 (Feb. 1920): 27.

42. "Hotel Man's Relation to His Community," *Hotel Monthly* 51 (Aug. 1943): 4.

43. Ibid.

44. "The Illinois of Bloomington," *Hotel Monthly* 10 (Dec. 1902): 23.

45. For example, see "Hotel Arrivals," *Roseburg [OR] Evening News,* July 3, 1913, 3, and July 11, 1913, 5; and "Hotel Arrivals," *Roseburg [OR] Review,* Nov. 4, 1913, 3.

46. Juacquetta Edwards, telephone interview with Keith A. Sculle, June 11, 2007.

47. Elise Scharf Fox, edited with additions by Harry Stokes, *Hotel Gettysburg: A Landmark in our Nation's History* ([Gettysburg, PA.]: Downtown Gettysburg, Inc., 1988), 67.

48. For example, see "Opening of Quincy's New Lincoln-Douglas Hotel Reveals Beauty and Convenience of Structure," *Quincy [IL] Herald-Whig,* Nov. 15, 1931, 10.

49. "The Warm Friend Tavern of Holland Michigan," *Hotel Monthly* 33 (June 1925): 38.

50. "Hotel Tallcorn of Marshalltown, Iowa," 53.

51. For example, see "Opening of Quincy's New Lincoln-Douglas Hotel Reveals Beauty and Convenience of Structure," *Quincy [IL] Herald-Whig,* Nov. 15, 1931, 10; and "A Tourist Hotel," *Lewiston (ID) Morning Tribune,* Sept. 24, 1922, 5.

52. "Lewiston Hotel Not Yet Named," *Lewiston (ID) Morning Tribune,* Nov. 21, 1921, 6.

53. Richard K. Francaviglia, *Main Street Revisited: Space, Time, and Image Building in Small-Town America* (Iowa City: Univ. of Iowa Press, 1996), 28, 31, 35.

54. "A Country Hotelman Talks to Rotary," *Hotel Monthly* 48 (July 1940): 36. Regarding the early uses of the Hotel Cherokee in Cleveland, Tennessee, see Snell, *Cleveland the Beautiful,* 346, 348.

55. John R. Stilgoe, *Outside Lies Magic: Regarding History and Awareness in Everyday Places* (New York: Walker and Co., 1998), 154.

56. "A Country Hotelman Talks to Rotary," 36–37.

57. Ibid, 39.

58. Ibid.

59. Ibid., 40.

60. "Looking Backward From Files of the Sedalia Democrat, Ten Years Ago," *Sedalia Democrat,* Aug. 27, 1937, 2.

61. "Over 200 Attend Standard Oil Company Dinner," *Sedalia (MO) Democrat,* Sept. 22, 1937, 4; Leslie G. Kennon, "Sedalia's Industrial and Civic Progress As Reviewed by a State Division Writer," *Sedalia (MO) Democrat,* Sept. 28, 1957, 2; "Building Sedalia Industrially," *Sedalia (MO) Democrat,* Oct. 3, 1957, 10.

62. Advertisement, *Sedalia (MO) Democrat,* Sept. 14, 1937, 8.

63. "Woman Finds Hotel Work Has Wide Variety of Experiences," *Sedalia (MO) Democrat,* Sept. 22, 1957, 3.

64. Howell, "The School of Hotel Administration at Cornell," 120; Edwin A. Boss, "History of Boss Hotels," unpublished typescript in author's possession (courtesy of John Patrick Reilly, grandson); John Patrick Reilly, e-mail to Keith A. Sculle, Jan. 11, 2007; "Hotel Whitney of Atlantic, Iowa," *Hotel Monthly* 39 (1931): 30; Edwin A. Boss, "'50 Wonderful Years of Hospitality,'" *Upper Midwest HOST* (Sept. 1966), 4; Larry Fruhling, "Edwin Boss, hotel owner, dies at 86," *Des Moines Tribune* Nov. 16, 1977, 5; John Patrick Reilly, e-mail to Keith A. Sculle, Feb. 15, 2007; John Patrick Reilly, email to Keith A. Sculle, Feb. 13, 2007; "How Ed. Boss Makes Boss Hotels Pay," *Hotel Monthly* 46 (Dec. 1938), 18–21; J. A. Dougher, "Refacing Hotel Anthes, Fort Madison, Iowa," *Hotel Monthly* 45 (Jan. 1937), 13–14.

65. Boss, "History of Boss Hotels."

66. Reilly, e-mail to Sculle, Jan. 11, 2007.

67. "The House of Van Orman," *Hotel Monthly* 48 (Dec. 1940): 20–21; "Heart Attack Causes Death of Van Orman," *Evansville (IN) Journal,* Nov. 18, 1927, 1. *Hotel Monthly* contradicted itself with claims for earlier chains: see "Pioneers of Early Hotel Chains of Today," *Hotel Monthly* 39 (Mar. 1931): 42. Also see Howell, "The School of Hotel Administration at Cornell," 96–97.

68. "Van Orman Sells Last Hotel in Once-Famous State Chain," *Evansville (IN) Post,* June 20, 1969, 6; "The House of Van Orman," 20–21.

69. "The Lord Jeffrey Inn of Amherst, Mass.," *Hotel Monthly* 35 (Dec. 1927): 41.

70. "A Chain of Ideal Inns," *Hotel Monthly* 37 (Mar. 1929): 43.

71. "Personalities in the Hotel Business," *Hotel Monthly* 51 (Nov. 1943): 26, 38.

72. "The Lord Jeffrey Inn of Amhersty, Mass.," 41.

73. "Hotels: The Colonial Innkeepers," *Time,* June 18, 1965, 65–66.

74. "The Colonial Hotels System," *Hotel Monthly* 30 (Nov. 1922), 25; "Personalities in the Hotel Business," *Hotel Monthly* 51 (July 1943): 14, 16.

75. "Personalities in the Hotel Business," *Hotel Monthly* 51 (July 1943): 17.

76. Ibid.

77. For a chain including towns of every size, consider The Eppley Hotels Company based in Omaha, Nebraska; see "Hotel Tallcorn of Marshalltown, Iowa," 53–54. The Tallcorn in Marshalltown, Iowa, was the smallest in the chain; see advertisement, *Hotel Monthly* 37 (Jan. 1929): 113. For a history of the Eppley chain, see "Pioneers of Hotel Chains of Today," *Hotel Monthly* 39 (Mar. 1931): 42–43. Also see the advertisements for Howard Dayton Hotels, *Hotel Monthly* 55 (Oct. 1947): 88; for the Anderson Hotels System, *The Official Hotel Red Book and Directory* (New York: American Hotel Association Directory Company, 1950), 917; and for the Fred Harvey Hotels, *Hotel Monthly* 49 (May 1941): 73. For the six-member Gateway Chain, see "Application for Registration[,] New Mexico State Register of Cultural Properties." For the chain that W. G. Hutson and Robert McCormick built, see Hagedorn, "Eldridge House Hotel," sec. 8, 1

78. For example, consider the Sterling Hotels System (advertisement, *The Official Hotel Red Book and Directory* [New York: American Hotel Association Directory Cor-

poration, 1950], 756); the Kaskaskia Hotel Company ("Hotel Kaskaskia of La Salle, Illinois," *The Hotel Monthly* 24 [Dec. 1916]: 43); Lamer Hotels (*The Official Hotel Red Book and Directory* [New York: American Hotel Association Directory Corporation, 1930], 270); DeWitt Operated Hotels, ("Ohio's New 75-Room Hotel Lancaster," *Hotel Monthly* 48 [July 1940]: 9); Sweet Hotels (postcard, circa 1930, in authors' possession); Grenoble Hotels, ("The Hotel Oneida of Oneida, New York," *Hotel Monthly* 35 [Aug. 1927]: 44); and Tennessee Hotel Operating Company ("James K. Polk Hotel of Murfreesboro, Tenn.," *Hotel Monthly* 41 [Aug. 1933]: 20).

79. "Hotel Chain with Dissimilar Links, Yet Prosperous," *Hotel Monthly* 38 (June 1930): 45.

80. Timothy R. Maloney, "The Small City in American History," *Indiana Magazine of History* 99 (Dec. 2003): 317.

81. "Small Towns and Large Hotels," *Saturday Evening Post,* May 15, 1926, 32.

82. "A Country Hotel That Caters for Man and Car," *Hotel Monthly* 31 (Aug. 1923): 52.

83. W. L. Hamilton, *Promoting New Hotels: When Does It Pay?* (New York: Harper and Brothers, 1930), 3–4.

84. "Illinois Hotel Assn's 27th Annual Meeting," *Hotel Monthly* 36 (Mar. 1928): 47.

85. James S. Warren, "The Present Status of the Hotel Business," *Architectural Forum* 51 (Dec. 1929): 714.

86. "Relation of Financing to Hotel Operation," *Hotel Monthly* 37 (Oct. 1929): 48.

87. Ibid., 52, 54.

88. "Small Towns and Large Hotels," 32.

89. Taylor and Bliss, *Hotel Planning and Outfitting,* 15.

90. Ibid., 13.

91. "Boom-Time Financing Explains Sad Plight of Hotel Business," *Business Week,* July 1, 1931, 18; "Happy Hotel New Year," *Business Week,* Jan. 23, 1937, 24; "Hotel Hopes Rise," *Business Week,* June 8, 1940, 22; "New Hotels Soon?" *Business Week,* Mar. 2, 1946, 33; "Hotel Hazard," *Business Week,* Sept. 7, 1935, 24; "Boom for Hotels," *Business Week,* May 31, 1941, 24; "Hotels Lose in '38," *Business Week,* Apr. 22, 1938, 56.

92. "Relation of Financing to Hotel Operations," 48; "Running Out of Hotels to Buy," *Business Week,* Aug. 11, 1956, 83, 88–89; Ingram, *The Rise of Hotel Chains in the United States;* Boss, "A History of Boss Hotels;" Reilly, e-mail to Sculle, Jan. 11, 2007; Boss, "'50 Years of Hospitality,'" 6; Fruhling, "Edwin Boss, hotel owner, dies at 86," 4.

93. "Van Orman Sells Last Hotel in Once-Famous State Chain," 6; Reilly, e-mail to Sculle, Feb. 15, 2007.

3. Hotel Management

1. Boss, "'50 Wonderful Years of Hospitality,'" 6; Paul Groth, *Living Downtown: The History of Residential Hotels in the United States* (Berkeley: Univ. of California Press, 1994), 169.

2. "The Dignity of the Hotel Profession," *Hotel Monthly* 43 (Jan. 1935): 23. Howell, "The School of Hotel Administration at Cornell," 77, attributes "mine host" to one of the terms for hotel manager used in the hotel press. Williamson, *The American*

Hotel, 5, likely reflects the hotel trade press writers' argot by introducing the term early in his text and without exploring its origins.

3. For Chicago's conversion to the "European Plan" and the claim that the shift occurred between 1883 and 1893, when hotels on the "American Plan" slipped from a ten-to-one ratio to a one-to-ten ratio, see "The Hotel Monthly's 35th Anniversary," *Hotel Monthly* 35 (Aug. 1927), 53. Regarding the preference among resorts for the "American Plan," see Williamson, *The American Hotel*, 207–8.

4. "Country Hotel Changing Over from European to American Plan," *Hotel Monthly* 28 (Aug. 1920), 41; "Hotel Pines of Pine Bluff, Arkansas," *Hotel Monthly* 30 (Apr. 1922): 29.

5. Lucius Boomer, *Hotel Management: Principles and Practice*, 2nd ed. (New York: Harper and Brothers, 1931), 2; Donald L. Lundberg, *Inside Innkeeping* (Dubuque, IA: William C. Brown Co., 1956), 96.

6. Fox and Stokes, *Hotel Gettysburg*, 51–52, 61, 66–67, 72.

7. "A Misfit Community Hotel," *Hotel Monthly* 36 (July 1928): 59.

8. "What They Say," *Hotel Monthly* 12 (Mar. 1904): 35.

9. John Willy, "Hotels of Illinois, 1818 to 1918," *Hotel Monthly* 26 (Feb. 1918): 82.

10. Ibid., 78.

11. "Work of Art," *Hotel Monthly* 42 (Feb. 1934): 23.

12. Lewis, *Work of Art*, 260.

13. Ibid., 94, 111.

14. "Work of Art," 23.

15. "We Visit a Lowry Hotel," *Hotel Monthly* 44 (Dec. 1936): 36.

16. "Hotel Lincoln-Douglas Will Be Open to Public Sunday for Inspection," *Quincy [IL] Herald-Whig*, Nov. 18, 1931, 18.

17. "The Country Hotel Keeper," *Hotel Monthly* 33 (Jan. 1925): 74. Also see "An Innkeeper's Diary," *Hotel Monthly* 41 (Oct. 1933): 51.

18. "The Illinois Hotel Association's 22nd Annual," *Hotel Monthly* 31 (Feb. 1933): 37.

19. "Country Hotelkeeper's Philosophy," *Hotel Monthly* 35 (Dec. 1927): 39.

20. Kenneth J. Lipartito, "The Hotel Machine: Management and Technology in the Skyscraper Hotel," in *Grand Hotels of the Jazz Age: The Architecture of Schultze and Weaver*, ed. Marianne Lamonaca and Jonathan Mogul (New York: Princeton Architectural Press, 2005), 99.

21. "The Country Hotel Keeper," 74.

22. [F. Harold Van Orman], *Van Orman's System of Hotel Control* (Chicago: The Hotel Monthly Press, 1934).

23. W. Vincent, "Famous Hotel Now College Dorm," *Negro History Bulletin* 27 (Mar. 1964): 140.

24. "Standard Depreciation Rates in Hotels," *Hotel Monthly* 36 (Feb. 1928): 64. Some set the useful life as low as ten years; see "The American Hotel Assn's 18th Annual," *Hotel Monthly* 36 (Oct. 1928), 49.

25. "Standard Depreciation Rates in Hotels," 65.

26. Ibid., 64.

27. Lundberg, *Inside Innkeeping*, 94.

28. Ibid., 97.

29. "Accountants Should Flag the Danger Signal," *Hotel Monthly* 35 (Aug. 1927): 44.

30. "Modern Accounting for a Small Hotel," *Hotel Monthly* 46 (June 1938): 12.

31. Theodore R. Nathan, *Hotel Promotion* (New York: Harper & Brothers, 1941), 59.

32. Ibid., 116–17.

33. Ibid., 55.

34. Walter O. Voegle, ed., "Take it for what it's worth," *Hotel Management* 64 (Dec. 1953): 54.

35. "Some Elementary Legal Principles Clarified," *Hotel Monthly* 36 (Oct. 1958): 58.

36. Sandoval-Strausz, *Hotel: An American History*, 101, 333 n45.

37. For example, see *Travelers Hotel Guide, July 1923* (Buffalo, NY: J. W. Clement [1923].)

38. For example, see "Hotel Jefferson of Iowa City, Iowa," *Hotel Monthly* 24 (Feb. 1916): 46.

39. "Hotel Business Promotion for Profit," *Hotel Monthly* 42 (June 1934): 50.

40. J. O. Dahl, *Advertising and Promotion for Hotels and Restaurants* (Stamford, CT: The Dahls, 1939), 9.

41. "Hotel Business Promotion for Profit," 50.

42. Ibid. For example of the components in detail, see Nathan, *Hotel Promotion*, 210–13.

43. "Hotels Lose in '38," 56–57.

44. "P.H.A. Sells Traveling Public on Hotels," *Hotel Monthly* 46 (Aug. 1938): 21.

45. Ibid., 22.

46. Nathan, *Hotel Promotion*, 44.

47. Dahl, *Advertising and Promotion for Hotels and Restaurants*, 11.

48. Ibid., 87.

49. "Co-operative Advertising by Hotels of the West," *Hotel Monthly* 48 (May 1940): 30–32.

50. "National Hotel Week Plans in High Gear," *Hotel Monthly* 49 (May 1941): 35–36.

51. For example, see advertisement, Detroit Publishing Company, *Hotel Monthly* 35 (Aug. 1927): 101. For a discussion and display of the themes in hotel postcards, see John A. Jakle and Keith A. Sculle, "The American Hotel in Postcard Advertising: An Image Gallery," *Material Culture: The Journal of the Pioneer America Society* 37 (Fall 2005): 2.

52. "Automobile Show in Hotel Lobby Brought Local Business," *Hotel Monthly* 42 (June 1934): 26.

53. "National Hotel Show Week in New York," 56; "The Park Hotel, Richland Center," *Hotel Monthly* 49 (Oct. 1941): 26.

54. "Terre Haute House Celebration," *Hotel Monthly* 46 (May 1938): 41–42.

55. "Terre Haute," *Hotel Monthly* 6 (Apr. 1898): 22.

56. "The Telephone's the Thing," *Hotel Monthly* 7 (Nov. 1899): 10; "The Bedbug," *Hotel Monthly* 21 (July 1913): 79.

57. "Good-by Old Register Book," *Hotel Monthly* 37 (Feb. 1929): 69; "The Hotel and the Automatic Stoker," *Hotel Monthly* 40 (Oct. 1932): 47–48.

58. See the following advertisements: "Roach Doom Free," *Hotel Monthly* 12 (Aug. 1904): 111; "Robert's Ovens," *Hotel Monthly* 12 (Apr. 1904): 13; "W. W. Wilcox & Co.," *Hotel Monthly* 11 (Jan. 1903): 47; "National Cash Register," *Hotel Monthly* 27 (Jan. 1919): 89; "Thesco Refrigerators," *Hotel Monthly* 31 (Nov. 1923), 98; "Carrier Air Conditioning," *Hotel Monthly* 45 (May 1937): 53–54; "Angelica Jacket Company," *Hotel Monthly* 36 (Feb. 1928): iii; "F. C. Huyck & Sons, Kenwood Mills," *Hotel Monthly* 49 (Feb. 1941): 55; "Lee Larson & Company," *Hotel Monthly* 49 (Aug. 1941): 55 [55]; "Good form Garment Hangers," *Hotel Monthly* 54 (Apr. 1946): 68; and "Honeywell," *Hotel Monthly* 76 (Sept. 1959): 16–17.

59. "Technocracy No Substitute for Personality," *Hotel Monthly* 42 (Mar. 1934): 37; "Using Employes' [sic] Slack Time to Inspect Rooms," *Hotel Monthly* 42 (Dec. 1934): 17–18.

60. "Anti-Tobacco Crusade," *Hotel Monthly* 29 (Mar. 1921): 52; J. B. Johnson, "Fire Insurance Problems," *Hotel Monthly* 48 (Feb. 1940): 35.

61. William J. Burns, "Hotel and Bank Crooks," *Saturday Evening Post*, June 6, 1925, 46 and 52.

62. Ludwig F. Grimstad, "Hotel-Room Prowlers and Sneak Thieves," *Saturday Evening Post*, June 30, 1934: 30–31, 33, 81–82.

63. Norman S. Hayner, *Hotel Life* (College Park, MD: McGrath Publish Company, 1969), 158–64.

64. For example, see *Travelers Hotel Guide, July 1923.*

65. "The Hotel Monthly's 35th Anniversary," 53. Also see [Willy], "We Celebrate 38th Anniversary," 33.

66. "New Lease of Life for American Hotel Association," *Hotel Monthly* 32 (Aug. 1924): 44.

67. For a history of the start of college training for hotel managers, see Howell, "The School of Hotel Administration at Cornell"; and Ingram, *The Rise of Hotel Chains in the United States 1896–1980*, 44–53.

68. Lewis, *Work of Art*, 70–71.

69. Howell, "The School of Hotel Administration at Cornell," 119; John Willy, "Country Hotels of the Future," *Hotel Monthly* 28 (Jan. 1920): 22–23. Specifically regarding the need for waiters, see "More Trained Waiters Needed," *Hotel Monthly* 31 (Apr. 1923): 23.

70. Howell, "The School of Hotel Administration at Cornell," 372–85; "Report of First Meeting of A.H.A. Executive Council," *Hotel Monthly* 32, (Aug. 1924): 50; "Michigan's Hotel Training School," 39; [Van Orman], *Van Orman's System of Hotel Control*, 18; "Hotel Whitney of Atlantic, Iowa," 44–45.

71. For example, regarding a manager's speech to the Rotary Club of Milwaukee, see "Hotel Operation and Economics," *Hotel Monthly* 27 (May 1919): 71–72. For two

hotel trade shows, see "National Hotel Show Week in New York," 52; and "Chicago's Second Annual Hotel Men's Show," *Hotel Monthly* 28 (June 1920): 26–31.

72. For example, see "Geography Classes for Hotel Employees," *Hotel Monthly* 31 (Apr. 1923): 23 [23]; "Know Your Geography," *Hotel Monthly* 39 (Mar. 1931): 59.

73. "Hotels," *Business Digest and Investment Weekly*, 22 (Dec. 24, 1918): 465; "Hotels: Management of," *Business Digest and Investment Weekly*, 24 (Sept. 23, 1919): 434; "Cooperation with Traveling Salesmen," *Business Digest*, 2 (Apr.–June 1917): 235.

74. "Principles of 'Hotel Management,'" *Hotel Monthly* 36 (May 1928): 31–35; untitled item, *Hotel Monthly* 36 (May 1928): 35; J[ohn]. K. W[illy]., "Ohio Hotels Association Hold 33rd Annual," *Hotel Monthly* 39 (Jan. 1927): 42; "Urge Uniform Hotel Laws," *Hotel Monthly* 30 (Aug. 1922): 83.

75. "Opportunities for Women in Hotel Work," *Hotel Monthly* 37 (Sept. 1929): 67.

76. Ibid.

77. *Behind the Scenes in a Hotel* (New York: Consumers' League of New York, 1922): 8.

78. Jane Van Ness, "The Executive Housekeeper of the Small Hotel," *Hotel Monthly* 44 (Sept. 1936): 17.

79. J.K.W., "Ohio Hotels Association Holds 33rd Annual," 43; "About Women Hotel Operators," *Hotel Monthly* 51 (June 1943): 25–27; "Answers Summons of Death," *Alaska Daily Empire*, Mar. 18, 1916: 1; Fox and Stokes, *Hotel Gettysburg*, 51–52; Lewis, *Work of Art*, 24, 37; Nathan, *Hotel Promotion*, 133.

80. "Training Cooks in Tuskegee Institute," *Hotel Monthly* 45 (Oct. 1937): 48.

81. For example, see "Hotel Operation in Wartime," *Hotel Monthly* 50 (July 1942): 52.

82. [Van Orman], *Van Orman's System of Hotel Control*, 15.

83. Edward C. Koziara and Karen S. Koziara, *The Negro in the Hotel Industry*, Report No. 4 in the series The Racial Policies of American Industry (Philadelphia: Industrial Research Unit, Wharton School of Finance, Univ. of Pennsylvania, 1968), 32

84. "Opportunities for Women in Hotel Work," 66.

85. "The Practical Hotel Steward," *Hotel Monthly* 21 (Jan. 1903): 51; Taylor and Bliss, *Hotel Planning and Outfitting*, 18.

86. "Hotel Keeping in Small Town," *Hotel Monthly* 29 (Nov. 1921): 30.

87. Lewis, *Work of Art*, 38.

88. Taylor and Bliss, *Hotel Planning and Outfitting*, 18.

89. Ibid.

90. "The Parkside Hotel of Kewanee, Ill.," 69.

91. "Fifty-six Ways to Cut Costs," *Hotel Monthly* 39 (Nov. 1931): 60.

92. See Matthew Josephson, *Union House, Union Bar: The History of the Hotel and Restaurant Employees and Bartenders International Union, AFL-CIO* (New York: Random House, 1956).

93. "The Code to Date," *Hotel Monthly* 41 (Nov. 1933): 37.

94. Frank Bering, "Report of A.H.A. Americanization Committee," *Hotel Monthly* 30 (Mar. 1922): 39.

95. "The Code Imposed on the Hotel Business," *Hotel Monthly* 41 (Dec. 1933): 42; "Returning to Profits," *Hotel Monthly* 42 (Oct. 1934): 52; "A Resolution of Protest," *Hotel Monthly* 41 (Dec. 1933), 43–44; "Mr. Boomer's 2nd Report on N. R. A. Activities," *Hotel Monthly* 41 (Dec. 1933): 44–47.

96. Hayner, *Hotel Life*, 155.

97. Dahl, *Advertising and Promotion for Hotels and Restaurants*, 28–29.

98. Nathan, *Hotel Promotion*, 25.

99. Lewis, *Work of Art*, 277.

100. H. V. Heldenbrand, "Bell Boy's Manual for the Country Hotel," *Hotel Monthly* 37 (Sept. 1929): 72.

101. Lewis, *Work of Art*, 84.

102. See "Personnel Problems," *Hotel Monthly* 50 (Apr. 1942): 23–26, 51–53.

103. "Returning to Profits," 52; "Laundry for 114-Room Hotel Cuts Cost Nearly in Half," *Hotel Monthly* 46 (Feb. 1938): 23–27; untitled item, *Hotel Monthly* 43 (Dec. 1935): 20; *Trends in the Hotel Business: A Statistical Review of the Year 1940* (New York: Harris, Kerr, Forster, and Company, 1941), 2, 14; "Hotel Hopes Rise," 21; Leslie Velie, "The Hotel Business Blooms Again," *Nation's Business* 25 (June 1937): 154.

104. Henry M. Scharf, "What Gasoline Rationing Did to and for Pennsylvania Hotels," *Hotel Monthly* 51 (Jan. 1943): 30.

105. Ibid., 31, 45.

106. Ibid., 46.

107. "Uses Cards in Street Cars and Busses to Build Up Food and Beverage Sales," *Hotel Monthly* 51 (Aug. 1943): 26–27.

108. "Hotel Operation in Wartime," 12.

109. Ibid., 13, 53.

110. Charles M. Stack, "Conservation and Care of Carpet," *Hotel Monthly* 50 (Apr. 1942): 27, 54.

111. "How Hotels Fared Under Army Rule," *Hotel Monthly* 51 (Oct. 1943): 28, 31.

112. "Innkeeper No. 1," *Business Week*, Oct. 9, 1943, 28, 30; "Resorts Go to War," *Business Week*, Aug. 13, 1944, 38.

113. For the regulations, see "Complete OPA Rent Regulation for Hotels and Rooming Houses," *Hotel Monthly* 42 (July 1942): 42–44.

114. "A Sale Prospectus of a Small Country Hotel," *Hotel Monthly* 51 (Sept. 1943): 4, 6, 8; "Can a Business Man Run a Hotel?" *Hotel Monthly* 51 (July 1943): 22–23; "New Hotels Soon?" 33; Scharf, "What Gasoline Rationing Did to and for Pennsylvania Hotels," 48.

115. "Hotels Fight to Stay in Black," *Business Week*, Oct. 9, 1948, 90.

116. For example, see "Hotel Kitchen Clock Turned to 1947 with New Equipment and Methods," *Hotel Monthly* 55 (Nov. 1947): 62.

117. For example, see *Requirements for Recommendations of Hotels, Motels, Resorts and Restaurants, 1960-61 Edition* (Washington, D. C.: American Automobile Association, 1960.)

118. For example, see advertisements, The American Laundry Machinery Co., *Hotel Monthly* 52 (Nov. 1947): 161; and *Hotel Monthly* 52 (July 1947): 213.

119. "Hotels Fight to Stay in Black," 90, 92; "Hotels Down, but Fighting," *Business Week,* May 10, 1958: 67.

4. Hotel Life

1. "The Hotel Problem," *The Nation* 73 (July 11, 1901): 25.

2. Ibid.

3. Ibid.

4. Ibid, 27.

5. Sam Walter Foss, "The House by the Side of the Road," in *Dreams in Homespun* (Boston: Lothrup, Lee & Shepard Co., 1897), 11.

6. Mrs. J. F. Tillman, "Main Street Maestro," *Hotel Monthly* 49 (Jan. 1941): 31.

7. G. C. Deetz, "The Hotel Man and the Commercial Traveler," *Hotel Monthly* 15 (Aug. 1907): 42.

8. Forrest Crissey, "The Modern Commercial Traveler," *Everybody's Magazine* 21 (July 1909): 12.

9. "Hotel Marting of Ironton, Ohio," *Hotel Monthly* 28 (Mar. 1920): 24–25.

10. William Maxwell, "The Traveling Salesman," *Collier's,* Sept. 5, 1914, 22.

11. Sinclair Lewis, *Free Air* (London: Cape, 1933), 31.

12. "Automobile or Railroad—Which is Better for Salesmen?" *Business Digest and Investment Weekly* 26 (Aug. 13, 1920): 131.

13. "Vanishing Americans," *Reader's Digest* 29 (Nov. 1936): 29.

14. "The Salesman and His Flivver," *Hotel Monthly* 32 (June 1924): 63.

15. Hayner, *Hotel Life,* 95.

16. J. R. Sprague, "On the Road," *Saturday Evening Post,* June 28, 1926, 34.

17. Don Marquis, "My Memories of the Old-Fashioned Drummer," *American Magazine* 107 (Feb. 1929): 20.

18. Williamson, *The American Hotel,* 124.

19. "Vanishing Americans," 30.

20. Rose Wilder Lane, *Old Home Town* (New York: Longmans, Green & Co., 1935), 159.

21. Review of Robert Tallant's *Southern Territories* (Garden City, NY: Doubleday & Co., 1951) by Robert W. Henderson (*Library Journal,* June 18, 1951, 1028), quoted in Donald L. Thompson, "Stereotype of the Salesman," *Harvard Business Review* 50 (Jan. 1972): 22.

22. Thompson, "Stereotype of the Salesman," 24.

23. "A Bible in the Room," *Newsweek,* Oct. 22, 1945, 102.

24. "New Patronage for Country Hotels," *Hotel Monthly* 15 (Aug. 1907): 24.

25. "Elyria, Ohio," *Hotel Monthly* 15 (Jan. 1907): 37.

26. "Readjusting for Automobile Catering," *Hotel Monthly* 25 (Jan. 1917): 30.

27. "Sampling Country Hotels in Northern Indiana," *Hotel Monthly* 27 (May 1919): 62.

28. "The Huron Hotel of Ypsilanti, Michigan," *Hotel Monthly* 31 (May 1923): 38.

29. "Make Friends with Auto Tourists," *Hotel Monthly* 32 (Apr. 1924): 27.

30. "Country Hotel Adjusting to New Travel Conditions," *Hotel Monthly* 32 (May 1924): 56.

31. "75-Room Hotel, 135-Car Garage and a Filling Station," *Hotel Monthly* 35 (Mar. 1927): 62.

32. "Future Trend in the Hotel Industry," *Hotel Monthly* 38 (July 1930): 82.

33. "Hotel 'Boom' Hampered," *Business Week,* Dec. 28, 1935, 38–39.

34. "Observations of Accommodations by a Motor Tourist," *Hotel Monthly* 40 (July 1932): 30.

35. G. K. Dahl, "Banquet Sales Promotion," in Nathan, *Hotel Promotion,* 171.

36. Ibid., 172.

37. Hayner, *Hotel Life,* 85–86.

38. "Hotel 'Boom' Hampered," 19.

39. Lundberg, *Inside Innkeeping,* 103.

40. See Lyell Henry, "Accommodations 'For Colored,'" *Journal, Society for Commercial Archeology* 23 (Fall 2005): 4–11.

41. For example, see Victor H. Green, ed., *The Negro Travelers' Green Book* (New York: Victor H. Green & Co. 1958).

42. See Juliet E. K. Walker, "Catering, Inns, Hotels," in *Encyclopedia of African American Business History,* ed. Juliet E. K. Walker, 128–34 (Westport, CT: Greenwood Press, 1999).

43. Henry, "Accommodations 'For Colored,'" 5.

44. Alfred Edgar Smith, "Through the Windshield," *Opportunity: Journal of Negro Life,* May 1933, 142.

45. Williamson, *The American Hotel,* 128.

46. "Do Hotels Want Women Guests?" *Hotel Monthly* 48 (July 1940): 44.

47. "The Forgotten Guest," *Hotel Management* 64 (Nov. 1953): 47.

48. Carolyn Brucken, "In the Public Eye: Women and the American Luxury Hotel," *Winterthur Portfolio* 31 (Winter 1996): 215.

49. Williamson, *The American Hotel,* 128.

50. Helena Judson, "The Hotel Guest Who Knows," *The Delineator* 95 (Nov. 1919): 78.

51. Emma Danforth, "On the Road," *Woman's Home Companion,* Mar. 1923, 44–45.

52. Dahl, *Advertising and Promotion for Hotels and Restaurants,* 26.

53. Fred C. Kelly, "Human Nature in the Lobby," *Hotel Management,* May 1922, quoted in Hayner, *Hotel Life,* 100.

54. Hayner, *Hotel Life,* 156.

55. Ibid., 157.

56. Allison Gray, "Queer Things that Hotel Guests Leave—and Take," *American Magazine* 97 (Jan. 1924): 49.

57. Lewis, *Work of Art,* 280.

58. "Hotel Detective Constantly Battling Smart Criminals," *Hotel World,* Mar. 3, 1923, 35.

59. Williamson, *The American Hotel,* 126.

60. "A Hotel Clerk Tells Why Baseball Players are not Usually Welcome Guests," *Gateway: The Quarterly Magazine of the Missouri Historical Society* 25 (Winter 2004–5): 72.

61. Hayner, *Hotel Life,* 6.

62. Ibid., 172.

63. Ibid., 182.

5. Food and Drink

1. Taylor and Bliss, *Hotel Planning and Outfitting,* 315.

2. "Family Style Dinner in a Country Hotel," *Hotel Monthly* 15 (Aug. 1907): 32.

3. Dreiser, *Hoosier Holiday,* 71.

4. "The Ballingall of Ottumwa, Iowa," *Hotel Monthly* 12 (Oct. 1904): 32.

5. E. F. Keller, quoted in "Logansport, Ind.," *Hotel Monthly* 12 (Jan. 1904): 37.

6. Edwin A. Boss, "The Country Hotel Dining Room," *Hotel Monthly* 30 (Jan. 1922): 41.

7. Charles C. Horton, "American Plan Advocated," *Hotel Monthly* 30 (Jan. 1922): 43.

8. "Simplicity of European Hotel Keeping, or, How to Change from the American Plan," *Hotel Monthly* 12 (Oct. 1904): 24.

9. John Tellman, *The Practical Hotel Steward* (Chicago: The Hotel Monthly, 1913), 3.

10. Nathan, *Hotel Promotion,* 52.

11. "The Stoddard of La Crosse, Wisconsin," *Hotel Monthly* 12 (Aug. 1904): 31.

12. "The Lowell Inn of Stillwater, Minnesota," *Hotel Monthly* 41 (Dec. 1933): 21.

13. "The Hotel Florence of Missoula," *Hotel Monthly* 49 (Aug. 1940): 23.

14. "You are Never Too Late for a Dinner at Schuler's," *Hotel Monthly* 49 (July 1940): 26.

15. "Yes!—A Satisfactory Country Hotel," *Hotel Monthly* 39(Feb. 1930): 38.

16. "Ohio's New 75-Room Hotel Lancaster," 14.

17. "Sociable Selling," *Business Week* (Mar. 10, 1934): 22.

18. "A Modern Fireproof Hotel," 59.

19. "The Otsego of Jackson, Michigan," *Hotel Monthly* 12 (June 1904): 31.

20. See Taylor and Bliss, *Hotel Planning and Outfitting,* 329.

21. Ibid, 327.

22. See "Safe Use of Carbonic Gas for Refrigerating," *Hotel Monthly* 29 (Aug. 1921): 39–51; and "The Story of Refrigeration," *Hotel Monthly* 59 (Dec. 1942): 29–32.

23. Lewis, *Work of Art,* 79–80.

24. W. B. Cleaves, quoted in "The Village Hotel," *Hotel Monthly* 24 (Nov. 1916): 74.

25. "The Hotel Harding of Marion, Ohio," *Hotel Monthly* 32 (Apr. 1924): 58.

26. "A Modern Coffee Shop for Hotel in 30,000 Town," *Hotel Monthly* 45 (Oct. 1937): 21.

27. Ibid.

28. Nathan, *Hotel Promotion,* 160.

29. Ibid, 162.

30. "Ohio's New 75-Room Hotel Lancaster," 13.

31. See Jakle and Sculle, *Fast Food.*

6. Changing with the Times

1. "Stoddart Hotel" reference file, Marshalltown Public Library, Marshalltown, Iowa.

2. Lipartito, "The Hotel Machine," 95.

3. "The New Livingston of Dwight," *Hotel Monthly* 11 (July 1903): 36–37.

4. "No Such Thing as a Fireproof Building," *Hotel Monthly* 55 (Aug. 1947): 24.

5. "The Rejuvenated Hotel Hildreth of Charles City, Iowa," *Hotel Monthly* 23 (Nov. 1915): 52.

6. "General Lewis Hotel of Lewisburg, W. Va.," *Hotel Monthly* 41 (Aug. 1933): 35–37.

7. "The Lamer, Salina, Kansas," *Hotel Monthly* 24 (June 1916): 56–57.

8. "Country Hotel Rental Idea," *Hotel Monthly* 30 (May 1922): 32.

9. For example, see "New and Remodeled Hotels," *Hotel Monthly* 29 (Sept. 1921): 81.

10. "A Country Hotel that Caters for Man and Car," 52.

11. For example, see "Hotel Supply Houses," *Hotel Monthly* 11 (June 1903): 62; and advertisement, "Vitrolite," *Hotel Monthly* 33 (Sept. 1925): 20.

12. Ed[win] A. Boss, "For Better Country Hotels," *Hotel Monthly* 49 (Feb. 1941): 32.

13. For an exception, see "Oneonta Hotel Modernized," *Hotel Monthly* 39 (Oct. 1931): 79.

14. Velie, "The Hotel Business Blooms Again," 81–82.

15. Ibid., 154; "Modern Coffee Shop for Hotel in 30,000 Town," 18.

16. Velie, "The Hotel Business Blooms Again," 56.

17. "A Country Hotel that Caters to Man and Car," 48–49.

18. "Hotel Marsh of Van Wert, Ohio," *Hotel Monthly* 42 (Jan. 1934): 29.

19. "Hotels Have Faces Lifted," *Hotel Monthly* 45 (Jan. 1937): 12; Dougher, "Refacing Hotel Anthes, Fort Madison, Iowa," 13.

20. "Hotels Have Faces Lifted," 12.

21. Ibid.

22. Paul Dorris, "Decorating for Profits," *Hotel Monthly* 49 (Apr. 1941): 5.

23. Robert P. Herzog, "Modernization Check Lists," *Hotel Management* 76 (July 1959): 36.

24. "Hotels Check Up," *Business Week,* Mar. 17, 1945, 24.

25. Ibid.

26. Herzog, "Modernization Check Lists," 36; "How Obsolescence is Being Defeated in a 200-Room Hotel," *Hotel Monthly* 55 (Aug. 1947): 21–25; "How Obsolescence is Being Defeated in a 200-Room Hotel," *Hotel Monthly* 55 (Sept. 1947): 30–34; "How Obsolescence is Being Defeated in a 200-Room Hotel," *Hotel Monthly* 55 (Aug. 1947): 21; "New Rooms with Bath Created from Old Hard-To-Rent Units," *Hotel Monthly* 55 (Oct. 1947): 28–33; Joyce Ring, Library Assistant, Burlington Public Library, e-mail to Keith A. Sculle, Apr. 2, 2007.

27. "How a 60-Year Old, 30-Room Hotel Is Kept on the Square," *Hotel Monthly* 54 (Mar. 1946): 41; Herzog, "Modernization Check Lists," 36.

28. "Thirty Years of Wear Wiped Away," *Hotel Monthly* 55 (Oct. 1947): 41.

29. Edward J. Russo and Curtis R. Mann, "Kewanee Hotel/Parkside Hotel," National Register of Historic Places nomination, signed by Ill. SHPO, Dec. 13, 2005, Section 8, 27 (Illinois Historic Preservation Agency, Springfield, IL).

30. Ibid., 27–30.

31. "The Hotel Bathroom," *Hotel Monthly* 49 (Aug. 1941): 48; Williamson, *The American Hotel,* 61–62.

32. "The McKinley Hotel of Canton, Ohio," *Hotel Monthly* 12 (Jan. 1904): 25.

33. "The Branham of Union City, Indiana," *Hotel Monthly* 14 (Jan. 1906): 26.

34. "The Parkside Hotel of Kewanee, Ill.," 70.

35. "Sidelights of Motor Tourist Accommodations," *Hotel Monthly* 35 (Jan. 1922): 80.

36. For example, see "Hotel Pines of Pine Bluff, Arkansas," 31.

37. For example, see "New Rooms with Bath Created from Old Hard-To-Rent Units," 30.

38. Ibid.

39. Fred Tetreault, "Col. Baker's 'Million Dollar' Hotel Granted Regular Status," *Historic Illinois* 1 (Apr. 1979): 8.

40. "$1,000,000 Investment in 60-Room Hotel," *Hotel Monthly* 36 (Sept. 1928): 27.

41. "Hotel Hayes of Jackson, Michigan, 200 Rooms," *Hotel Monthly* 35 (Mar. 1927): 35.

42. "Practical Hotel Construction," 55.

43. "Hotel Bothwell," http://www.hotelbothwell.com/index.cfm?section=roomsuite (accessed Aug. 22, 2008).

44. For example, see "Hotel Kaskaskia of La Salle, Illinois," 46.

45. Light equaled bright in "The Hotel Harding of Marion, Ohio," 58. Regarding light colors, see, for example: "Hotel Kaskaskia of La Salle, Illinois," 43. Regarding hallways, see, for example "The New Gilder of Danville, Kentucky," *Hotel Monthly* 25 (May 1917): 63; "Hotel Marting of Ironton, Ohio," 24.

46. "Hotel Marting of Ironton, Ohio," 24; "The Hotel Reich of Gadsden, Ala.," 38.

47. For example, see "The McKinley Hotel of Canton, Ohio," 24.

48. "Northern Hotel," *Hotel Monthly* 50 (Aug. 1942): 18.

49. Lewis, *Work of Art*, 7. Without attributing feeling or using derogatory adjectives, John H. Hopkins, a "designer and color expert" with the architectural firm of Holabird and Root in Chicago similarly described for *Hotel Monthly* a room in a Victorian style, albeit a room in a house; see "How We in America Have Arrived at Modern Decoration," *Hotel Monthly* 45 (Mar. 1937): 38, 40.

50. "The Benwalt of Philadelphia, Mississippi," *Hotel Monthly* 37 (Aug. 1929): 52.

51. "The Hotel Harding of Marion, Ohio," 58.

52. For example, see "The New Irwin Cobb of Paducah, Kentucky, is Prolific of New Ideas," *Hotel Monthly* 37 (Aug. 1929): 32; and "The Hotel Harding of Marion, Ohio," 59.

53. "To Increase Revenue from Large Rooms," *Hotel Monthly* 42 (Feb. 1934): 20–21.

54. Lee McCann, "The Metamorphosis of the Hotel," *Country Life* 61 (July 1931): 97.

55. "Why Go Modern?" *Hotel Management* 29 (Mar. 1936): 192.

56. [John H. Hopkins], "How We in America Have Arrived at Modern Accommodations," 42.

57. "Ohio's New 75-Room Hotel Lancaster," 14.

58. "Package Rooms," *Hotel Management,* 76 (Sept. 1959): 69–70; "The Room of Tomorrow; 1960," *Hotel Management* 76 (Oct. 1959): 85–88.

59. "Radio Rental to Hotel Guests," *Hotel Monthly* 33 (Mar. 1925): 68.

60. "Hotel Maytag of Newton, Iowa," *Hotel Monthly* 35 (Jan. 1927): 72–73.

61. Boss, "For Better Country Hotels," 31.

62. For example, see advertisement, RCA Victor, *Hotel Management* 64 (Oct. 1953): 37; and advertisement, Westinghouse TV, *Hotel Management* 64 (Oct. 1953): 161.

63. For example, see advertisement, "Hunter Fans[,] 49th Season," *Hotel Monthly* 45 (June 1937): 12.

64. "The First Complete Air Conditioned Hotel," *Hotel Monthly* 42 (Aug. 1934): 31.

65. "The First Air Conditioned Hotel," *Hotel Monthly* 47 (Jan. 1936): 6–7.

66. "Can Small Hotels Afford Air Conditioning?," *Hotel Monthly* 43 (Mar. 1935): 23–26.

67. For example, see advertisement, American-Standard, *Hotel Management* 76 (Sept. 1959): 139.

68. For example, see "The Fowler of Lafayette, Indiana," 59.

69. "A Tour of the World's Biggest Hotel Supplies House," *Hotel Monthly* 27 (Apr. 1919): 60–62.

70. "Poor Hotels Drive Trade to Tourist Homes," *Hotel Monthly* 42 (Aug. 1934): 29.

71. "The Code Versus Borderline Competition," *Hotel Monthly* 42 (Oct. 1933): 47–48; James Warren Belasco, *Americans on the Road: From Autocamp to Motel, 1910–1945* (Cambridge, MA: MIT Press, 1979), 126–27.

72. J.K.W., "Ohio Hotel's Association Holds 33rd Annual," 42.

73. John Willy, "A Week-End Motor Ride Thru Rock River Country," *Hotel Monthly* 30 (Sept. 1922): 63–64.

74. John Brunner, "We Beat the Tourist Camps by Meeting Their Competition," *Hotel Monthly* 29 (May 1936): 374.

75. "Record of a 2,000-Mile Automobile Journey," *Hotel Monthly* 41 (July 1933): 17.

76. J.K.W., "Ohio Hotel's Association Holds 33rd Annual," 42.

77. "The Code to Date," *Hotel Monthly* 42 (May 1934): 45.

78. "A.H.A. Silver Anniversary," *Hotel Monthly* 43 (Dec. 1935): 24.

79. "Out-Selling the Tourist Camp," *Hotel Monthly* 41 (Oct. 1933): 19.

80. "Country Hotel Adjusting to New Travel Conditions," 56.

81. J. Knight Willy, "The Code Versus Borderline Competition," 48.

82. "Normal Hotel Operation," *Hotel Monthly* 39 (Aug. 1931): 66, based on a paper delivered to the American Hotel Association by John Courtney of the Cornell University Hotel Administration Course, July 22, 1931.

83. Lewis, *Work of Art,* 398.

84. Ibid., 399.

85. "Hotel with Tourist Camp Annex," *Hotel Monthly* 42 (Feb. 1934): 13; "A New Arlington Inn for Santa Barbara, California," *Hotel Monthly* 38 (Aug. 1930): 67; "Pulling Guests from Highway to Hotel," *Hotel Monthly* 42 (Nov. 1934): 12–15; and Brunner, "We Beat the Tourist Camps by Beating Their Competition," 375–76.

86. "Will a Cottage Annex Solve Your Cabin Competition?" *Hotel Monthly* 43 (Mar. 1935): 17–19; "A Hotel-Operated Tourist Camp That Creates Business," *Hotel Monthly* 44 (July 1936): 14–15; Keith A. Sculle, "A Landscape Divided: The 'Danish Village' as Microcosm," *P.A.S.T.* 20 (1997): 45–54.

87. M.P.H., "Trailers No Substitute for Hotel Comfort and Security," *Hotel Monthly* 45 (Jan. 1937): 21.

88. Ibid.; "Poor Hotels Drive Trade to Tourist Houses," 29–30.

89. Boss, "For Better Country Hotels," 32.

90. "Co-operative Advertising," 32.

91. Keith A. Sculle, "'Our Company Feels that the Ozarks are a Good Investment. . .': The Pierce Pennant Tavern System," *Missouri Historical Review* 93: 3 (Apr. 1999): 293–307; "Proposed Chain of 40-Room Hotels Along U.S. Highways to Link New York and Los Angeles," *Hotel Monthly* 37 (Sept. 1929): 62–64.

92. "Make Friends of the Good Tourist Courts," *Hotel Monthly* 49 (Jan. 1941): 33.

93. Frank Cannon, "Advocates Good Motor Courts to be Members of Hotel Association," *Hotel Monthly* 50 (Feb. 1942): 8.

94. Don Nichols, "Publisher's Page," *Hotel Management* 64 (Nov. 1953): 5.

95. For TraveLodge, see Jakle, Sculle, and Rogers, *The Motel in America,* 156–60; Keith A. Sculle, "Tracking TraveLodge: An Inquiry After the Origins of a Roadside Chain," *SCA Journal,* 19 (Spring 2001): 16–21; and James Joseph, "TraveLodge," *Hotel Management* 64 (July 1953): 46–47, 102, 106–7. For Holiday Inn, see Jakle, Sculle, and

Rogers, *The Motel in America*, 261–85; and Jefferson S. Rogers, "Wilson, (Charles) Kemmons, Jr.," in *The Scribner Encyclopedia of American Lives* (Detroit: Thomson Gale, 2007), vol. 7: 577–78.

96. Keith A. Sculle, "Production of the Downtowner Motel Chain in Memphis," *West Tennessee Historical Society Papers* 54 (2000): 94–108.

97. Jakle, Sculle, and Rogers, *The Motel in America*, 45.

98. Robert P. Bryant, "More and More Tourists are Turning to Motels," *Hotel Management* 52 (Aug. 1947): 33–36.

99. "Small Hotel in Contemporary Design," *Hotel Management* 76 (July 1959): 28–33.

100. "The better hotels are doing the best," *Business Week*, Dec. 7, 1972, 29.

101. Fox and Stokes, *Hotel Gettysburg*, 122.

102. "Monon Hotel opened in 1927," *Montgomery County Magazine*, Aug. 1978, 23.

103. "Hotels Shaken By Change—New Names and New Styles," *U.S. News and World Report*, Sept. 8, 1975, 40–42.

Epilogue

1. For example, see "Terre Haute House Commemorative Section," a twenty-eight-page commemorative section inserted in the *Terre Haute (IN) Tribune-Star*, Nov. 16, 2005. The personal tributes included are numerous, as both young and old among the *Tribune-Star*'s readership appear fondly endeared to a landmark about to vanish.

2. For example, see "Landmark Means Different Things to Different People," *Terre Haute (IN) Tribune-Star*, Nov. 16, 2005, 6; and Dona Rains, "Renovators of Cobb Hotel are Seeking Black Tenants," *Paducah (KY) Sun*, Feb. 25, 1982, A-2.

3. "History of the General Morgan Inn," in *Guide to Enhancements* (Greeneville, TN: n.p., n.d.), 29.

4. Lee Ann Woods, "Greeneville's General Morgan Inn Where Genteel Meets Gorgeous," *Appalachian Life* (Oct.-Nov. 2002), 3; "History of the General Morgan Inn," 3.

5. Woods, "Greeneville's General Morgan Inn," 41.

6. Dan Costello, "Transportation Enhancements: Historic Preservation and the Community Revitalization," *Historic Preservation Forum* 11 (Fall 1996): 38–39.

7. Eugenia Estes, "Niswonger Buys General Morgan Inn," *Greeneville (TN) Sun*, Nov. 29, 2000, A-7.

8. "History of the General Morgan Inn," 4; Douglas Watson, "General Morgan Inn Achieves An Upswing in Business," *Greeneville (TN) Sun*, Benchmark Edition, Mar. 11, 2004, A-16.

9. "History of the General Morgan Inn," 4.

10. Eugenia Estes, "Morgan Inn, Other MSI Properties Begin New Phase with New Owner," *Greeneville (TN) Sun*, Nov. 30, 2000, A-7.

11. Costello, "Transportation Enhancements," 38, 40–41.

12. "History of the General Morgan Inn," 5.

13. Watson, "General Morgan Inn Achieves An Upswing," A-16.

14. Douglas Watson, "GMI's General Manager Leads Discussion on Greenville's Potential for Tourism," *Greeneville (TN) Sun,* Mar. 2, 2007, A-11.

15. Dana L. Pratt and Karen L. Kummer, "Hotel Bothwell," unpublished National Register Nomination Form, Dec. 14, 1988, section 8, 6–7 (Missouri State Historic Preservation Office, Jefferson City, MO).

16. Inhauser, *All Along Ohio Street,* 214.

17. Ron Jennings, "Furnell Leaves Mark on Sedalia," *Sedalia (MO) Democrat,* Feb. 20, 2001, 1.

18. David C. Furnell, interview with Keith A. Sculle, Sedalia, Missouri, May 24, 2006.

19. Ibid.

20. "Good Nights," *Midwest Living,* Aug. 2001, 26.

21. David C. Furnell, quoted in Bob McEowen, "Grandeur Restored," *Rural Missouri,* June 1999, 8.

22. Furnell, interview with Sculle.

23. McEowen, "Grandeur Restored," 9.

24. Furnell, interview with Sculle.

25. Ibid.

26. Sam Carter, "Rich Past, Hopeful Future," *Staunton (VA) News Leader,* Dec. 23, 1992, C-1.

27. Ibid.; Jeff Greenough, "20s Hotels Roar Again," *Virginia Living,* Oct. 2006, 140.

28. Greenough, "20s Hotels Roar Again"; Sam Carter, "'Pearl of the Valley' May Shine Again," *Staunton (VA) News Leader,* Dec. 23, 1993, C-1.

29. Maria Longley, "Officials Release New Rendering of City Project," *Staunton (VA) News Leader,* Dec. 4, 2003, A-1.

30. Tim Harrington, "Hotel Meant to Bring Big-City Feel to Small Town Virginia," *Staunton (VA) News Leader,* Jan. 19, 2003, A-4.

31. Tim Harrington, "Relocating Hotel Residents No Easy Task," *Staunton (VA) News Leader,* Feb. 20, 2003, A-1.

32. Tim Harrington, "Hotel Residents to Leave in 30 Days," *Staunton (VA) News Leader,* Feb. 1, 2003, A-1 and A-8.

33. Maria Longley, "Landmark Sign Staying on Hotel," *Staunton (VA) News Leader,* Dec. 12, 2003, A-1.

34. David Fritz, "Hotel Project Built on Fragile Foundation," *Staunton (VA) News Leader,* Sept. 7, 2003, A-9.

35. Maria Longley, "Staunton Keeps Chasing $2 Million in Tax Credits for Hotel Project," *Staunton News Leader,* Sept. 17, 2003, A-1.

36. Maria Longley, "City Wins Stonewall Jackson Hotel Fight," *Staunton (VA) News Leader,* Nov. 14, 2002, A-1, A-10.

37. Maria Longley, "Plans for Hotel's Future Elicit Questions," *Staunton (VA) News Leader,* Nov. 28, 2002, A-1.

38. Greenough, "20s Hotels Roar Again," 142.

39. Maria Longley, "Conference Center May Benefit Motels," *Staunton (VA) News Leader,* Feb. 12, 2003, A-1 and A-10.

40. "There's a Small Hotel," *Newsweek,* Dec. 25, 1950, 63; "F-M Hotels Plays Part in Area's History," *Fargo (ND) Forum,* July 14, 1987, p. 1 of "Heartbeat" section.

41. Sveen, "FM Hotel was Catalyst for Moorhead Improvements," C-2.

42. "80 Expected for Dinner Honoring Chef Escoffier," *Moorhead (MN) Daily News,* Jan. 5, 1952, 1.; "Minneapolis Man Named Manager of Martin Hotel," *Moorhead (MN) Daily News,* Dec. 30, 1949, 1; "FM Hotel Gives New Concept to City's Banquet Business," *Moorhead (MN) Daily News,* Mar. 10, 1952, B-1.

43. Virgil Larson, "Kahler Sells Moorhead's FM Hotel," *Fargo (ND) Forum,* May 6, 1971, 1–2.

44. C. Joseph Molinaro, "Ten Reasons Why People Buy Motels," *Motel/Motor Inn Journal* 38 (Dec. 1974): 49.

45. "FM Hotel Plays Part in Area's History"; Randolph E. Stefanson, interview with Keith A. Sculle, Jan. 29, 2008.

46. Jonathan Knutson, "Tree Top Raising and Its Rooots, Moorhead Eatery Plans Transplant," *Fargo (ND) Forum,* Jan. 29, 2000, B-1; Gerry Gilmour, "Developers: Hotel Construction Could Begin Immediately," *Fargo (ND) Forum,* Sept. 30, 2000, C-1.

47. Gerry Gilmour, "702's View Keeps Improving, Local Telecom Company Moves Headquarters to Former Tree Top Space," *Fargo (ND) Forum,* Sept. 7, 2002, E-1, E-6; "New Locations, Vtrenz Opens New Moorhead Location," *Fargo (ND) Forum,* Oct. 12, 2002, E-7.

48. Stefanson, interview with Sculle.

49. Hal Crocker, interview with Keith A. Sculle, Jackson, Tennessee, July 10, 2007; ·John Linn Hopkins and Marsha Oates, "New Southern Hotel," National Register of Historic Places nomination form, Feb.1, 2002 (Tennessee Historical Commission, Nashville, TN). For the personal recollections of Nora Noe Alexander, whose parents owned the hotel and who lived with her parents in the hotel's penthouse, see "New Southern Reclaims Glory Days," *Jackson (TN) Sun,* Sept. 26, 2004, 30-D, 40-D.

50. Crocker, interview with Sculle; Hopkins and Oates, "New Southern Hotel"; Hal Crocker, e-mail to Keith A. Sculle, June 21, 2007.

51. Crocker, interview with Sculle and e-mail to Sculle.

52. Ibid.; also see Jamie Page, "The New Southern," *Jackson (TN) Sun,* Jan. 8, 2004, 1-A, 2-A.

53. Harold B. Fairchild and Ross W. Fairchild, "Milton John Wolford, Danville Businessman and Civic Leader," *Heritage of Vermilion County,* Summer 1989, 8–9.

54. Ibid.; Dan Olmstead, "Wolford to Host Celebrities," *Danville (IL) Commercial News,* Oct. 2, 1975, 29.

55. Dan Olmstead, "Hotel Wolford to End Battle, Close Nov. 1," *Danville (IL) Commercial News,* Oct. 2, 1975, 1; Les Smith, "Wolford May Get New Life," *Danville (IL) Commercial News,* Nov. 13, 1975, 1.

56. Les Smith, "Firm Defends Bid for Help from City," *Danville (IL) Commercial News,* May 3, 1975, 7; Olmstead, "Wolford Host to Celebrities"; "City Takes Option to

Buy Wolford," *Danville Commercial News,* Sept. 14, 1976, 24; Les Smith, "Hotel Missing Loan List," *Danville (IL) Commercial News,* Apr. 23, 1976, 1–2.

57. Smith, "Hotel Missing Loan List," 1–2.

58. Mary Beth Balika, "Plan to Refurbish Wolford Unveiled," *Danville (IL) Commercial News,* Dec., 17, 1977, 1–2; Mary Beth Balika, "Developer: Wolford Work Could Begin in '80," *Danville Commercial News,* Aug. 24, 1979, 9, 18.

59. Carl Young, "New Era is About to Start for Wolford," *Danville (IL) Commercial News,* Oct. 25, 1981, 9, 20; *The Wolford* (brochure; Danville, IL: ca. 1981), 1.

60. "Fate of Field Home at Stake," *Monterey Peninsula (CA) Herald,* Jan. 26, 1940, 1; "Field Home Acquisition Discussed," *Monterey Peninsula (CA) Herald,* Jan. 27, 1940, 1–2.

61. "Field Home Acquisition Discussed," 1; "Preservation of Casa Munras is Council Topic," *Monterey Peninsula (CA) Herald,* Mar. 6, 1940, 1.

62. "Casa Munras to Open Tomorrow," *Monterery Peninsula (CA) Herald,* Sept. 26, 1941, 6.

63. Jeri Bostwick, "This is the House that Jack Built," *Game and Gossip* 8 (Nov. 11, 1955): 3; Earl Hofeldt, "Famed Old Casa Munras Hotel Changes Hands," *Monterey Peninsula (CA) Herald,* Aug. 13, 1965, 1–2.

64. Hofeldt, "Famed Old Casa Munras Hotel," 1–2.

65. Davis S. Mullaly, "Casa Munras—An Amazing Evolution," *Alta Vista Magazine,* Oct. 13, 1996, 5.

66. Kirk and Associates, *The Marshall Downtown Luxury Residences* [Marshall, TX: circa 2003], n.p.; "Will Award Contract for New Hotel Monday," *Marshall (TX) News Messenger,* Jan. 18, 2004, 6-A.

67. Nancy Canson, "Hotel Deal is Signed," *Marshall (TX) News Messenger,* Mar. 18, 2003, 1-A, 3-A; Mike Elswick, "Getting Closer," *Marshall (TX) News Messenger,* Jan. 18, 2004, 6-A.

68. Elswick, "Getting Closer," 6-A.

69. Robin Y. Richardson, "Flowers for Lady Bird," *Marshall (TX) News Messenger,* Dec. 23, 2005, 1-A; Kirk and Associates, *The Marshall Downtown Luxury Residences,* 1.

70. Charles L. Hall, "Waldorf of the Prairies," *Kansas Country Living,* Feb. 1972, 12-D.

71. "Landmark Becomes Vacant," *Manhattan (KS) Mercury,* June 3, 1985, 1.

72. Windsor Hotel Restoration Project, Finney County Preservation Alliance, http://www.gardencity.net/windsor/status/executive_seminary.html (accessed June 29, 2005).

73. Diane Lewis, "Windsor Significant to State, Nation," http://www.getelgram.com/new/2003/jaunary/10/story1.html.

74. Manya A. Brachear, "A Decade of Dreams Abruptly Check Out," *Chicago Tribune,* Jan. 2, 2007, A-4.

75. "Legacy Started With Far-Fetched Vision," *Terre Haute (IN) Tribune-Star,* Aug. 25, 1996, 1; Joretta Roloff, "Terre Haute House Brought People, Business From Miles Around," *Terre Haute (IN) Tribune-Star,* Nov. 16, 2005, 20.

76. Roloff, "Terre Haute House Brought People, Business From Miles Around," 20; "Old Hotel Property in Good Hands," *Terre Haute (IN) Tribune-Star,* Oct. 26, 2005, 8-A.

77. The *Terre Haute (IN) Tribune-Star,* the city's only daily newspaper, is owned by the same family that for many years owned the Terre Haute House. The newspaper's seven-store office building, located across the street from the Terre Haute House, had also stood empty for many years, a replacement facility having been built several blocks to the south. In 2008 the building was undergoing refurbishing as still another new motor inn for downtown Terre Haute.

78. Mike Matherly, "Understandable Fate for Terre Haute House," *Terre Haute (IN) Tribune-Star,* Nov. 16, 2005, 9.

79. See Victoria Southwood, "Its Time to Save What's Left of Downtown," *Terre Haute (IN) Tribune-Star,* Nov. 16, 2005, 9-A.

80. Sara Medina, "Cozy Homes Away from Home," *Time,* Sept. 7, 1981, 65–66; Subrata N. Chakravarty and Anne McGrath, "Room at the Top?" *Forbes,* Mar. 12, 1984, 58, 60.

INDEX

Pages numbered in **boldface** refer to topically-relevant illustrations.

African Americans: as hotel employees, 45, **82**, 84, **85**, 86, 89, 110–11; as hotel guests, 4, 45, 82, 110–11, 120; as hotel managers and owners, 74, 86, 111

Ahmanson, Roberta Green, 177

Albert Pick-Barth Co., 30, 34, 48, 65–66, 152, 168

Albuquerque, NM, 52

"American plan" hotels, 7–8, 70, 120–22, 192n

Amherst, MA, Lord Jeffrey Inn, 63

arts and crafts movement, 35

Art Deco style, 121–25, **135**

Asheville, NC, 55

Ashtabula, OH, Hotel Ashtabula, 41–42, 48

Athens, OH, 74

automobile clubs, 3, 43, 107; American Automobile Assoc., 94, 109

automobile-convenience, xiii, xv, 14, 22, 107, 136, 139, 178

automobiles and automobility, xv–xvii, 3–4, 14, 17, 21–22, 24, 48–49, 64–66, 77, 79, 98, 102–9, 122, 137, 140–41, 160, 164, 180–81

Atherton, Louis, 18

Baker, Don T., 156

Ball, C. N., 73

Bartholomew, Fred, 154

Bassett, Charles N., 50

Baur, Charles, 19, 79–80, 130, 177

Baur, Jacob, 130

Bay City, MI, 92

Beaux Arts style, 35–36

Bedford, IN, Greystone Hotel, **160–61**, 162

Beloit, WI, 63

Bergmann, Marle E., 85–86

Berry, Edward Cornelius, 74

Billings, MT, Northern Hotel, 149

Binghamton, NY, 24

Bjorklund, Knute, 54

Bliss, Vincent R., 30–34

Bloomington, IL, Illinois Hotel, 55; Tilton-Hall Hotel, 87

Bloomington, IN, Hotel Graham, 39, 125

Boarding houses, 8–9, 111

Boomer, Lucius, 89

Boone, IA, Hotel Holst, **72**

Boorstin, Daniel, 7

Boss, Edwin A., 61, **62**, 63, 66, 81, 122, 140–41, 151, 155

Boston, MA, **129**; Tremont House, 145

Bothwell, John, 51–53, 165

Boutique Hotels, Inc., 166

Bozeman, MT, Baxter Hotel, 132

Bristol, TN, General Shelby Hotel, 72

Brucken, Carolyn, 112

Brunner, John, 154–55

Bryant, Robert P., 156

Buffalo, NY, Hotel Statler, 147

Burlington, IA, Hotel Burlington, 49–50, **144**, 145

buses and travel by bus, 107; hotel waiting rooms, 39, 45; terminals, xiii–xvi, 39, 45

Cannon, Joseph G., 42

Canton, OH, Hotel McKinley, 147

Canyonville, OR, 10

Cargill, Jerry, 174–75

Carson, Pirie, Scott & Co., 151

central business districts, xiv, xvi–xvii, 11, 138, 156, 163–64, 166–68, 172–73, 176, 179–80; business blocks, 11–12, 22–23, 35, 57

Champaign, IL, Hotel Beardsley, 88

Chandler, GA, Hotel Chandler, **49**

Charles City, IA, Hotel Hildreth, 139

Charleston, MO, Russell Hotel, 54

Chicago, IL, xx, 19, 24, 35, 70, 98, 104, **109**, 172; convention business, 110; Drake Hotel, 151; Graesmere Hotel, 88; Great Northern Hotel, 54; Hotel Sherman, 61; Plymouth Hotel, 88

Chicago Title & Trust Co., 60

Churchill, Winston, 71

Cincinnati, OH, 104

Civil Rights Movement, 111

Civil War, the, 10, 23, 37, 70, 84, 110, 163, 174

Clare, MI, Hotel Doherty and Cottage Annex, 154–55

Clark, Martha Haskell, 18

Clark, O. A., 141

Clarksville, TN, Hotel Montgomery, 99

Clearwater Beach, FL, 66

Cleaves, W. B., 131

Cleveland, OH, 81, 106

Cleveland, TN, Hotel Auditorium, 155; Hotel Cherokee, 52, 155

Clinton, IA, La Fayette Hotel, 122

Colonial Revival style, 35, 124, 139

Columbia River Highway, 14

Colt's Patent Fire Arms Manufacturing Co., 125

Cook, John W., 55

commercial strips, xiii, xvi, 179–80

Commercial Traveler's Mutual Accident Insurance Association of America, 104

community and community hotels, see: locality-based community and hotels, community-sustaining implications of

convenience stores, xiv

Corning, IA, Hotel Maywood, 58–59

Cornell University, School of Hotel Management, 87, 156

Corre, Joseph, 5–6

Council Bluffs, IA, Chieftan Hotel, 56–57

Crawfordsville, IN, Monon Hotel, 156

Crissey, Forrest, 100

Crocker, Hal, 172

Crocker, Morris, 169

Cumberland, MD, 10

Dahl, G. K., 109–10

Damon, J. Linfield, 64

Danforth, Emma, 112–13

Danville, IL, Hotel Wolford, 93, 172–73; Lincoln Hotel, 42, 44–45

Denver, CO, 66, 176; Albany Hotel, 52

Decatur, IL, Hotel Orlando, 86

Des Moines, IA, 63, 141

Detroit Publishing Co., 79

Dixon, IL, Nachusa Tavern, 10

Dorris, Paul, 141

Doherty, Fred, 154–55

Dougherty, Jack, 174

Dougherty, P. J., 172–73

Dreiser, Theodore, 24, 121

Dubuque, IA, Hotel Julien-Dubuque, 38

Duparquet, Hunt & Moneuse Co., **129**

Dwight, IL, 139, Hotel Livingston, 139

Egyptian Trail, 11

Eisenhower, Dwight David, 56, 70

El Centro, CA, 154; Hotel California, 152; Las Palmas Court Hotel, 154–55

Elkhart, IN, 93; Hotel Bucklen, **77**, 106

Elmira, NY, 24

El Paso, TX, 50

Elyria, OH, Andwar Hotel, 106

Emmetsburg, IA, Waverly Hotel, 61

English Revival style, 35–36, **37**, **130**, 131–32

Erwin, TX, Erwin Hotel, 55

"European Plan" hotels, 8, 70, 120, 122, 192

Evansville, IN, McCurdy Hotel, 63, 77; Vendome Hotel, 88

Fargo, ND, 168; Hotel Gardner, **140**; Hotel Powers, 132, **133–34**

Fisher, Claude S., 21

Fort Campbell, KY, 55

Fort Madison, IA, Hotel Anthes, **143**

Foster, William J., 74

Francaviglia, Richard, 57–58

Fred Harvey Co., 10, 52, 190n

Fremont, OH, 80; Hotel Fremont, 83

Furnell, Doyle D., 165

Gadsden, AL, Hotel Reich, 149

Galena, IL, 10

Galesburg, IL, Hotel Custer, 88

Garden City, KS, Windsor Hotel, 175–76

gas stations and service garages, xiii–xiv, 24, 107, **108**

geographical knowledge of one's locality, 83, 107; maps and atlases in hotel reading rooms, 107

Georgian Revival styling, 35

Gettysburg, PA, Hotel Gettysburg, 56, 70, 79, 86, 147, 156

Gideon Society, 104–5

Goist, Park Dixon, 21

Goshenville, NY, Central Hotel, 105–6

Grafton, WV, 10; Grafton House, 10

Grand Forks, ND, 154

Grand Island, NE, Hotel Yancey, **85**

Grand Rapids, MI, Pantlind Hotel, 81

Great Depression of the 1930s, 8, 20, 22, 61, 65–66, 69, 73, 84, 87–88, 95, 102–3, 108–9, 138, 140, 155–56, 160, 181

Great Plains, the, 176

Green Bay, WI, Beaumont Hotel, 107, 153

Greene, NY, Sherwood Hotel, 131

Greeneville, TN, 162–65; General Morgan Inn and Conference Center, 162–65; Morgan Square and Olde Town Development Corp., 164

Grey, Allison, 114

Harrisburg, IL, Horning Hotel, **71**

Harrisburg, PA, 54

Harris, Kerr & Foster, Inc., 74

Hartford, CT, 125

Harvard, IL, Ayers Hotel, 11

Hayner, Norman, 91, 103, 114, 115

Hazelton, PA, Hotel Altamount, 33–34

Hennepin, IL, Cecil House, 120

highway associations, xiv

highways, xiii, xv–xvi, 4, 24, 48, 63, 73, 99, 102, 106–8, 181; interstate highways, xiv–xv, 1, 11, 50–51, 94, 154, 179; named, xiv, 11, 14, 49, **77**, 154; parkways and tollways, xiv

historic preservation planning, 1, 161–77; National Register of Historic Places, 162, 167, 176; National Trust for Historic Preservation, Main Street Project, 163, 177

Holland, MI, Warm Friend Hotel, 56

Hopkins, John H., 202n

Horwath and Horwath, Inc., 65, 74, 89

hospitality, 7–8, 21, 61, 69–70, 73–74, 76, 89–91, 98, 113, 115, 131, 134

hotel adaptive reuse, 159–81; for conference center, 160, 164, 167, 179; for elderly housing, 3, 10, 160, 165, 169–73, 181; for offices, 3, 160, 167–69, 181

hotel associations, 17; American Hotel Assoc., 4, 74, 79, 81, 83, 86, 89–90, 110, 144, 153, 155; Associated Hotels of the West, 79; Illinois Hotel Assoc., 65, 71, 73; Kansas-Missouri-Oklahoma Hotel Assoc., 17, 147; Northwestern Hotel Men's Assoc., 54, 73, 148; Ohio Hotels Assoc., 89; Pennsylvania Hotels Assoc., 79; Texas Hoteliers' Assoc., 74

hotel auto entrances and parking garages, xv, 3, 15, 22, 24–25, **32**, 45, 49, 105–7, **108**, 141, **142**, 153, 167

hotel chains, 2, 4, 15, 25, 42, 55, 61–67, 94, 116, 153, 179, 190–91; Albert Pick Hotels, 168; American Hotels Corp., 64; American Hotel System, 190n; Boss Hotel System, 61–62, 81, 122, 141, **150**, 151, 165; Capitol Associates, 172–73; DeWitt Operated Hotels, 191n; Eppley Hotels, 191n; Gateway Hotels, 190n; Grenoble Hotels, 191n; Hilton Hotels, 66; Hockenbury Systems, Inc.,

hotel chains (cont.)
54; Kahler Hotels, 167; Knox Hotels, 66, 86,156; Lamar Hotels, 191n; Radisson Hotels, 166, 178; Sheraton Hotels, 66, 156; Sterling Hotels System, 190n; Sweet Hotels, 191; Tennessee Hotel Operating Co., 190n; Treadway Inns, 63, 145, 151; United Hotels Co., 64; Van Ormand Hotels, 66, 71, 74, 81, 86

Hotel Credit Letter Co., 80

hotel design and construction, 3, 23–46, 53, 56–57, 63, 66, 125, 202n; architectural styling, 35–44, 48, 63, 120, 124–25, 135; building types, xvii, 11–18, 56–58; fireproofing, 30, 34, 51, 80, 139; hiring an architect, 24–25, 30–35; planbooks for floor layout, 4, 25, **26–29**, 48; "theming," 25

hotel financing, xiii, 4, 9–10, 14–16, 30–31, 47, 50–57, 64–66, 94

hotel guest rooms, xiii, xvi, 6, 11, 18–19, 24–31, **32**, 33–34, 48, 105–7, 119, 145, 147, **148**, 149, **150**, 151–52, 154, 163; air conditioning of, 151; furnishings for, xvii, 101, 113, 115, 125; layout of, 147, **148**, 149; number nationwide, 20; private toilets and baths in, 6, 27–29, 63, 106, 139, 145, **146**, 147, **148**; radio and television in, 151

hotel industry, xx–xxi, 19–20, 65, 88–89, **90**, 100, 157; directories for, 11, 76, 82, 104, 111; over expansion of, 65–66, 108; size of, per number of hotels and annual revenue, 4, **5**, 20; supply houses for, xx, 24, 30, 126, **129**, 140, 151–52; trade journals, xx–xxi, 4, 24, 31–33, 51, 53, 69, 71–72, 94, 105, 111–12, 114, 150, 183n; training manuals, 4, 71, 90–91

hotel life, xiii–xvii, 54, 97–102, **103**, 104–17; behavior and dress codes, 39, 119–20; commercial travelers, xvi, 18, 29, 31, 48–49, 59, 61–65, 83, 97, 99, **100–1**, 102, **103**; conventions and conventioneers, xvii, 2–3, 97, 109–10; guest expenditures, **79**; problem guests, 80, 91–92, 106, 113–16; tipping, 104, 122; transients and transiency, xiii–xvii, 5–6, 8–9, 18, 20–27, 46, 59, 86, 97, 135, 166, 181; vacationers, xvi, 1–2, 97, 105–9

hotel logistics, 32–34, 54; boiler rooms and heating, 29–34, 80, 86, 92; gas lighting, 18, 115, 149; electric lighting, 6, 19–20, 34, 115; elevators, 6, 11, 27, 34, 41, 127; employee lounges and bedrooms, 3; housekeeping 30, 84–85; janitorial supply rooms, 30; kitchens, 19, 25, 27, 33–34, 41, 72, 86, 123, 126, **127–29**, 130–31, 165; laundries, 29–30, 34, 86, 92; pest control, 80; plumbing, 34 ; refrigeration, 19, 29, 31, 34, 43, 86, 92, 126; telephones, 18, 34, 36 , 39, 80, 86, 106; trunk storage, 29–30, 115

hotel management, xviii, 7, 14, 19, 21, 25, 54, 64, 69–88, **89**, 96–98, 109–11, 117; accounting services, 65–66, 74, **75**; business planning, 16–17, 30–32, 53, 93–94; labor issues, xviii, **75**, 83–89, 140; management companies, xx, 54, 63–65, **75**; market analyses, 48–49, 53; occupancy levels, 108–9; office functions, 36, 38–39, 72, 98, 102; publicity and promotion, 50–52, 60–61, 72–74, 76–80, 93, 126–27, 152–53; setting room rates, 9, 91, 100–1, 108, 113, 153; standardization through scientific methods, 19, 69–75, 79, 81, 83, 89–92, 98, 100, 115; technical innovation, 19, 62, 79–80, 92–93, 127–28, 157

Hotel Monthly, xx–xxi, 4, 8, 10, 17, 24–29, 36–39, 41–43, 48–49, 54, 56, 58, 63, 65, 70–71, 79–81, 83–84, 86–89, 92–94, 102, 105–9, 120, 122, 124, 126, 131–32, 136, 139–41, 144–45, 147–49, 151–54, 183, 190n; design contests, 25–29

hotel obsolescence and disinvestment, 1–2, 18–19, 98, 114–15, 146, 156, 160–61, 165, 168, 178, 181

hotel public spaces, 6–7, 11, 21, 24, 31, **32–33**, 34–35, 76, 139, 181; ball, banquet and event rooms, xvii, 6, 27, 32, 35, 40–42, **58–59**, barber and beauty shops, xvii, 25, **32**, 34, 37, 39–40, **43**, 44, 86; bars and cocktail lounges, 3, 22, 31, 70, 104, 109, 119, **130**, 131, 134, **135**, 136, 141, 149, 174; checkrooms, 27, 36, 40; cigar and newspaper stands, xvii, 36, 42, 86; coffee shops and lunch counters, 11, 25, 27, **32–34**, 136, 141, 154, 163, 174; dining rooms, xvi–xviii, 3, 6–8, 11, 14, 18, 21, 23, 25, 31, **33**, 34, 39, 47,

89, 105–6, 109, 115, 119–20, **121**, 122, **223–24**, 125–27, 136, 141, 149, 154, 164–65, 174, 181; ladies waiting rooms, 4, 27, 40, 112; lobbies and mezzanines, 3–8, 14, 25–26, 31, 33, 36, 38–44, 48, 50, 61, **100–1**, 102–3, 120, 126, 135, **140**, **144**, 149, 154, 165, **170–71;** men's grills, 24, 37, **130**; porches, 14–15, 18, 26; reading rooms, 6, 107; registration desks, 3, 26, 37–39, **72**, 87, 121; retail rental spaces, 11, **12**, 16–17, 31, **32**, 34, 39, 42–43, 54, 87, 91, 120; roof gardens, 41; sample rooms, 18, 23, **32**, 101; shoeshine stands, 86; public toilet and bath rooms, 27–30, 37, **146**; waiting rooms, 39, 44; writing rooms, 26, 37

hotel receivership and refinancing, 65–66

hotel renovation and rehabilitation, 52, 63, 94, 105, 138–39, **140**, 141–42, **143**–44, 145, 152, 159–78

hotels, 145, 147, 151; community-sustaining implications, xv–xviii, 1, 3, 5–9, 19–22, 24, 44–46, 50–61, 64–65, 67, 117, 153, 160–61, 174–75, 179, 181; defined, xvi, xviii, 4–9; early history of, xvi, xviii, 4–9; geographical distribution of, 4, **5**, 20, 62–63

hotel work, 84, 88–92; bar tenders, 130–31, 134; bellhops and porters, 87–88, 91–92, 107, 113–16; cashiers, 88; chamber maids, 87–88, 92, 114–15; chefs and cooks, 81, 127; desk clerks, 61, 87–88, 91–92, 113, 115; dining room stewards, 81, 122–23; dishwashers, 87; doormen, 15, **85**, 88, 107; electricians and engineers, 87; elevator operators, 87; head housekeepers, 87; house detectives, 87, 115; housemen, 82; parking valets, 22; scrub women, 87, 112; waiters and waitresses, 86, 92, 114, 120, 122, **123**; watchmen, 87

Hungerford, Edward, 15–16

Hutson, W. G., 52, 54;

Illinois Housing Development Agency, 173

inns and taverns, 5–6, 8, 10, 14, 74, 98, 108, 120

Ironton, OH, Hotel Marting, 101, 149

Iron Mountain, MT, Superior Hotel, 105

Italian Renaissance style, 178

Jackson, John Brinckerhoff, xiii, xvii

Jackson, MI, Hotel Hayes, **43**, 44, 147–48; Hotel Otsego, 127, **128**

Jackson, TN, New Southern Hotel, New Southern Apartments, 168, **169–71**,172

Jacksonville, IL, Hotel Dunlap, 74, 92

Jakle, John A., 1, 180

Janesville, WI, 104

Jennerstown, PA, White Star Hotel, 154

Johnson, Lady Bird, 175

Jones, Gregg, 163

journey to shop, xv

journey to work, xv, 44

Juneau, AK, Bergmann Hotel, 86; Circle City Hotel, 86

Kansas City, MO, 176; Victoria Hotel, 6, 147

Kansas Preservation Alliance, 176

Keeley, Leslie A., 139

Keller, Suzanne, 21

Kenmore, ND, Irvin Hotel, 48

Kessinger, Harold, 19

Kewanee, IL, Kewanee Hotel, 145, 147

Kincaid, James Leslie, 64, 141

Knoxville, TN, 48

Knutson, Donald T., 53

Kroller Manufacturing Co, 149

Kurtz, Wilbur H., 74

labor unions, 88–89, 110; Hotel & Restaurant Employees Union, 110

La Crosse, WI, 103, Stoddard Hotel, 124

La Fayette, IN, Hotel Fowler, 41–42

Lancaster, OH, Hotel Lancaster, 126, **135**, 151

landscape as built environment, xiii–xiv, 57, 137–38; automobile-oriented landscapes and places, x iv–xvi, 1, 22

Lane, Rose Wilder, *Old Home Town*, 104

Lansing, MI, 43

Lawrence, KS, 52, Eldridge Hotel, 54

Lewisburg, WV, General Lewis Hotel, 139

Lewis, Sinclair, 18, 23, 47; *Free Air*, 102; *Main Street*, 23, 47, 50, 102; *Work of Art*, 18, 72–73, 81, 86, 88, 91–92, 94, 114, 149, 153

Lewiston, ID, Lewis-Clark Center, 57

Lexington,, VA, 15–16; Robert E. Lee Hotel, 15, **16**

Liquid Carbonic Co., 130

Lincoln, Abraham, 120

Lincoln Highway, **77**, 154

livery stables, 18

locality-based community, 19–22, 44–45, 162, 181

Logansport, IN, Barrett House, 122

Lordsville, NM, Hidalgo Hotel, 50

Lundberg, Donald, 110

"Main Street America," xiv, 3, 5, 11–12, 16, 21, 57, 86–87, 94–95, 99, 108–9, 137–38, 164, 177

Manchester, NH, 155

Mansfield, OH, 111

Marshall, MI, Hotel Schuler, 125

Marshall, TX, Marshall Hotel, 174–75

Marshalltown, IA, Stoddard Hotel, 138; Hotel Tallcorn, **42**, 56, 190

Mason City, IA, Eadmar Hotel, 48

Mattoon, IL, Hotel Byers, 11, **12**

Maxwell, William, 101–2

Memphis, TN), 155; Peabody Hotel, 156

Michigan State College, 81

Middlebury, VT, 63

Midwest, the, 3, 18, 109, 122, 165

Minneapolis, MN, 54, 167

Missoula, MT, Florence Hotel, **124**, 125

modernity and modernization, 46, 53, 71, 106, 132, **133–35, 140**, 141, **143–44**, 150–51

"mom and pop" hotels, 87–88

Monterey, CA, Casa Munras, 173–74

Moorhead, MN, Frederick Martin Hotel, 53, 167–68

Morgan, John Hunt, 163

motel chains: Downtowner Inns, 155–56; Holiday Inns, 155–56; Travelodge Motels, 155; Voyager Inns, 66–67

motels and motor inns, xiii–xvi, 3, 8, 24, 66, 83, 94, 105, 136, 139, 144, 152–56, 160, 167–68, 177, **179**, 180

motorists and motoring, xiii–xviii, xxi, 4–5, 8, 14–15, 19, 21–22, 24, 44–45, 64–65, 93, 97–99, 105–6, 117, 137, 153, 166, 169, 181

Mount Carroll, IL, Hotel Glen View, 145

Murfreesboro, TN, James K. Polk Hotel, 16

Naperville, IL, 140

Nashville, TN, 48

Nathan, Theodore, 123, 135

National Hotel Week, 79

National Recovery Act, NRA, 8–9, 88–89; NIRA Codes, 89, **90**, 153

Negro Traveler's Green Book, 111

New England, 63–64

New Philadelphia, OH, Hotel Reeves, 89

Newton, IA, Hotel Maytag, 151

New York City, NY, 24, 73, 98; City Hotel, 6, **129**; Coree's Hotel, 5–6; Holt's Hotel, 6; Hotel Everett, 6; Metropolitan Hotel, 8; St. Regis Hotel, 15; Waldorf-Astoria Hotel, 6, 25

Nichols, W. C., 89

Niswonger, Scott, 164

Nolan, David J., 54

Oconomowoc, WI, Majestic Hotel, 12, **14**

Official Hotel Red Book and Directory, **82**, 83

Ohio State University, 85

Okmulgee, OK, Hotel Okmulgee, 54

Olympia, WA, Olympia Hotel, 51

Omaha, NE, 70, 190n

Ostrow, John, 73–74

"other-directed houses," xiii

Ottumwa, IA, Ballingall Hotel, 122; Hotel Ottumwa, 40

Paducah, KY, Irving Cobb Hotel, 188n

"palaces of the people," 7

Pantlind, Fred, 81

Paragould, AR, Hotel Van Dervoort, **26–29**, 30

parking, xiv–xv, 15, 22, 109, 138, 153, 163, 171, 179–80; see also: hotel auto entrances and parking garages

Pensacola, FL, San Carlos Hotel, 79

Peoria, IL, 10; Hotel Jefferson, 93

Perkins Brothers Co., 174

Perry, IA, Hotel Patee, 176–77

Persinger, Allen, 166–67

Philadelphia, MS, Benwalt Hotel, 149

Philadelphia, PA, Bellevue-Stratford Hotel, 25, 70

Phoenix, OR, 10

Pierce, John, 51

Pierce Petroleum Co., 155

place and sense of place, xiv, 25, 44–45, 48, 64, 162, 179

Pocahontas, AR, 12, **13**; Banks' Hotel, 12, **13**; Bigger's Hotel, 12, **13**; Imodea Hotel, 12, **13**; St. Charles Hotel, 12, **13**; Turner's Boarding House, 12, **13**

Portland, ME, Danish Village, 155

Portland, OR, 10

postcards, **2**, **12**, **14–17**, **71**, **79**, **83**, **146**, 193n

Poughkeepsie, NY, 140; Nelson House, 141, **142**

Prairie style, 177

Prohibition, 22, 31, 42, 116, 119, 131, 134, 141

Quincy, IL, Lincoln-Douglas Hotel, 72–73

railroad era, xiv, xvi, 4, 8, 10–11, 18, 22–24, 35, 98, 100, 105, 160, 166

railroad hotels, 10–11

railroads and railroading, xiv, xvi, 10–11, 14, 17, 22–24, 61–63, 65, 67, 101, 103–4, 109, 137–39, 165, 169, 174; Atchinson, Topeka & Santa Fe RR, 10–11; Chicago & Northwestern RR, 10; Erie RR, 10; Illinois Central RR, 11; Union Pacific RR, 14; Wabash RR, 57

railroad stations, xiii–xvi, 10–12, 15, **17**, 31, 52, 93

Rand Mc Nally & Co., 107

Red Wing, MN, St. James Hotel, 52

Renaissance Revival style, 176

residential or apartment hotels, xviii, 3, 9

resort hotels, xviii, 14, 70, 93

restaurants, 122, 136, 165; fast food restaurants, xiii–xiv

Richmond Center, WI, Park Hotel, 79

Ritchey, David, 16

"Roadside America," xiii–xiv, xvii, 76, 99, 105, 152

Robinson, IL, Woodworth Hotel, 52–53, 88, **101**

Rochester, MN, 167

Rockford, IL, 63

Rock Island, IL, 173

Rock Rapids, IA, Marietta Hotel, 73

Roosevelt, Franklin, 8, 88

Roseburg, OR, 55, Umpqua Hotel, 53

Royer, J. W., 36

Russell, Joseph J., 54

Rutledge, TN, Rutledge Inn, 152

Salina, KS, Lauer Hotel, 139

Salisbury, MD, Hotel Wicomico, 35, **36**

San Diego, CA, 155

San Francisco, CA, 10

Santa Barbara, CA, Arlington Inn, 154

Sault Ste. Marie, MI, 153

Scharf, Elsie, 86

Scharf, Henry, Jr., 70, 93–94, 147, 156

Scharf, Henry, Sr., 56, 70, 79

Scott, Roy, 79

Sculle, Keith, 1

Sedalia, MO), 168; Hotel Bothwell, 38–39, 51–53, **58–60**, 61, 148, 165–67

Seguin, TX, 51

service and fraternal organizations, 47, 49–50, 56, 58–59, 97, 99, 100, 126, 174; Ancient Free & Accepted Masons, 58; Benevolent & Fraternal Order of

service and fraternal organizations (cont.)
  Elks, 58; Daughters of the American
  Revolution, 110; Exchange Club, 174;
  Lions Club, 58, 174; Kiwanis Club, 42,
  50, 110; Order of Odd Fellows, 58, 110;
  Rotary International, xiii, **60**, 65, 110,
  140

shopping centers and shopping malls, xv,
  156

signs, 42, 76–77, **78**; along roadsides, xiv,
  76, **77**, 79–80

Simmons Co., 151

"skyscraper hotels," 1–2, 15–17, 35–38, 53,
  170, 174

small towns and small cities, xvi, 9–10,
  17–18, 21, 23, 50–51, 98–99, 102–4,
  116–17, 125, 181; boosterism in,
  xvi–xvii, 5, 10, 12, 14–16, 43, 50–53, 66,
  161; courthouse squares in, xvi, 10–12,
  13, 145, 169, 174; defined, xviii; trade
  hinterlands surrounding, xiv, xvi, 10,
  23–24, 79, 100, 137

Smiler, Si, 105

social values and social proclivities in the
  United States: "Americanization," 89;
  anonymity, 115–16; class mobility, 7;
  "democratization," 20; egalitarianism,
  7, 20; freedom, xv; gentry respectability, 6–7; gregariousness and
  collegiality, 7, 26, 50; individualism,
  xv, 7; materialism, 7, 50; privacy, 7;
  republicanism, 7

South, the, 4, 20, 85, 104, 161

Southwest, the, 35, 74

Spanish Revival style, 35, 50

Sparta, IL, 61

Sprague, J. R., 103

Springfield, IL, Leland Hotel, **130**, 131

St. Charles, IL, Hotel Baker, 147

St. Clair, MI), St. Clair Inn, 151–52

St. Joseph, MO, Hotel Robidoux, **41**

St. Louis, MO, 104, 155; Maryland Hotel,
  61; Hotel Statler, 55

St. Petersburg, FL, 64

stage coach era, 8, 10

Statler, Ellsworth M., 74, 145–46, 177

Staunton, VA, 168; Stonewall Jackson
  Hotel and Conference Center, 166–67

Stefanson, Randolph, 168

Stevens, H. L., 17

Stilgoe, John, 58–59

Stillwater, MN, Lowell Inn, 124

strangers and the "stranger's path," xiii–
  xiv, xvi–xvii, 20–21, 59, 115–16, 181

Streamline Modern style, 132, **133–35**, **144**,
  145, 151

streetcars, xiii, 44, 105

suburbia, xvi, 156, 178

Sullivan, Louis, 35

Susquehanna, PA, Starrucca House, 10

Syracuse, NY, 125

Tallant, Robert, *Southern Territory*, 104

Tampa, FL, 64

Taylor, C. Stanley, 30–34, 120

taxi cabs, xiii, 48, 56, 88, 93, 107

Tellman, John, 123

Temple, TX: Doering Hotel, **57**; Hawn
  Hotel, **57**; Kyle Hotel, **57**

Tennessee Valley Authority, 164

Tennessee Historical Commission, 172

Terre Haute, IN, 1–2, 19, 208n; "Crossroads
  of America," 1, 177–79; Terre Haute
  House, 1, **2**, 3, 19, 79–80, 130, 177, **178**,
  179–81, 208n; Hilton Garden Inn, **179**,
  180

Texarkana, AR, Hotel McCartney, 15, **17**

The Dalles, OR, Hotel Dalles, ix, **15**

Tillman, Mrs. J. F., 99

Toledo, OH, Boody Hotel, 54

Tourists and tourism, xiii–xiv, 14, 31, 44,
  102, 105–9, 117, 152, 164; pleasure trips,
  xv–xvi, 1–2, 18, 166

tourist homes, 8–9, 111, 152

transiency, see: hotel life, transients and
  transiency

Travelers Hotel Credit Letter Co., 76

Treadway, Laurens G., 63–64, 69, 145

trucks and trucking, xiv–xv, 18

Tuskegee Institute, 86

Twin Falls, ID, Rogerson Hotel, 100

Union City, IN, Braham House, 147

Union Grove, WI, Hotel Shepard, **12**

United Commercial Travelers, Inc., 104

U.S. Bureau of the Census, 9

U.S. Department of Agriculture, 80

U.S. Department of Housing and Urban Development, 169–70, 172–73

U.S. Department of Transportation, Intermodal Surface Transportation Efficiency Act, ISTEA, 164

U.S. Internal Revenue Service, federal income tax codes, 156, 168–72, 181; Federal Tax Reform Act of 1986, 156, 162, 167–68

Urbana, IL, Urbana-Lincoln Hotel, 35–36, **37**

Van Orman, F. Harold, 55, 63, 81

Van Orman, W. H., 63

Vicksburg, MS, Hotel Vicksburg, 37, 40, 126, **127**

Vietnam War, 56

Virginia Department of Housing and Community Development, 166

Warsaw, IN, 63

Washington, George, 38

Washington, PA, George Washington Hotel, 36–37, **38**

Waterbury, CT, 125

Waterloo, IA, Hotel Russell-Lamson, 30

Wellsboro, PA, Cone House, 52; Penn-Wells Hotel, 52

West, the, xv, 10, 137

Williamson, Jefferson, 6, 104, 111

Williamson, WV, Raymond Hotel, 83

Willy, John, xx–xxi, 8, 71, 83, 152

Wolf Creek, OR, Wolf Creek Tavern, 10

women in hotels, 27, 29–30, 50, **58–59**, 111–13; as employees, 61, 70, 83–88; as guests, 6, 21, 40, 61, 99, 111–13, 117, 120, 132, 135; as managers and owners, 9, 85–86; their impact on hotel maintenance and service, 112–14

Woodson, Warren, N., 58–59

Woodworth, Abner Palmer, 52–53

Wooster, OH, Ohio Hotel, 107, **108**

World's Columbian Exposition of 1893, 70

World War I, xvi, 10, 14, 24, 31, 62, 81, 85, 89, 102, 105, 111, 120, 125, 160, 181

World War II, 55, 59, 66, 86, 93, 105, 111–12, 136, 138, 144, 147, 155, 163

America's Main Street Hotels was designed and typeset on a Macintosh computer system using InDesign software. The body text is set in 9.25/14 Mercury and display type is set in ITC Franklin Gothic. This book was designed and typeset by Chad Pelton and manufactured by Thomson-Shore, Inc.